THE POETICS OF ROCK

THE POETICS OF ROCK

Cutting Tracks, Making Records

ALBIN J. ZAK III

University of California Press

Berkeley · Los Angeles · London

University of California Press
Berkeley and Los Angeles, California

University of California Press, Ltd.
London, England

Library of Congress Cataloging-in-Publication Data

Zak, Albin.
  The poetics of rock : cutting tracks, making records /
Albin J. Zak III.
     p.   cm.
  Includes bibliographical references (p.   ) and index.
  ISBN 0–520–21809–4 (cloth : alk. paper)—ISBN 0–520–
23224–0 (paper : alk. paper)
     1. Rock music—History and criticism.   2. Composition
(Music)   3. Sound—Recording and reproducing.   I. Title.

  ML3534 .Z35 2001
  781.66'149—dc21   2001001835

Manufactured in the United States of America
10 09 08 07 06 05
10 9 8 7 6 5 4 3 2

For Victoria and Sophia

Contents

Acknowledgments

This book, like many others, began as a Ph.D. dissertation. Credit for insisting on the viability of the topic goes to my musicological mentor, Leo Treitler, whose personal warmth, scholarly example, and enthusiasm for the project were, and continue to be, so greatly appreciated. Other faculty members at the City University of New York Graduate School also offered support and helpful criticism along the way, especially Stephen Blum, Allan Atlas, Peter Manuel, Joseph Straus, and Joel Lester, all of whom were more than forthcoming with their time and attention. I was fortunate as well to receive a generous dissertation fellowship from the American Musicological Society.

At the University of California Press, several people have helped this project make its way to publication. Lynne Withey believed in the project from the start; Mary Francis guided me through some of the early stages; and David Gill has attentively overseen production. I have also been extremely fortunate to have as an editor Carolyn Bond, whose sensitive ear and careful hand brought the manuscript to a new level of refinement.

In the years that I've spent in recording studios, mastering rooms, rehearsal halls, and clubs, I have encountered a great many fine musicians, engineers, producers, arrangers, and songwriters. Though our interactions were in the realm of practice rather than scholarship, all have affected my thinking in one way or another. Scholarly colleagues who have helped me develop and refine the intellectual nuances of that thinking include Joseph Darby, Richard Kassel, and Shaugn O'Donnell in New York, and Richard Crawford and Mark Clague in Ann Arbor. All read and commented on some part of some version of the manuscript, and their input invariably led to improvements. I am grateful as well for their friendship and for their willingness to listen and to share their ideas freely. Special thanks go to another Ann Arbor colleague, Travis Jackson, who read the entire manuscript, allowed me the run of his record collection, and during many evenings spent listening to records well into the morning hours was a willing partner in lively discussions of music, musicians, and mixes.

The notion of rock scholarship as a subspecialty of academic musicology is a young one, and there are still places in academia where it is considered questionable, if it is considered at all. At the University of Michigan I have had full support for writing about and teaching rock music from the former dean of the School of Music, Paul Boylan, and from his successor, Karen Wolff. I have also had the good wishes and encouragement of my colleagues, especially Richard Crawford, Joseph Lam, and Roland John Wiley. For any needed research materials I have always been able to turn to Charles Reynolds, Calvin Elliker, and the entire library staff. With Mr. Elliker's recent passing we have lost a skilled and sympathetic colleague.

I am also grateful to my students, who are always happy to share their knowledge and their records and to turn me on to new bands and new sounds. While rock musicology may be in its infancy, it has already attracted a number of committed and imaginative thinkers. The groundwork laid by scholars such as Robert Walser, Richard Middleton, Walter Everett, John Covach, Allan Moore, Theodore Gracyk, and David Brackett, to name only a few, has contributed to a change in the academic climate without which my own work hardly seems possible.

Finally, I would like to thank my family—my wife, Victoria; my daughter, Sophia; my mother and father, brother and sisters—a group of remarkable people whose deep embrace of life and of beauty reminds me continually of why art matters. In countless ways they inspire, excite, motivate, and challenge me. Their confident support and loyal cheering have been a great help throughout the writing of this book.

Introduction

In a small and unremarkable building on the west side of Manhattan, I walk down a narrow hallway that leads past a line of cramped offices to a recording studio. The walls are hung with gold- and platinum-colored discs in frames, commemorating the commercial successes of artists who have worked here. At the end of the hallway I cross through a small, simply furnished lounge area—a couch, a television, a backgammon board, some magazines—and open a heavy door leading into a room of peculiar character. Its walls and ceiling are angled and covered with a combination of oddly shaped wood and fabric-covered panels. There is no natural light, no view of the world outside. The dimness within is dotted with bright spots of colored light, some shining steadily, some flickering on and off, some shooting up and down or back and forth on various display panels, all emanating from one or another of the many machines that fill the room. The acoustic atmosphere is concentrated. Sounds have a focused presence about them quite unlike the diffuse quality of normal sonic experience. They seem to be closer to the ear and tightly framed. The air is filled with musical sound. Though there are no musicians in the room, I hear the full and satisfying sound of a band—drums, guitars, bass, and keyboards—rocking steadily. Two people are sitting before a large console filled with knobs, buttons, lights, and faders. As they listen, they watch through a large window on the other side of the console, which looks through to another room where a musician wearing headphones is playing a bass guitar. She appears to be completely absorbed—eyes closed, head bobbing rhythmically, face contorting expressively. As I watch and listen, it becomes apparent that she is playing the bass line for the music I'm hearing. Alone in the studio, with previously recorded music filling her ears, she pours herself into the performance, while in the control room the engineer goes about capturing the expressive moment on tape and the producer follows along with a critical ear.

When the song ends, the bass player enters the control room, the tape is rewound, and playback begins. All listen intently, scrutinizing every detail and nuance of the sonic image. After some discussion, it is agreed that the general direction is good, but the part could use some refinement and a few aspects of the performance need to be tightened up. The bass player reenters the studio, and communicating through microphones, the team begins a collaborative effort to hammer out a part and a performance that will stand as a record. The bass player spends much of the next hour playing her instrument, always with the same absorption and expressive focus, but it's clear that what is going on here is not musical performance for its own sake. With an ear not only to its momentary appeal but to its durability, the performance is treated to the same sort of considered deliberation and decision making as musical composition. What's going on here is not simply recording, but record *making.* Performance is simply the means of inscription through which fully embodied musical essences—musical idea and musical action—are captured by the electrical tracings in particles of iron oxide.

It is also clear that everything the team does is part of an inclusive process and that all involved are contributors to the compositional project in some way, for all have some effect on its outcome. All employ both intuition and deliberation in a collective effort to produce the record, and all are responsible in some way for the sonic inscriptions that form the record's essential identity. While their roles vary considerably, all of them fall under the rubric of "recordist," a term whose original meaning has been extended in common usage to include the work of songwriters, arrangers, performers, engineers, and producers and to account for the frequent overlaps among roles. For in a production process that is complex and often unpredictable, roles that start out discretely defined may become quite fluid.

This book is about recordists and their creative process, which centers on the practice of shaping musical ideas and performances into permanent sounding form. The aim is to present a picture of a compositional milieu by exploring its elements and giving an account of issues and concerns faced by artists. It is not, in any conventional sense, a book of musical analysis, criticism, or history, though at one time or another all of these come into play. Even less is it a how-to book of the sort that appear with increasing frequency— a product of the "project studio" phenomenon—though there is necessarily some discussion of technical matters. It is first of all an extended encounter with artists—their words and their works—within a framework that uses their testimony to illuminate the nature of record making and of records themselves. While a number of records are cited for the purpose of illustration, far more are represented by the collective experience of the recordists whose comments are collected in these pages.[1] As Stephen Blum reminds us, in the study of musical practices musicians themselves are our best guides. For "wherever we turn, we can find skilled performers engaged in the exercise of their musical knowledge."[2] It is from this knowledge that I have fashioned my account.

The first two chapters map out some conceptual terrain. Chapter 1 provides a brief historical sketch of the changes that sound recording has brought to our conception of music and how these affected the development of rock. Chapter 2 takes apart the common conflation of elements that so often distorts our view of what a record actually is. Records are often equated with their song or performance, but these are only aspects of what is actually a more comprehensive work, the track. Keeping in mind the nature of the track sets us on course toward thinking about issues surrounding its making.

In Chapter 3, I begin my exploration of the compositional process by positing five broad categories that account for all the sounds that one hears on a record: musical performance, timbre, echo, ambience, and texture. Each of these represents both concrete elements and associated activities that go into making a record, and each is explored in terms of its place in the overall compositional concern. Chapter 4 brings into the discussion the influence of electronic devices and architectural spaces on both the creative process and the finished work. Because records are musical works wrought in sound, their full meaning is imparted by a particular sensory experience whose every detail counts. The factors affecting those details are a matter of aesthetic concern, for, as the frequent references to the "musicality" of certain pieces of electronic equipment indicate, recordists' tools and sonic environments have the potential to shape musical style.

Chapter 5 looks at issues surrounding the process of getting music onto tape, from initial performance to mixdown. The successful transferal of musical energy from a moment of human expression into a fixed mechanical state is, as recordists say repeatedly, something of a magical process. Still, there is a range of strategies and approaches that artists bring to the task, and these are explored here. Chapter 6 considers some of the social aspects of record making, namely, the dynamics of collaboration as seen in the roles of engineers and producers. I have singled out these two members of the recording team because, unlike songwriters and performers, their functions—their "performances," their "voices"—remain mysterious to most people, yet their contribution to the compositional project is profound and indelible.

In Chapter 7, I offer some final thoughts, which center on the language and rhetoric of record making. Throughout the book to this point, implications have accumulated concerning the workings of convention, style, association, and so forth. In this final chapter I go about addressing these in an explicit way that serves also as an open-ended conclusion. The appendix includes a glossary and discographical information. Because in this book the primary focus is on sounding—rather than written—music, illustration must be in the form of listening. All of the recordings cited in the text are listed at the back of the book. In addition, there is a listing of engineers and producers cited, along with a representative sample of their work.

I came to this project as a recordist myself, with long-time friends and acquaintances in all areas of record making. But other than my general knowledge of the field, I largely set aside my own experience to make a report based on a body of easily accessible material. Most records cited are widely available, and many are no doubt already in readers' record collections. I have drawn on an array of printed sources—biographies, histories, reviews, interviews and feature articles, technical books and articles, liner notes, encyclopedias, and discographies. The common availability of this body of data provides a broad context of cultural relevance. The use of material gathered from popular recording magazines, for instance, can be viewed on a secondary level as a report on the state of discourse informing the ever-growing project studio constituency. And the focus on recordists working within the mainstream music business presents a picture of a recording culture that spans most of the world and the entire history of rock. Moreover, because the issues engaged here concern not only the *practice* but the *language* of record making, their significance is tied to the records that have participated in the formation of that language. The language of record making has developed over the years through the accumulation of associations and resonances as individual works carved out their own cultural space and then gradually coalesced into a larger cultural field. This field has served as the referential frame for both practice and reception.

There are many approaches to record making, reflecting differing aesthetic stances, commercial pressures, logistical contingencies, and so forth. In attempting to sketch broadly what is by now a long-standing and widespread compositional practice, it seems necessary to present a range of approaches and examples. Not wishing to imply any particular priority—indeed, believing that it would be foolish to do so—I have cast eye and ear in various directions both historically and aesthetically. Great records have been made under all sorts of conditions—from the most primitive to the most luxurious—in all styles of rock, and using all sorts of techniques. I have chosen examples that illustrate clearly the principles and topics covered, but they are in no way exclusive. Sometimes an example is suggested by the testimony of a recordist, sometimes it is simply one that comes to mind. But for any given issue, there are at least hundreds, often thousands of other examples, and readers are invited to substitute their own favorites.

"Poetics" is a word with several meanings, which is appropriate in the context of the present study. "Poetics" may refer to poetic production or to a treatise on aesthetics. Its association with "poet" and "poetry" suggests also poetic feeling, intuition, and imagination. In connection with musical composition, "poetics" turns up in German music treatises beginning in the late sixteenth century. The designation *musica poetica*, representing written musical works, was added to what had previously been a two-part scheme—*musica theorica* (abstract theory) and *musica practica* (musical activity). As Edward Lippman has pointed out, the notion of *musica poetica* augmented the conception of musical composition—represented in earlier treatises mostly by the craft of counterpoint—with a concern for rhetoric and aesthetics.[3] The term "poetics," then, came to include both compositional principles and aesthetic beliefs, as, for example, in Bernard Germain Lacépède's opera treatise, *La poétique de la musique* (1785).

In the series of six lectures that he gave at Harvard University in 1939–1940, Igor Stravinsky spoke about composition only in a general way, avoiding technical specifics. Nevertheless, the views he expressed on various musical topics reflected the aesthetic beliefs he had formed through his experience as a composer. Thus he called the series *Poétique musicale sous forme de six leçons*, published later as *Poetics of Music in the Form of Six Lessons*. In his introductory talk he explained his choice of title:

> And it is no secret to any of you that the exact meaning of poetics is the study of work to be done. The verb *poiein* from which the word is derived means nothing else but *to do* or *make*. . . . The poetics of music is exactly what I am going to talk to you about; that is to say, I shall talk about *making* in the field of music.[4]

The Poetics of Rock, too, is "about making in the field of music." It is an exploration of musical composition in the recording studio—cutting tracks, making records. The title's resonance with aesthetics is fitting, for the aesthetic stances of those involved in the record-making process are inseparable from the compositional choices that they make.

In calling this a study of the poetics of *rock*, I am to a certain extent flirting with vagueness. For as a marker of stylistic distinction, "rock" threatens to become a meaningless designation. The stylistic diversity that has long been a hallmark of the idiom has burgeoned exponentially in the past twenty years, and increasingly we have monographs devoted to a particular rock style, genre, scene, or historical period. There are books on doo wop, heavy metal, garage rock of the sixties, funk, rap, punk, techno, Motown, Stax, the electric guitar, girl groups—to say nothing of biographies, oral histories, and specialized essays of criticism and analysis devoted to a band, an album, or a single track. My account, on the other hand, moves freely among historical periods, styles, and artists, roaming back and forth from 1950s rockabilly to 1990s hip-hop. In taking such a wide-ranging and somewhat generalized approach, however, I hope not to minimize the richness of the differences among rock styles, but rather, to call attention to the pervasiveness of compositional consciousness in the recording processes that they all share. Just as we refer to both Earl Hines and Cecil Taylor as jazz pianists—sharing, as improvisers, a similar basic approach to musical creativity though with very different-sounding results—so are Buddy Holly, Sly Stone, Prince, and Trent Reznor all rock musicians, for they, too, share a common attitude toward musical creativity. For all these musicians, records are not simply carriers of their songs and performances but artworks in themselves whose crafting requires a particular sort of consciousness. For them, stepping into a recording studio means entering a world where the challenge is not simply to play music well, but to use musical performance as a vehicle for the creation of an aesthetic object. And this attitude is shared by recordists of all sorts: Sam Phillips, Phil Spector, Chuck Berry, Brian Wilson, Jimi Hendrix, the Beatles, Stevie Wonder, Marvin Gaye, the Sex Pistols, Abba, Daniel Lanois, Frank Zappa, George Clinton, Kate Bush, Tony Visconti, Led Zeppelin, Chic, George Martin, Bruce Springsteen, Janet Jackson, Rick Rubin, Björk, Soundgarden, Massive Attack, Sheryl Crow, Babyface, Pink Floyd, Public Enemy, Beck, Dr. Dre, Brian Eno, Lou Reed, Bruce Swedien, and Lauryn Hill—an admittedly arbitrary and tiny list. Whatever the stylistic differences that account for the conventional distinctions among genres and historical periods, artists in all categories share a preoccupation with record making.

Even after a hundred years of recording, records remain mysterious to most people who listen to them. They hold a fundamental place in the dynamics of modern musical life, but what do they represent? Indeed, what are they? Are they documents? Snapshots? Artworks? Fetishes? Commodities? Conveniences? They are, of course, whatever we make them to be, and one's answer is always bound up with one's own beliefs. My aim has been to approach the question from the recordists' perspective, to gain from their insights into the aesthetic and practical facets of the process a fuller appreciation of rock records and the artistry of those who make them.

1

Writing Records

> Here is a new art. For a few decades it seemed like nothing
> more than a new technical device . . . a new way of pre-
> serving and retailing . . . performances. But today its
> development has already belied this assumption. . . .
> [I]t exhibits—quite beyond any doubt, I think—not only
> a new technique, but a new poetic mode.
>
> Susanne Langer

In a series of scenes from Michael Radford's film, *Il Postino*, the post-man Mario Ruopollo gathers aural images of his island home with a recording machine left behind by the poet Pablo Neruda. "Small waves. . . . Big waves. . . . The wind on the cliffs," he says to the microphone, pointing it at waves and cliffs in turn and smiling in wonder. As he takes hold of the power to record selectively the sounds that make up his world, Mario is overcome with excitement. Wherever he points the microphone, it seems not only to capture sound but to register his feelings about the world he perceives. Finally, he points the microphone at the night sky. "Starry sky over the island," he says. He has become intoxicated with the magic of this machine and in the process has forgotten that it can record only sound. To Mario, the machine seems capable of capturing and replaying anything that engages his emotions or leaves a trace on his imagination. In these scenes, Radford portrays the interface between human consciousness and mechanical recording as one of poetic col-laboration. The magical machine inscribes an image of whatever sound is set before it, but the choice of image is a matter of human agency; the talking machine can repeat only what it has been given to hear. Thus, as it performs its mechanical task it makes a record not only of sound but of the recordist's intention.

Mario's childlike wonder is understandable, as is his sense of empowerment. Sound recording *is* a kind of magic, conferring on the recordist the power to capture temporal phenomena, to make permanent what is by nature fleeting. To a great extent, this power and the disembodied aural images that it produces remain as mysterious to us now as they were to Nipper, the bull terrier in Francis Barraud's painting that became the ubiquitous symbol of recorded sound as the trademark for the Gramophone Company Ltd., and later, RCA Victor. Barraud represents the new technology with an image of puzzlement, the dog in a suspended state of wonder at the sound of "his master's voice" (the painting's actual title) emanating from the phonograph's horn. The mystery, however, lies not so much in the technological feat of recording, but rather in the art that has been its unimagined consequence. Although invented to record the spoken word, sound recording's greatest cultural impact has been through music; and music itself has changed as its production and reception processes have become permeated by technology.

Like musical notation before it, sound recording has had a profound influence on the way music is made, heard, and thought about. With the ability to transform the ephemeral act of musical performance into a work of art, it has altered the conceptual landscape of our musical culture in many ways, and its influence has made itself felt in all musical idioms. Jazz improvisations, once recorded, are treated like fixed musical works—collected, studied, learned, played over and over again. While spontaneous performance is central to the idiom, preservation of performances on records has been essential to its influence, its pedagogy, and the development of its historiography. In the realm of Western concert music, already a "museum of musical works," performers are able to make their interpretations part of the permanent record of a work's history.[1] Their recorded performances are as much a part of the historical archive as the musical texts that they represent. When we want to buy a recording of Mahler's Ninth Symphony, it is not simply Mahler's music that we shop for, but Bruno Walter's interpretation of it, or Otto Klemperer's, or Bernard Haitink's. For that matter, we often have a choice of interpretations by a single performer, each of which is shaped in various ways by its own particular set of circumstances, which are themselves part of the record. Will it be Walter's 1961 recording with the Columbia Symphony Orchestra—which gives us the benefit of Walter's long-standing association with the piece and with Mahler himself, presented here in relatively modern high fidelity—or his 1938 performance with the Vienna Philharmonic, a recording of lesser quality in terms of sound, but whose historical significance is forever etched into its grooves?[2] Either way, it is the record buyer's choice to make, a choice that itself represents a shift in the musical landscape.

For musics that had been confined historically to a particular region or audience, recordings and the radio stations that played them provided a conduit into the cultural mainstream. If down-home blues, for instance, was originally a music of black people in the rural South, its exposure in the form of recordings eventually brought it to the attention of a wider audience. The records crossed geographical distances and lines of social demarcation that individual performers could not, and as a consequence the blues influence, both overt and subtle, turns up in all kinds of places throughout the musical culture of the United States. Blues is perhaps the single most influential musical idiom in twentieth-century American music, and it's hard to imagine that this would have been possible were it not for records.[3]

The recurring themes of possibility and opportunity reflected in these examples, however, are only part of the story. Woven throughout the history of sound recording is an ideological conflict that has resulted in varying degrees of ambivalence toward the machine's presence in our midst. The technology of sound capture and manipulation has confronted traditional notions of music making with a new kind of musical ontology. While this has meant new possibilities for musical expression and reception, the realization of these possibilities has been a very gradual process over the course of the twentieth century. For if, in an ideal sense, sound recording opened up to music an unprecedented world of exploration, technical limitations and ideological resistance meant that the course of exploration would be slow and that the consequences would take some time to emerge.

FUSION

"We only begin to really hear *about* sound as a cultural entity," writes Douglas Kahn, "with the introduction of Cros' paleophone and Edison's phonograph right into the midst of ascendant modernist and avant-garde culture. The timing of the two was perhaps no coincidence, for here was a machined fusion of orality and literacy . . . the totalizing cornu/copia of all and every sound."[4] The phrase "fusion of orality and literacy" is as good a formulation of sound recording's impact as there is, I think. The ramifications of such a fusion, both conceptual and practical, spread out in all directions like the shock waves from an explosion, for each of these terms—"oral," "literate"—stands for heretofore distinct modes of human experience. They are often viewed as opposing dualisms, which include such basic distinctions as body/mind, process/structure, improvisation/composition, performance/work. It is often noted as well that exaggerating or oversimplifying the differences between the elements of these pairings can be misleading, falsely obscuring the ways in which they may overlap and interact. But while such contrasting types of experience are in no way mutually exclusive, they do represent different kinds of attitudes. Thus, the fusion of orality and literacy occasioned by the catalytic medium of sound recording provided the potential for a kind of artistic expression and response encompassing a wide range of cultural ideas, beliefs, and practices. Though the shock waves from this fusion would emanate in slow motion over the years of the twentieth century, its eventual consequences for culture would be profound.

In his essay Kahn outlines some of the ways in which recording technology, from its inception, fed a curiosity about sound and a desire to use it as artistic material. If at first technological capability—the ability to "phonograph sounds," as Edison put it—lagged behind conceptual implications, it nevertheless fired many artistic imaginations among avant-garde artists, most of whom were not musicians. Before turning to film, for example, the Russian director Dziga Vertov attempted to "transcend the limits of ordinary music" by making aural artworks using any and all sounds in the "audible world."[5] In the late 1920s, the "great adventurer of modern art," Laszlo Moholy-Nagy complained that "[c]ontemporary 'musicians' [had] so far not even attempted to develop the potential resources of the gramophone record, not to mention the wireless,"[6] and he urged the development of an "acoustic alphabet of sound writing"—whereby "visual signs can be translated into acoustic phenomena"—to create film sound tracks "without reproducing any existing music."[7] In an experiment that he called *The Sound of ABC*, he employed a technique of direct inscription similar to the one others had used on wax discs, scratching images and letters on the sound track of optical sound film that produced sounds with "the character of whistling and other noises."[8]

Indeed, most musicians were not so adventurous. Among composers, Igor Stravinsky was happy to have signed a contract with "the great Columbia Gramophone Company," but he regarded his recordings simply as "documents." Their "most important object" was "safeguarding [the] work by establishing the manner in which it ought to be played." For all their "instructional value," Stravinsky cautioned that the "indisputable advantages" of recordings were "attended by serious danger," which included "the musical deception arising from the substitution for the actual playing of a reproduction," which was "the same difference as that between the *ersatz* and the authentic."[9] Composers had for centuries relied upon the encryption of musical ideas in symbolic notation to fashion and preserve their works. And while musical ideas could now be embodied as concrete aural images, most composers of concert music continued to use musical notation exclusively. For they belonged to a tradition of written musical expression that had developed in such a way that musical relationships and ideas could be represented in great detail through writing alone. The notational system was of such refinement that scores could serve both as practical blueprints and as texts that contained and transmitted all that was thought to be musically essential. Throughout the nineteenth century, composers included more and more of the details of their musical thought in the scores that they wrote, and by the early twentieth century the written score had attained an unprecedented degree of specificity and authority. Like Stravinsky, Béla Bartók considered sound recording's principal value to be "pedagogic," offering "the possibility for composers to pass on to the world their compositions not only as musical scores but in the form of their personal appearance or in a presentation which conforms to their ideas."[10] In other respects, the record was merely a "surrogate." It had "the same relation to the original music out of which it was made as canned fruit to fresh fruit; one does not contain vitamins, the other does."[11]

On the other hand, there were some composers who viewed the confluence of music and technology as inevitable, and as potentially good. In his essay of 1926, "Radio and the Restructuring of Musical Life," Kurt Weill envisioned a "special type of radio art" that would ultimately "go far beyond a more or less perfect 'reproduction' of earlier artistic achievements."[12] Weill argued that rather than simply offering reproductions of live concerts, radio had the potential to become an altogether new part of musical life, which would involve new ways of composing and performing. "A special technique of singing and playing for radio purposes will develop," he predicted, "and sooner or later we will begin to find special instrumentations and new orchestral combinations suited to the acoustic requirements of the broadcast studio."[13]

Similarly, Carlos Chavez reckoned that "the electric apparatus of sound production will facilitate the constant and inevitable development of music."[14] Surveying the state of music technologies in the 1930s, Chavez saw a vast field of opportunity. "The effect was that of sound extraordinarily well outlined, balanced, and accentuated," he enthused about the famous 1933 broadcast performance from the Academy of Music in Philadelphia to loudspeakers before an audience seated in Constitution Hall in Washington, D. C. Chavez recognized that with technological mediation "classical music conceived within the limits of direct human performance . . . undergoes a manifest alteration, if compared with the composer's original conceptions," and that, for many, this was a source of objection. But for him, the debate over whether such treatment was "traditionally 'proper'" was of far less consequence than what it implied: "What is needed is the new music conceived in terms of these new resources."[15] Such music would soon emerge, but in the world of concert music, it would take the form of Pierre Schaeffer's *musique concrète*, and then electronic and computer music. The tradition of musical performance would carry on much as it always had.

Rather than as a fusion of orality and literacy, most performance traditions—from Italian opera to American country music—saw recording simply as a way of capturing and preserving what already existed. A fusion would have meant that the machinery had to engage actively in the music-making process, rather than simply record what was set before it, and there was no basis for that in any performance tradition. Musicians of all sorts worked for years to develop their skills in order to seize the performative moment with the power of their musical expression. Using machinery to tamper with the performance was looked upon as dishonest trickery, rendering the performance inauthentic or worse. Altering the sound quality of musical performances—adding a layer of technological

patination—could be forgiven on the grounds of technological prim-
itivism. But allowing the machine to invade the integrity of the musical moment was unacceptable.

Jazz clarinetist Mezz Mezzrow, for example, characterized Sidney
Bechet's 1941 one-man-band recording of "The Sheik of Araby" and
"Blues of Bechet"—on which Bechet played soprano and tenor saxophones, clarinet, piano, bass, and drums—as an "engineering
stunt." Although he praised the high quality of Bechet's playing,
the nature of the project represented for Mezzrow the "neurotic and
bestial" product of a ruthless individualism, a sad lack of communal
interaction, "the final and most eloquent comment on the level to
which our jazz had sunk."[16] Another jazz musician, Lennie Tristano,
having used and been criticized for overdubbing and tape speed
manipulation on his 1955 album, *Lennie Tristano*, felt the need to
reassure fans and critics with the following notice on the album
cover of *The New Tristano* (1962): "Lennie Tristano is heard on this LP
in unaccompanied piano solos. No use is made of multi-tracking,
overdubbing, or tape-speeding on any selection." In jazz, the integrity of the musical moment is a central tenet of the music, and
musicians' creative energy and technical discipline, both individually and collectively, is aimed at making the most of that moment as
it is happening. Altering it after the fact challenges the traditional
ideology of authenticity in jazz. While records were extremely
important in the development of the jazz tradition, the art of jazz
recording up until the emergence of jazz-rock fusion was focused on
the quality of the sonic presentation and on capturing a good—and
complete—take.

In classical music we find a somewhat broader range of stances as
to acceptable recording practices and authenticity, but the general
aim was still a more or less transparent documentary representation.
The difficulties of recording forced musicians to perform differently
in recording sessions than in the concert hall, but this was largely a
matter of practical contingency. While the effect on performance
practice was real, it was simply a necessary compromise.[17] Leopold
Stokowski stands out as one who grasped early on the potential of
the new technology. When he began to make radio broadcasts with
the Philadelphia Orchestra in 1929, he "noticed in the wings there
was a man sitting at a sort of keyboard with dials"—the sound engineer, whose job it was to control the sound picked up by the micro-

phones. "Then you're paying the wrong man," he insisted when he found out what the stranger sitting at the side of the stage was doing. "He's the conductor and I'm not. I don't want this to be broadcast under my name if I'm not controlling the pianissimo, the mezzo forte, and the fortissimo."[18] Stokowski turned the orchestra over to assistant conductor Alexander Smallens and worked with the production team on microphone placement and balances, resuming his place at the podium only after he was satisfied with the sound. The "extraordinarily well outlined, balanced, and accentuated" sound that so impressed Chavez at the Constitution Hall concert was mixed by Stokowski, who sat at the rear of the balcony in Washington while Smallens conducted the orchestra in Philadelphia. Stokowski went on to make extensive experiments with engineers such as Harvey Fletcher, Arthur Keller, and Joseph P. Maxfield to do with tone color, balance, and even, in 1931, stereo, which he found to be "better in every way than monaural listening."[19] And in an address to a joint meeting of the Institute of Radio Engineers and the Society of Motion Picture Engineers on December 9, 1931, he offered the following prediction:

> Eventually all sounds may come under the classification of music. Methods of writing down sound on paper are tremendously imperfect. I believe the composer of the future will create his harmonies directly in tone by means of electrical-musical instruments which will record his idea exactly.[20]

Another classical musician who was famous for exploiting the resources of the recording studio was Glenn Gould, himself a great admirer of Stokowski.[21] For Gould, the recording and postproduction process offered the opportunity to "transcend the limitations that performance imposes upon the imagination." As an example, he tells the story of his recording of J. S. Bach's Fugue in A Minor from volume 1 of *The Well-Tempered Clavier*. After making several takes of the fugue the tapes were put away, with two takes, numbers 6 and 8, deemed "satisfactory." Some weeks later, at an editing session, "it became apparent that both had a defect . . . : both were monotonous." One take treated the fugue's subject "with Teutonic severity," the other with "unwarranted jubilation," neither of which "could be permitted to represent our best thoughts on this fugue." The decision was made to use parts of both takes, splicing them together to create an interpretation that was never actually played, or even conceived as a performance. Only the possibility of "post-taping afterthought" allowed the production team to arrive at this version.[22]

Today, over a century after recording began, most performers use the editing capabilities of the recording studio at least to make things presentable. After all, recordings can help in building a career—and anyway, who will know? With any luck, the record will be played again and again, and it must be able to withstand prolonged scrutiny on a number of fronts. Still, the technological mediation is to be kept as transparent as possible—as though it never really happened. It seems safe to say that classical recording artists such as Stokowski and Gould remain what they were in their own time, iconoclastic innovators on the periphery of the mainstream, because of their willingness to integrate musical expression and technological means.

One particular group of musicians, unhampered by ideological restraints, found that technology offered them great practical benefits. In the 1920s, breakthroughs in electrical amplification technology, which included the microphone, gave singers of blues, country, jazz, and pop songs the ability to project their vocal stylings as never before. Singers were no longer required to have operatic voices in order to fill a large hall or to be heard above an ensemble. Electrical amplification provided popular singers with a new set of possibilities, and they embraced the microphone both as an aspect of vocal technique and as an expressive tool. The singing style known as crooning—famously exemplified by Bing Crosby—owed its very existence to the microphone, which gave singers the power to dramatize their subtlest vocal inflections. Embracing the microphone as an artistic accomplice, crooners developed a performance style that was inseparable from technology. Over the next several decades American popular music continued to develop performance practices and recording techniques that incorporated technological mediation as an element of musical style. Among the electronic innovations that contributed to this development were the electric guitar, the tape recorder, and the mixing console. Each of these played an important part in the gradual change of attitude toward electrified music, and each would have a central role in shaping defining stylistic features of the musical idiom that would come to be known as rock and roll— a music that, from its inception, embraced technology and wove its influence into the musical fabric. In doing so, rock and roll took advantage of several decades of musical and technological development. One of the central figures in this development was Les Paul, who, though not a rocker himself, was a pioneer of both recording technology and compositional method in the recording studio.

ROCK AND ROLL

The tape recorder saw its most rapid development in Germany in the 1930s. After the war, returning GIs brought these machines home with them, and sound recording in the United States gained a flexibility and convenience far surpassing what disc recorders could offer. Again, although the main motivating force for technological change was the spoken word—in this case, Nazi propaganda—the results were eagerly embraced by those involved with recording music. One of the techniques improved and facilitated by tape recorders was overdubbing, an additive process whereby successive performances are combined or overlaid with one another within the unitary time frame represented by a disc or a piece of magnetic tape, creating the illusion of an ensemble performance. Overdubbing was used from the early 1930s on in film, but the only medium available at the time was the lacquer disc, on which sound quality quickly diminished with successive transfers. Thus the use of overdubbing for recordings of music was rare, a novelty, like the Bechet recordings. For Les Paul, however, overdubbing seemed like a great opportunity to single-handedly build records layer by layer, and he set out to find ways of improving the sound quality and increasing the number of possible overdubs. Although he had no formal training as an engineer, Paul was a tireless and creative experimenter, and working in his garage, he managed eventually to devise equipment modifications and recording techniques that allowed him an unprecedented number of overdubs. Using his own disc-cutting lathe made from a Cadillac flywheel, Paul made records containing many more generations of disc transfers without serious degradation than had previously been thought possible. According to his son, Gene, he accomplished this by recording the least important parts of the arrangement first and by minimizing his use of microphones, using them only toward the end of the layering process. Plugging his electric guitar directly into the recording console eliminated the accumulation of successive layers of room and microphone noise, while saving the most important musical elements for last meant that they would retain the greatest clarity.[23] His breakthrough hit came in 1947: a recording of Rodgers and Hart's "Lover" arranged for eight guitars, all of which he played himself.

Paul acquired a tape recorder in 1948—a gift from Bing Crosby, who in 1947 at Paul's urging had begun taping his weekly radio show (and whose Crosby Enterprises had subsequently become the worldwide distributor of Ampex tape recorders). Paul immediately saw in the recorder an opportunity to record even more overdubs with greater fidelity. This was, however, a difficult proposition. The machine had only one track, and each new recording pass had to be laid over the existing material—rather than simply combining the two, as in the disc method—so that a mistake meant starting the whole process over from the beginning. Paul and his wife and partner, Mary Ford, rose to the challenge—"It made us real pros," he boasted later—and in 1950 they made a recording that contained twelve overdubs.[24] The recording was an intricate arrangement of "How High the Moon," with all parts recorded by Paul and Ford. They followed the same reverse order they had become accustomed to, Ford singing her least important harmony parts first and saving the lead for last. Released on March 26, 1951, it reached the number one spot on *The Hit Parade* in less than a month.

Bruce Swedien, a recording engineer and record producer who has worked for almost half a century with recording artists ranging from Fritz Reiner's Chicago Symphony to Michael Jackson, points to "How High the Moon" as the "one record [that] changed pop music forever. . . . There wasn't a shred of reality in it—and it was wonderful."[25] For Swedien, the record "broke through like a shining light," and it dawned on him that "it was no longer necessary to present popular music in concertlike form."[26] Now a record could take its own form, which would develop in the course of the recording process. In Paul's efforts we see and hear the beginnings of the oral/literate fusion in the field of conventional music making. Indeed, Paul did not use any musical notation for his elaborate arrangements. He relied instead on oral modes of music making—a combination of memory and improvisation—to create a unique work represented by inscriptions in the iron oxide particles of the magnetic tape. As recording moved away from the "reality" of "concertlike form," the process and its end result became very different from what they had been. The process became one of deliberate composition, and its product, an original musical work.

From our vantage point it is easy to appreciate both the technical and the conceptual importance of Paul's innovations for rock recording. In time, they would constitute its normative procedure. But at first his work had little direct impact on rock and roll, an emerging idiom that was drawing from sources far from the centers of cosmopolitan pop, New York and Los Angeles. Though the style in which he and Ford worked was still popular with an older audience, teenagers now had a music of their own and money to spend, and differences of musical style became celebrated in part as markers of generational difference. For his part, Paul, like many other established popular artists, seems to have neither liked nor understood the new music, which he considered inept at best. On the other hand, most musicians and producers associated with what came to be called rock and roll had little interest in constructing recordings systematically. Rock and roll emerged as an eclectic, unruly mixture of various musical styles and idioms—blues, R&B, gospel, country, jazz. And in all of these, records were conceived not as works but as snapshots of live performances.

Even if rock and roll had its roots in live performance traditions, it was nevertheless, and unlike any of its precursors, first and foremost a recorded music. Its rapid rise in popularity was a result not of live performances but of mass radio exposure, which was fed by records—primarily the new and affordable 45-rpm singles that were the staple of teenagers' record collections. Because of their affordable price, their accessibility, and the sheer numbers of customers, rock singles had a commercial potential that was unprecedented in the music business. A hit single, one song, could turn an unknown musician into a celebrity almost overnight even if, like Elvis Presley, he or she had had little or no experience or exposure as a live performer. Records were the life blood of the music, spinning over the air on the radio and showing up in stores and on juke boxes from coast to coast, and their power to generate fame and wealth held an irresistible attraction for musicians and businessmen alike.

Many writers have pointed to this emphasis on records as a key element in the constellation of rock's distinguishing features. As early as 1969, in one of the first historical accounts of rock, Carl Belz made the "fundamental assumption . . . that rock has existed primarily on records.... Records were the music's initial medium."[27] While Belz acknowledged that rock was not the first musical idiom to "*use* records and radio, it was the first to express itself *primarily* through these ... media [emphasis in original]." Moreover, with rock, "records became the primary, common bond among artists and listeners."[28] Assuming this to be self-evident, Charlie Gillett's *The Sound of the City: The Rise of Rock and Roll*, which was first published in 1970, goes about telling the story almost entirely in terms of records, weaving together the workings of art and commerce as strands in a single multidimensional cultural process.[29] Writing in the 1980s, Peter Wicke argued, again, that rock "was the first form of music to be distributed in mass quantities on record"; that it "found its basic conditions of existence" in records and in the mass media of "radio, television, and film"; and that it "accepted this fact without compromise as a prerequisite for artistic creativity."[30] The case has been made most recently, and most comprehensively, by Theodore Gracyk, who writes that rock "is essentially dependent on recording technology for its inception and dissemination."[31] For no matter how much or how little electronic mediation is involved in the recording process, it is through records that "artists *announce* and *stipulate* new works."[32]

With the performer's actual presence becoming secondary—at least chronologically—to his or her disembodied sonic presence emanating from loudspeakers, recordings began to take on a different sort of identity. The "artistic creativity" that Wicke refers to went into the creation of a recorded voice. With this change of attitude, recording moved almost inevitably from a process of collecting, preserving, and disseminating to one of making. The aesthetic criterion shifted from the sound of the actual performance to the sound of the recording. When Sam Phillips wanted to audition Elvis Presley, he did not simply want to hear him sing. He left that to guitarist Scottie Moore. It was only after Moore had determined that Presley had "good timing" and "a good voice"[33] that Phillips invited Elvis to his studio to "see what he sound[ed] like coming back off of tape."[34] Presley's recorded voice was to be the central character in a dramatic production, and what concerned Phillips was the transmutation of the young singer's physical presence into an electronic persona.

While the verb "to record" can have a passive sense to it, meaning something like "to register," "to archive," or "to document"—all implying the preservation of something that already exists—rock and roll records do not simply capture and make portable an image of a performance. Presenting a transparent representation of some natural acoustic reality was never the point. Records were meant to be distinctive worlds of musical sound with the power to make their way into the consciousness of a mass audience, and the record-making process was a matter of building those worlds. Still, the aesthetic terms inherited from its precursors—especially the expressive spontaneity of unedited performances—stood as guiding principles. In the sessions that he ran at his own Memphis Recording Service, Sam Phillips was quite conscious of *making* records. He was willing to use electronic distortion and artificial echo to create distinctive sounds, and he was willing to control the relative levels among the musical parts at his mixing console, but he didn't use the kind of layered construction process that Les Paul did. Rather, he aimed to create a unique sonic setting for a real-time performance that was in itself somehow extraordinary. Recordists in general strive to "bottle lightning," as Quincy Jones puts it, to capture the energy released in the recording process and to use it to imbue the record with a life of its own.[35] In early rock, although the focus was on making records, it was the tradition of live performing that served as the model for producing the "lightning" required to cut the grooves.

Les Paul's success with overdubbing led eventually to the development of multitrack tape machines and recording techniques. In 1954, pleased with the results of his and Ford's efforts but not with the cumbersome recording process, Paul became involved in the development of a machine that would record eight separate parallel tracks on a single piece of tape. He commissioned Ampex—whose engineers had already come up with seven-track flight data recorders for airplanes—to build it, and by 1957 he had the first fully operational Ampex Model 300–8 in his Mahwah, New Jersey, home. One of the chief obstacles the Ampex engineers had to overcome was the time delay between recording and playback that resulted from the gap between the machine's record and playback heads. The delay made synchronized recording with a previously recorded track impossible. They solved the problem by devising a method whereby a single head could provide both record and playback functions simultaneously. With this machine, which Paul dubbed "the Octopus," recording gained an unprecedented degree of control over individual elements.

Overdubbing no longer involved real-time mixing with preexisting material; rather, each overdub could be stored separately on its own track and the accumulated tracks mixed together at some later time, when decisions could be reconsidered and further sound processing and balance refinements could take place.

Thus the technology of 1957 already allowed for twice the number of tracks used to create the Beatles' *Sgt. Pepper's Lonely Hearts Club Band* a decade later. *Sgt. Pepper's* is considered a watershed in rock recording in part because of its elaborate multitrack composition.[36] After the mid-sixties, the demand grew for recorders and tape formulations with more and more tracks. Four became eight, became twelve, then sixteen, twenty-four, and so on. But during the first decade of its existence, the possibilities of multitrack recording remained mostly unexplored. Resistance to the new technology ranged from musicians' fears of being put out of work to the machine's $11,000 price tag and added tape noise. But most importantly, there seems to have been a general consensus that the kind of piecemeal recording that Paul and Ford had mastered would diminish the vitality of music making. The only record label to acquire and use the machine extensively in the 1950s as a tool for enhancing record production was the fledgling Atlantic Records, where chief engineer Tom Dowd became one of the first to master the new machine. But the enhancements were in the realm of balance control and sonic clarity, rather than compositional method. Separate tracks were dedicated to each instrumental section and overdubbing was available as a production convenience; but the focus at Atlantic, as at all other labels, remained on capturing the dynamic energy of complete performances. "It all had to do with capturing the spontaneity of the moment," recalled songwriter and producer Mike Leiber, for in this there "was an interaction that was irreplaceable."[37]

Rock recordists' initial indifference to the eight-track machine is instructive, for it tells us something about their sense of what the artistic project was all about. Although sound recording was used as a creative medium and performances were treated to various kinds of sonic manipulations that altered the sense of literal representation, the musical energy released in the "spontaneity of the moment" was at the heart of things.[38] To put it another way, while the rock and roll records of the 1950s were not simply documentary snapshots, neither were they analytic constructs on a par with "How High the

Moon." While multitrack recording would eventually be valued as a boon to the artistic process, at first it seemed like a violation of the expressive line. Also, the sensibilities of rock and roll recordists were influenced by the practices that they knew from the various musics they had grown up with and their previous experiences with recording. Bruce Swedien recorded the Chicago Symphony. Sam Phillips recorded early sides by Howlin' Wolf and B. B. King. The Chess brothers in Chicago and the Erteguns in New York recorded R&B and jazz. In none of these musics was there a precedent for putting the recorded artifact before the live performance. But rock and roll was a nascent thing, and the spirit of exploration was in the air. "Every time engineers went into the studio, we were feeling our way, trying to find out what rock and roll was,"[39] recalls Stan Ross, the owner of Gold Star Sound Studios in Hollywood, which was to be the home of Phil Spector's "wall of sound." Thus, even while early rock shared some of the same ideological tensions as other musical idioms about the intrusion of technology into the musical moment, focusing on records made for a greater willingness to experiment with the medium and the process.

Over time, as it became clear to many that multitracking in itself need not diminish the passion of musical performance, recording practices became increasingly elaborate. In fact, the more performers focused on making records, the more aware they became that their performance had to be extraordinary, for the traces that they left on the tape would forever be the persona of the record. The development of the methodical multitrack techniques pioneered by Les Paul, however, represented an increase in the analytic detail of the compositional process rather than a conceptual shift. For although the aesthetic of live musical interaction so prevalent in early rock and roll recording had little place for piecemeal overdubbing, the practice of combining multiple sonic images into a single composite was always part of the recording process. If recordings from the fifties and early sixties are rarely multitrack, almost all are multi-*channel*. The multi-channel mixing console provided several discrete inputs, which could be fed by different sound sources, including separate microphones, added ambience, and tape echo effects. These were combined at the console using its controls. Although the performance was live, the relationships that defined the configuration of the recording were controlled electronically at the console.

The electronic shaping of the performance ensemble's sound represents the other half of the record-making process—what George Martin calls "building musical images."[40] While musicians leave the traces of their emotions, experiences, and the sounds of their musical expression on tape, the composite sound image that we recognize as the musical work is fashioned by recording engineers and producers—"performers" in their own right. They are the musicians' artistic collaborators, and their actions and aesthetic choices, too, are represented in the form of the finished work. Microphones are chosen and placed, balances are set, frequency content is shaped, performances are coached, coaxed, coerced—these are a few of the many techniques used to fashion the sound world of the recording. As such, these techniques generate musical content and are thus elements of compositional craft with their own language and rhetorical practices. Using both technical skill and aesthetic sense, engineers and producers participate in forging the connections that draw together a recording's three principal elements: musical parts (song and arrangement), performances, and sounds. The relationships represented by these connections—which are essential elements of identity and musical style—are explored in some detail in succeeding chapters. But first, a little more needs to be said about what records represent.

AUTHENTICITY

Walter Benjamin's 1936 essay "The Work of Art in the Age of Mechanical Reproduction"[41] is often cited by scholars who work with recorded music, even though Benjamin had almost nothing to say about sound recording. He simply included it as an analogue to the visual media with which his argument is mostly concerned. But the essay remains a valuable source for its critical engagement at a particular historical moment with certain general aesthetic issues raised by the interface of the technologies of reproduction with art making and reception. One of the ideas that Benjamin put forward was that in their high degree of technological sophistication the mechanically reproducible arts of photography, sound recording, and, above all, film had "transformed the entire nature of art." Speaking to long-standing debates about the artistic validity of these media, he insisted that the question they raise is not *whether* but *how* they manifest artistic impulses and functions, and he began his answer with a sketch of traditional notions of an artwork's authenticity, which he defined as follows: "The authenticity of a thing is the essence of all that is transmissible from its beginning, ranging from its substantive duration to its testimony to the history which it has experienced." The authority of such testimony relies on the artwork's "presence in time and space, its unique existence at the place where it happens to be." Benjamin called this unique presence the work's "aura," and argued that only the original work could claim it: "there can be no replica of it." For the arts that were "founded in" and "designed for reproducibility," however, such a concept of authenticity had little meaning. Because "mechanical reproduction is inherent in the very technique of film production . . . it not only permits in the most direct way but virtually causes mass distribution." As a result, Benjamin argued, what he calls the "cult value" of artworks gave way to their "exhibition value." The ritualistic function that artworks had performed, and which required a unique presence, yielded to "public presentability," for which refinements in reproduction techniques made them increasingly fit. Thus, "that which withers in the age of mechanical reproduction is the aura of the work of art." On the positive side, "for the first time in world history, mechanical reproduction emancipates the work of art from parasitical dependence on ritual."

Benjamin insists that aura is dependent on the direct perception of some unique physical presence. It could be "a mountain range on the horizon or a branch which casts its shadow over you." In the case of art, the presence is that of an original work or agent. The "shriveling of the aura," therefore, is an inevitable consequence of film, where the actor is never physically present before the audience. The actor performs "not for the audience but for a mechanical contrivance," and "the audience's identification with the actor is really an identification with the camera." With film, "man can represent his environment" in new ways. Like Freudian psychoanalysis, with which Benjamin compares it, "film has enriched our field of perception" by placing the unconsciously observed detail into "a space consciously explored by man." But while he recognizes that the new methods of art production lead to new modes of perception, Benjamin never allows the film an aura of its own. It remains, as Richard Middleton puts it, an "analytic critique of reality,"[42] a representation of an original presence.

In the end, Benjamin, like so many others in his time and after, is both fascinated by and ambivalent toward the new media. He is enthusiastic about technology's potential to move art away from the nineteenth-century "theology" of *l'art pour l'art* and to replace its ritual function with a political one, to bring about for "the masses" a "direct, intimate fusion of visual and emotional enjoyment with the orientation of the expert." Yet he seems to regret what he views as the passing of the traditionally authentic, what everyman might call "the genuine article." Initially, he articulates the problem of the film actor using the words of Luigi Pirandello, who writes in his novel *Si Gira* that the actor "feels as if in exile—exiled not only from the stage but also from himself."[43] Benjamin himself, however, is in full agreement that in film "the aura that envelops the actor vanishes, and with it the aura of the figure he portrays."

Records, too, have produced this sort of ambivalence—and because of conventional ideas about musical performance, probably to a greater degree than film. After all, film has a much longer history of critical discourse, which stretches back practically to its beginning; by comparison, speculation about records as artworks in themselves has been taken up only recently. However, as rock recording developed, it rapidly dispelled such ambivalence, and a new kind of poetic process emerged. While Benjamin's basic terms are useful in thinking about rock records, in order to understand what records are and how they come to be, the argument needs to be rearranged. The notions of presence, aura, and authenticity must be transferred, as with film, to the work itself. For records and films represent not a shriveling of aura, but rather, a transferal of aura. And it is this transferal that is at the heart of the poetic process in the technologically mediated arts. The "audience's identification" is not with the camera—which "is the mind's eye and nothing more," as Susanne Langer puts it—but with the film itself.[44] If the aura of the performer is missing, the aura of the work—whose making has involved a transferal and translation of the performer's aura in the context of an articulated composition—is quite apparent. In this case, authenticity does not rely on the presence of a unique instance but on a unique arrangement of elements. All instances of the work are equally original as far as the audience—from the amateur to the connoisseur—is concerned. The permeation of the artistic process by machinery creates a new set of terms that affect both artists and audience—both production and reception. The presence of the artwork "designed for reproducibility" is experienced by perhaps millions of people around the world, and the work's aura lies not in a unique physical existence but in the space it makes for itself in the collective consciousness of cultural discourse and the witness that it bears to all that went into its making. For therein lies its transmissible "testimony to the history which it has experienced."

What I am calling "transferal of aura" is often referred to by recordists simply as "magic." The word comes up again and again in interviews, and it seems a fitting one for the life-giving process it describes. For records represent more than the expression of their creators' talent, ideas, emotions, and influences; they also capture physical presence and action. The performative acts of all those involved in the record-making process form the substance of the work, the sinews of its being. While the process has its mundane, even tedious, aspects, at some point in the making of a successful record there is a magical transferal of aura from artists to artifact. Recalls Jerry Leiber of his 1950s recording sessions at Atlantic Records:

> We would rehearse for three weeks before a session, eight hours a day. Every lick was planned. The only thing we would leave to chance on the session was the feel, and the tempo. . . . So we knew pretty much what to expect. The only thing we were looking for was that magic, that thing that comes together when everything is cooking.[45]

Similarly, Quincy Jones speaks of "waiting for those special moments, trying to produce magic from a chemistry between people."[46] It is from this "chemistry," the "thing that comes together when everything is cooking," that records are made. The dynamics of this chemical process produce, in turn, a transmutation: the record takes on a life. It becomes infused with energy imparted from the interactions of human personalities, embodied now in the form of an artifact with powers of its own. Acknowledging the mystical aspect of such a transferal, Jones sums up: "There's also a saying we have in the studio that goes: you have to leave space, after you've done your homework, to let the Lord walk through the room."[47]

The work of many early rock recordists shows signs of doing with music what film had done decades before with narrative drama, namely, transforming the nature of authenticity as it traditionally had been conceived. "We didn't write songs, we wrote records," claimed Jerry Leiber and Mike Stoller.[48] Of course, Leiber and Stoller did write songs, but more importantly in their own minds, they produced the records for which the songs were only starting points. For them, as for many others, the sound of the recording represented the ultimate form of the artwork, and their compositional intention was to have a hand in shaping the sonic relationships that made up its identity. The character of their production practices and their intention to make, rather than simply to record, records forces us to think about their work in its totality. For their records are not reproductions of anything; they are "realities in themselves."[49]

AUTOGRAPHY

In his monograph on rock aesthetics, Theodore Gracyk makes the claim that rock records are "autographic musical works," and that "such works are the standard end-products and signifiers in rock music, and have been as far back as Elvis Presley's Sun sessions."[50] This portion of Gracyk's argument speaks to the issue of ontology, discussions of which have been more common among philosophers (of which he is one) than musicians or musicologists. But in addition to their philosophical significance such musings also have practical implications, for in contemplating the nature of an artwork's identity we are forced to deal also with the nature of its medium and the workings of the interface between medium and artistic practice. This is Gracyk's aim. He borrows the category "autographic" from Nelson Goodman, who in his book *Languages of Art* develops his own ideas about the nature of authenticity in the arts. Drawing a distinction between what can and cannot be forged, Goodman posits two general categories of media: those that are autographic, and those that are allographic. Painting is an example of an autographic art because "even the most exact duplication of it does not thereby count as genuine." A painting that is "genuine" is one that exhibits the actual marks that the artist made. Music represented in a score, on the other hand, is, like a book, allographic, for "all accurate copies . . . are equally genuine instances" of the work.[51] That is, particularity of inscription is not an attribute of an allographic work's identity. "Art," adds Goodman, "seems to be allographic just insofar as it is amenable to notation."[52] Thus, autographic works are those that carry with them the physical traces of their making, while allographic works are represented by a set of relationships—stipulated through some form of notation—from which the authentic work can be recovered any number of times. Musical performances of a scripted piece are equally authentic so long as they "comply" with the score. In terms of musical sound, then, the autographic is actual, the allographic is virtual.

Gracyk goes to some trouble to prove that records are autographic. Using Goodman's criterion of forgeability, he sets up a "thought experiment" to show that a record, like a painting, could in theory be forged. The exercise takes us into the realm of philosophical abstraction, which is some distance from the practice of record making. Yet the goal of the experiment is to prove precisely what I have been getting at here, namely, that "precise details of timbre and articulation can be essential properties of a musical work."[53] What is interesting about Gracyk's dialogue with Goodman in a book on rock is, again, what it says about rock composition, this time from the side of aesthetics. An autographic artwork is by nature a fusion of idea and action. The medium registers both. While Gracyk acknowledges that the particulars of Goodman's argument have been challenged many times over the years, he also notes that "there is little challenge to the position that music is always allographic."[54] For music to be *autographic*—for every single detail of its sound to be a fixed element of its identity—requires both recording machinery and an intention on the part of artists to use that machinery as a medium for producing artworks. This, in turn, presents audiences with new standards or terms of perception. Furthermore the informed audience is thereby challenged to form an appreciation of the panoply of diverse skills and talents required to bring the work into being.

For anyone who thinks seriously about records, the claim that particular sounds are essential aspects of the musical work might seem self-evident. Yet while recordings quite obviously invite us to think about them in a holistic way, rock criticism has traditionally leaned most heavily on interpretation of lyrics and, to a lesser extent, on musical performances, while the growing body of scholarly analysis tends to focus on elements of musical syntax such as harmony, meter, melody, form, and so forth. The record's most essential character, its sound, remains, even at this late date, its least-talked-about aspect. But the testimony of recordists leads us in another direction. Recurring analogies to visual media and perception—terms such as "image," "canvas," "sculpture," and "color"—are a tip-off to a pre-occupation with the sounding musical surface. Like a visual artist, the recordist handles the actual material of which the piece is made. "I *see* music," says George Martin. "[P]art of my life has been painting pictures in sound."[55] "It's all just paint, right?" says Nile Rodgers of the elements that make up a recording.[56] And Brian Eno puts it this way:

> If you start thinking of music as something you don't have to do in real time but something that can be built up, like a painting, that gives you a different way of working. You can think about it on, shall we say, the atomic level. The other level you can think at, through working with the kinds of processing equipment that studios have, is as a way of making atmospheres, landscapes, whatever you like.[57]

While it is common in discussions of rock recordings to talk about what records *contain*, rather than what they *are*, the notion of writing records invites us to broaden the discourse, keeping the focus squarely upon the record itself. For while it contains words, musical syntax, and performances, it is far more than merely their sum. Its essential and irreducible element is sound. In the essay from which this chapter's introductory quote was taken, Susanne Langer claims that film "creates a virtual present, an order of direct apparition." Because of the nature of its appearance, she labels this "the dream mode" (the dreamer, like the filmgoer "is always 'there,' his relation is, so to speak, equidistant from all events") but notes that unlike an actual dream, a film "is a poetic composition, coherent, organic, governed by a definitely conceived feeling."[58] Rock records, too, are "an order of direct apparition." They, too, represent a "new poetic mode," the traces of which are evident in their content and form—about which I have more to say in the next chapter. Wittingly or not, we grasp the image that they present as a whole. Every nuance of their sound, which includes the history of the sound's original moment and all that went into its production, informs our understanding of what they are. Records are both artworks and historical witnesses. In short, they are all that they appear to be.

2

Tracks

You design the experience to be a record rather than just a
song. It's the record that people listen to.

Brian Wilson

While I have begun by arguing for the significance of sound recording's poetic role in rock, records obviously have components that
represent other kinds of compositional activity, namely, songwriting
and arranging. To sharpen the focus on the autographic aspect of the
process, it will be useful to think of a recording as containing three
distinct compositional layers: the song, the musical arrangement,
and the track. The song is what can be represented on a lead sheet; it
usually includes words, melody, chord changes, and some degree of
formal design. The arrangement is a particular musical setting of the
song. It provides a more detailed prescriptive plan: instrumentation,
musical parts, rhythmic groove, and so forth. The track is the recording itself. As the layer that represents the finished musical work, it
subsumes the other two. That is, when we hear a record, we experience both song and arrangement through the sounds of the track.

While the song and the arrangement are integral aspects of the finished work, both retain an ontological independence. They have
modes of representation—lead sheets, scores, performances—other
than the recording. Even if songwriting and arranging take place
during the recording session, when the record is finished they can be
extracted from it and treated independently. They may be altered in
any number of ways while still retaining their basic identity. This is
not true of the track. Its identity lies in its actual sound, and while
that may change somewhat from one reproduction system to
another—like a painting hung in different kinds of light or space—
it is essentially a fixed set of relationships.

Cutting tracks, then, is a stage in a multifaceted creative process.
It is the point at which musical ideas become concrete material, that

is, specific performances and sounds. Where this stage begins in relation to songwriting and arranging varies considerably. Sometimes it begins only after song and arrangement have been completed, while in other cases the three compositional layers operate simultaneously and interactively. The wide range of approaches to record making requires allowance for all sorts of overlap, even in the course of a single project, for the relationships among the three modes of creative activity are themselves subject to a process of ongoing development. In any case, how songwriting and arranging fit into the overall process of record making is a question worth asking. The answer may be an important part of a work's compositional history because it delineates the compositional parameters involved in a particular recording project and provides insight into the creative roles of those involved in the sessions and the nature of their collaborative interactions. It may also reveal ways in which the more traditional activities of songwriting and arranging were influenced by the autographic process.

SONGS

Making up songs must be one of the world's oldest arts. Whenever people gather together in communal activities there is liable to be singing, and it's easy to imagine that the impulse is as ancient and universal as the human voice. Songs are among the most robust and durable of musical entities. As long as its basic features remain intact, a song can be reconfigured in various ways yet still be recognizable. Words, pitches, rhythms, chords, arrangements can all be modified without changing the song's essential identity. As such, a song is easily separated from any particular recorded rendering.

In rock it is understandable that songs are often taken to be the essence of the musical work rather than simply an aspect of it. After all, rock records almost always contain songs, though the rest of their features can vary a great deal. Songs are the common link among records across the wide and varied field of rock styles. They are certainly the most easily remembered aspect of a recording; singing a half-remembered song fragment can call a half-remembered impression of the recording to mind. Moreover, songwriters are always named on a record even when they have had nothing to do with its making, while until relatively recently musician and engineer credits have been treated in a cavalier fashion at best and have often been omitted altogether.

At first sight, the privileging of songwriters, like the privileging of songs, seems reasonable enough. Historically, songwriters have a celebrated place in American music. When George Gershwin lay dying of a brain tumor in a Hollywood hospital, two Navy destroyers were sent out in search of leading neurosurgeon Dr. Walter Dandy, who was vacationing aboard a yacht on Chesapeake Bay: an important man, a beloved songwriter, required urgent attention.[1] Songwriters have provided some of our most memorable and enduring cultural symbols, and many have attained great wealth and prestige, commanding respect at all levels of society. Record making, by contrast, is a recent art form, and many of its artistic roles belong to no prior tradition. We know what songwriters do, but what about sound engineers? Even now, after a century of sound recording, the process of making records remains at least a partial mystery to the majority of those who listen to them.

In the first half of the twentieth century most urban popular singers relied on professional songwriters like the Gershwin brothers for their material. Exceptions to the writer/performer dichotomy—artists like Hoagy Carmichael, for instance, who wrote many of his own songs—were relatively rare. But in some regional musical idioms, like blues and country music, writer/performers were common. Jimmie Rodgers and Hank Williams were fine songwriters, as were Robert Johnson and any number of other Southern bluesmen. Many early rockers who grew up listening to blues and country—Carl Perkins, Chuck Berry, Buddy Holly, for example—were themselves songwriters, and eventually it became common practice for recording artists to write the songs for their records. Thus they were known not simply for how they played and sang, but for what they had to say.

Given the emphasis on making records, many rock and roll songwriters became increasingly aware of and involved in the recording process—Chuck Berry and Buddy Holly were both notable in this regard—and the creative interface between songwriting and recording brought about an increasing interdependence between songs and sounds. Songs became linked with their recorded versions to an unprecedented degree, their meaning mediated by specific performances and sonic settings. Part of what makes "Long Tall Sally" or

"Tutti Frutti" work so well is the sound of Little Richard's manic howl. The problem with Pat Boone's cover versions of these songs—both hits in 1956—is not simply that he "cleans up" the lyrics, or that his white middle-class proto-suburban image clashes so annoyingly with the spirit of the songs; the real problem is that it *sounds* all wrong. On the other hand, when Paul McCartney sings "Long Tall Sally," his vocal timbre emulates the original. For McCartney, rendering the song means not only playing its chords and singing its melody and lyrics but also evoking its sonic impression. Similarly, the only Beatles recording of a Buddy Holly song, "Words of Love," bears a striking sonic likeness to the original. The chiming guitar and the tone of Holly's voice, both of which the Beatles emulate, were clearly as important to them as the song itself. Further, the pat-a-cake effect of the eighth-note handclaps is a reference to another Holly track, "Everyday" (1958). So while the Beatles track is at one level a cover version of a Buddy Holly song, it is also a more extended allusion to Buddy Holly's sound. Complaints, usually voiced by Tin Pan Alley aficionados, about the dumbing down of the popular song in rock miss the point: through this linkage, rock records actually represent an expansion of the concept of "song." "I make the best demo I can, singing and playing guitar, bass, piano and drum machine," writes Sting about introducing a new song to his fellow band members in the Police. "I get a good version so that people will see its potential."[2] Tin Pan Alley songs, though they benefited from the performances of "song pluggers," were represented fairly by lead sheets, which contained all that was essential—words, tune, chord changes. Rock songs, on the other hand, often rely on specific recordings to demonstrate their "potential." And that's because the songs may be only sketches for records, their words and tunes awaiting the next stage of production, which will add further layers of musical meaning.

While the linkage between songs and recording sets the stage for bringing them together into a single compositional process, the choice of whether or not to do so is a matter of personal preference and logistical possibility. Though recordists work with songs as sound and listeners experience both simultaneously, songwriting and recording have historically been treated as sequential stages. One of the main reasons for this is financial. Writing songs while the studio clock is ticking can get expensive, and prior to the advent of affordable high quality recording equipment, which has given rise to the "personal studio," the practice was rare. Brill Building songwriters worked much as their Tin Pan Alley predecessors had,[3] writing at pianos in small cubicles and then passing the songs on to record producers. At Motown Records in the 1960s, a stable of songwriters, including Lamont Dozier, Eddie and Brian Holland, Smokey Robinson, and Norman Whitfield, passed along a steady stream of songs to the next link in the production chain. And at Atlantic Records in the 1950s, the union-mandated three-hour recording session was used as efficiently as possible to produce and record performances, not to write songs. Even though recording technology has become more and more accessible outside of professional studios, having songs in hand before embarking on a recording project is preferred by many recordists simply because it allows the project to focus more intensely on a smaller range of tasks. Producer Rick Rubin, for instance, is "a great fan of pre-production." From his point of view, "the most important thing a producer can do is spend time getting the songs into shape before recording," and this "should be done at home or in a rehearsal studio."[4]

Some recordists, on the other hand, are more willing to allow the recording process to influence the songs. While the songs may be written prior to recording, they are always susceptible to rewriting as the recording process unfolds. British producer Steve Lillywhite allows that "as much pre-production as you do, it all sort of goes out the window when you get into the studio."[5] John Leckie, whose production credits include XTC, the Stone Roses, and Radiohead, believes that shaping the ultimate content of the song and the arrangement is "an ongoing decision-making process all the way through to the final mix." Since "your personal approach may vary slightly or radically from inception to finish . . . [y]ou shouldn't decide that a song is going to be . . . of a very specific nature before you begin piecing it together."[6] In other words, the song's ultimate form should be allowed to emerge over the course of the record-making process as the song absorbs the influences of the process itself. In this approach the song/track relationship is somewhat like that of a screenplay to a film. The song or screenplay provides a genesis and a guide for the work's ultimate form, but it remains malleable throughout the production process. As words and music are manifested in sound, they become subject to a new round of evaluation—one based upon an expanded set of criteria that includes all of the elements of the sounds' sonic particularity and the associative meanings that the sounds convey.

Because a song need not be completely finished until the final mix, songwriters who perform on and perhaps even produce their own records have a fluid situation in which to work. Those with the resources to do so may integrate the songwriting and track creation processes to one degree or another. For Lindsey Buckingham, the "writing process is very intertwined with the process of making a record. Sometimes I have a whole track and don't have a melody yet."[7] If songwriting is "intertwined" with record making, the concrete aural shape of the track may influence the song in any number of ways. "You've got a canvas, and you start off with a certain intent. But because it's a quiet and intuitive process, you put strokes on the canvas, and the work starts to speak to you, taking you off in a direction you didn't expect."[8] The influence of specific sonic textures can open new doorways to the songwriter, expanding the context within which the song develops. Thus, lyrics and melodies are evaluated from the beginning in terms of their suitability to the track as a whole.

Tony Asher, who collaborated with Brian Wilson on the songs for *Pet Sounds* (1966), recalls that Wilson "used to go in and record [instrumental] tracks. We didn't know what they were going to be. They didn't even have melodies. They would just be a series of chord changes that Brian liked. . . . Then, we would bring these back (to the house) and play them and kind of write a melody to them and then write some lyrics."[9] Once the basic "feel," as Wilson called his sketches, was in some kind of concrete form, the aural impression it made informed and furthered the songwriting process. "Once they [the "feels"] are out of my head and into the open air, I can see them and touch them firmly," says Wilson. "Then the song starts to blossom and become a real thing."[10]

According to producer Tony Visconti, David Bowie seldom came to a recording session for his 1970s albums with a "finished lyric or melody. . . . Bowie is the only artist I've worked with who actually writes on mic." The song "Fashion," for example, from *Scary Monsters* (1980) "was conceived as nothing more than a riff. . . . All the little musical 'tastes' were recorded simply because they sounded good; they weren't embellishing the vocal melody because there wasn't one."[11] The song was finished only months later when the vocal was being recorded, and some of the lines were written on the spot. Chris Thomas tells a similar story about producing Roxy Music's *Stranded* (1973). Initially, the band "just put down backing tracks of keyboards, bass, and drums. 'What's this one called?' 'Number 3.' 'Oh, okay, that's inspirational!' Half the time there were no lyrics written for these songs."[12] Phil Manzanera would then put down guitar tracks, which were followed by more layers of musical arrangement. Finally, with the track all but finished, the song would appear as Bryan Ferry came into the studio to record his vocal and reveal to all what the song they had been working on was about.

In his account of U2's working methods on the *Zooropa* (1993) project, Bill Flanagan describes a songwriting process where the group begins by jamming freely with tape recorder rolling:

> [Producer Brian] Eno or Edge then go through the tapes, finding sections they like and editing them into proper song form. Then the band listens, suggests alterations, and tries coming up with words and melodies to go on top of the edited tracks. Bono or Edge will then sing these lyrical and melodic ideas into a Walkman while the track plays back. When a song has taken shape that way, U2 listens to the tape, goes back into the studio, and tries to play it.[13]

Once again we have an example where lyrics, melody, and vocal character develop as responses to the sound of a recorded track. Feel, sound, and groove all precede "proper song form." As the song elements are fitted to the affective character of the track, however, they may, in turn, shift the track's existing arrangement in new directions. In short, the formation of track and song constitutes a continual interaction.

Over the course of rock history—and as it has become more feasible technically and economically to do so—an increasing number of artists have adopted synergistic creative approaches where songwriting, arranging, and recording proceed simultaneously. Peter Gabriel is an example of an artist whose songs are conceived and developed as recordings from the start, for as he puts it, "if a sound is a great one it almost has a song within it."[14] Working always with a tape recorder, he deals with recorded sound from the earliest sketch stages and is guided throughout the compositional process by his responses to aural images. On Gabriel's *Us* album (1992), engineer David Bottrill recalls that "the 'writing process' continued right through until the end of the recording process. . . . We run DATs all the time as we're recording just for a reference, so that if a great performance happened about 15 minutes ago, we'll just spin the DAT back."[15] Though the DAT is only a documentary "reference," the medium is of sufficient quality that even performances and sounds thought initially experimental or "throw away" might find their way onto the master tape and become part of the finished project. Thus, as Bottrill's conflation of "writing," "recording," and "performance" suggests, Gabriel's approach makes for a seamless process where song, sound, and musical performance flow together in a steady stream of raw creative expression. Analytical assessment and decision making can wait. As Gabriel sees it, "if you don't have some recording device on all the time you're playing, you're going to miss some of your best moments."[16]

Gabriel characterizes his sketch ideas not as themes or motives, but as "little snatches of sound"[17]—akin to Brian Wilson's "feels"— for these are what guide his compositional course. On "Digging in the Dirt," for example, after deciding on a rhythmic groove, his usual departure point, Gabriel improvised chord changes and vocal melodies—using only nonsense vowel sounds—in a succession of experimental forays. Every attempt was recorded and had the potential to eventually turn up as part of the finished track. At the very least, each attempt led to the next one in a series of related steps, each informed by those that preceded it. Throughout the process, Bottrill recalls, "Peter would basically be building up sections until he'd have a tentative structure of a song."[18] The song, however, remained in a formative state even as the recording/mixing process moved into later stages. "The structures were constantly changing. . . . In effect, the song was constantly being molded and built up over the two-and-a-half-year period."[19]

Rock songs, then, are written in all kinds of ways. The relationship of their genesis to that of the track varies considerably. Because songs are associated so closely with records, and because they are written so often by their performers, songwriting may be wholly integrated with recording. But even if songwriting is an entirely separate stage, a rock song assumes the fullness of its meaning only as it is uttered. Songs may be performed in multiple versions, but their primary identity and their place in the galaxy of rock works is fixed by an original recording. However many cover versions I may hear of "Be

My Baby," I can never separate what the song means to me from the image I hold in memory of Ronnie Spector's voice and Phil Spector's lavish production. Somehow, the cover performance resonates with the memory, and though the sound is all different, the meaning imparted by the original recording still comes through.

ARRANGEMENTS

While most recorded songs can easily be separated from their specific contexts and performed in any number of ways, arrangements are often more dependent upon the particularities of the recording, and an analytical division between track and arrangement may sometimes be artificial and misleading. For in the context of record making, arranging involves more than the fitting together of instrumental parts; in many cases a track's arrangement develops according to criteria that are specific to recorded sound. That is, some of an arrangement's most characteristic features may come about as a result of electronic sound processing, frequency manipulation, or various mixing techniques. As Hugh Padgham puts it, "When we're putting parts down in the studio, I have a quick realization whether the parts are going to work against each other musically and from an audio point of view. When I produce or mix a record, I hear the music in a sort of sonic spectrum."[20] The simultaneous consideration of music and audio amounts to an integrated kind of arranging where musical parts and actual sounds are interdependent. Mitchell Froom calls this the "overall noise." It is a mistake, he believes, "to separate sonics from the musical arrangement."[21] Still, while the exact effect produced by the recording may be impossible to reproduce in a live performance, *some* version of the arrangement can be extracted from the recording. And, as with songwriting, the way arranging fits into the recording process tells us about the scope of the compositional project that the recording represents.

Rock arrangements usually start out as head arrangements created by the members of the band—what Ruth Finnegan calls "the rock mode of collective prior composition," which is an "oral and active group learning mode." As additional parts are added during recording—as session players are brought in, say, to add string parts—a second "mode" involving musical notation often comes into play: the "classical mode of prior written composition by an individual."[22] The arrangement may also include improvisations captured on tape. Furthermore, engineers, with an ear to the sonic logic of instrumental combinations as they make their way to tape, may use electronic resources to modify some aspects of the arrangement's texture. Thus, anyone involved in making a record is a potential contributor to the arrangement, which may, in its final form, represent many "modes" of musical creativity.

Of course, the nature of arrangements has a lot to do with aesthetic philosophy and musical style. Because Rick Rubin is such a proponent of pre-production, for example, the instrumental arrangements for the Red Hot Chili Peppers' *Blood Sugar Sex Magik* sessions (1991) developed in rehearsal as live performances. Although their particular manifestation as recorded tracks involved further editing and overdubbing, they were essentially formed prior to beginning the recording process. Indeed, Rubin reckoned that if he had left the project at the end of pre-production, the album would have sounded substantially similar, since the recording stage of the project was focused on capturing the specific details of a sound whose general shape had already been developed.

Many of the arrangements on Los Lobos' *Kiko* (1992), on the other hand, were developed during the recording process as constructs of recorded sound. As producer Mitchell Froom puts it, "the songs didn't suffer under the tyranny of their being a live representation of what was going to happen [in concert. The band] wanted to get cool noises and make it a cool record; then they could reinvent it live later."[23] With the sole aim of making a "cool record," the palette of sounds from which the album's arrangements were made included unusual instrumentations and sound processing techniques. In the song "Angels with Dirty Faces," for example, an Optigan—"a cheesy-sounding keyboard that was sold at Woolworth's and Penney's in the late '60s and early '70s"—provides a gritty, scratching sound that permeates the center of the track, creating a grainy sonic texture that underscores the emotional texture of the song's theme of homelessness. This sound is an important affective feature of the track, but it has nothing to do with the live sound of Los Lobos. The Optigon scratches are an element of the arrangement specific to the track, a "cool" sound chosen purely for its effect in the context of the recording.

The Beatles' records exemplify a variety of approaches to arranging, as they do with most other aspects of record making. As a live band the Beatles had long been accustomed to making head arrangements, but when George Martin, the classically trained "fifth Beatle," joined on, scripted arrangements became a readily available resource. Then, as things developed—as technology advanced and as the band's enormous popularity persuaded EMI, their record company, to allow them unlimited studio time—the Beatles and Martin experimented increasingly with sounds and recording techniques, using the resources of the recording studio to color and shape their arrangements in unusual ways.

However arrangements come about, their full sense, as with songs, lies in their sound, which is a product of particular instruments tuned and played a particular way in a particular room on a particular day. Consider Paul McCartney's recording of "Yesterday" (1965). The track features an arrangement for voice, acoustic guitar, and string quartet. The string parts, arranged by Martin, are completely notated; the guitar part, invented by McCartney, functions as a continuo. The vocal melody is clearly articulated. The entire arrangement can be represented convincingly by conventional musical notation, and as such it can be easily reproduced in a concert setting. Because it was created separately from the track, it has a solidly independent identity.

Yet even in a case like this, it would be inaccurate to say that the recording simply documents a performance of the song as arranged by McCartney and Martin. The track is a composition in its own right, and as its recording history confirms, although the recording process did not come into play in the writing or arranging of the song, it clearly shaped both of them in the version by which "Yesterday" is, and will always be, known. According to Martin, who produced the session, the first step in the process was to capture a simultaneous guitar/vocal performance by McCartney. "Then we overdubbed the strings while Paul had another go at the vocal. But because we didn't use headphones there was leakage from the studio speaker into his microphone, giving the impression of two voices or double-tracking."[24] The doubled voice—the image of a person singing with himself—moves things into a sound world that is unique to recording. Furthermore, the fact that the track consists of performances played at different times and overlaid one on top of the other makes it something quite distinct, both conceptually and practically, from a recording of a live performance. The string performances are regulated by a prerecorded tape, and the process of combining the different performances requires the collaborative efforts of the recording engineer. Of course, even without overdubbing, the hand and ears of the latter are apparent in any sound captured on tape. Martin's arrangement of McCartney's "Eleanor Rigby" (1966) is a fully scripted piece for double string quartet, but the close miking of the instruments—a creative decision made by engineer Geoff Emerick, much to the doubting bemusement of the string players—creates a sonic image that is unique to the recording.

The year 1966 marked a turning point in the Beatles' career. No longer touring, and with virtually unlimited studio budgets, they began to work exclusively in the studio, creating works that were never intended for live performance. In this setting diverse arranging techniques became increasingly integrated into a single process. Although the first album to emerge from the new approach was *Sgt. Pepper's Lonely Hearts Club Band*, the project began with the recording of a song that did not appear on that album: "Strawberry Fields Forever." The recording began on November 24, 1966, and continued for a month, during which time the arrangement underwent several changes. Originally presented by John Lennon to the other Beatles and Martin in a gentle guitar and vocal rendition, the song was subsequently arranged by the entire band and recorded in a version that in Martin's estimation "started to get heavy."[25] Aside from the mellotron flute sounds, this arrangement is cast in the guitar/bass/drums texture that one might expect to emerge from the Beatles' head arrangement process.

Lennon then decided that he wanted a different approach, and he asked Martin to write something. Martin came up with a score for trumpets and cellos whose effect is quite different from the band arrangement. The texture of the verses is spare and dry: voice accompanied by trumpets, cellos, and the strange, sucking timbres produced by recording various percussion instruments with the tape reversed.[26] In the choruses the band joins in with an electric guitar slide and a dense percussion texture—an ensemble of percussion instruments played by all of the Beatles plus road manager Mal Evans—which creates an enveloping sound of murky darkness that contrasts sharply with the crystalline texture of the verses. Though it comes later in the song, the percussion was actually recorded prior to the trumpet and cello parts. The result at this point was a confluence of head arrangement and score—both of which took place at some stage of pre-production—a layering of nonsynchronous performances through overdubbing, and, in the backwards percussion, timbral characters produced by the recording medium itself. Lennon's next idea would use the medium to shape the essential structure of the arrangement. He decided that both versions had merit and that somehow they should both be used. According to Martin's account, Lennon told him, "I like the beginning of the first one, and I like the end of the second one. Why don't we just join them together?"[27] The two were in different keys—A and C—in their original versions prior to any tape speed manipulation[28] and in slightly different tempos, but Lennon by now had complete faith in Martin's abilities. "You can fix it, George," he said.

Martin's solution was to slow one version down and speed the other up using the variable speed control on the tape machine—matching the pitches and tempos sufficiently to make a credible, if not altogether unobtrusive, edit. Martin then selected "precisely the right spot" to cut and splice the two tapes, which was determined to be one minute into the track at the beginning of the second chorus. Geoff Emerick, who was working as the Beatles' engineer at the time, recalls gradually changing the pitch of the first version just before the edit point to make the splice as smooth as possible. This can be heard on the word "going" from the line "Let me take you down 'cause I'm going to," just over one minute into the track. The effect is slightly surreal and well in keeping with the overall atmosphere of the track. Thus, with an arrangement that includes backward tape effects, altered tape speed, a false fade in the coda, and a crucial splice that joins two conceptions in a single gesture, "Strawberry Fields Forever" brings together head arrangement, script, and studio manipulation in a multifaceted collection of compositional modes.

Karl Wallinger is a great Beatles fan and a master recordist. Much as a composer of scores might copy out a favorite piece by another composer, Wallinger remade "Penny Lane" note for note and sound for sound, including reverb. He reckons that his effort is "pretty realistic," though "it's not quite Paul McCartney singing."[29] What he learns from such an undertaking he uses in making his own records, which in turn bear the sonic influence of, among other things, the later Beatles albums he is partial to. Like Gabriel, Wallinger works to tape as a matter of course. He does his own engineering and production work, as well as the writing, arranging, and most of the playing. In the course of developing a track he records all sorts of ideas, most of which do not make the final mix. But curious bits and pieces remain from the process that are not only unusual for a musical arrangement; they are explicit acknowledgments of the nature of the process and the art form. At the very beginning of the *Goodbye Jumbo* album (1990), for example, he announces over a repeating drum machine pattern, "Okay, rolling." It is at once a recognition of artifice and an invitation to enter the sound world of the artificer. It is also a reference to another record. "Is it rolling, Bob?" Dylan asks producer Bob Johnston at the beginning of "To Be Alone with You" on his *Nashville Skyline* album (1969). Similarly, the strange beginning of "Is It Like Today?" from *Bang!* (1993)—something like the sound of a tape recorder being turned on in the midst of some ongoing music making—announces that the machinery and techniques of the recording studio are central to what this music is about. The principle is illustrated again and again on Wallinger's World Party records. With dense textural layerings whose proportions are dependent upon balances created at a mixing console, with the treatment of the stereo panorama as a dramatic stage, and with the liberal use of backward tape and other electronically processed sounds, Wallinger creates musical arrangements that are shaped from the beginning in terms of recorded sound. Working directly to the medium, he is no longer an arranger in the traditional sense, but rather, a composer of tracks.

TRACKS

I have based much of my discussion up to now on an implicit claim: that record making is a compositional process that produces musical works. I need now to be explicit about this claim and to frame the context within which it is being made. For both the terms "composition" and "musical work" have histories in which rock has no part. Furthermore, musicological studies of compositional process themselves have a particular history, also having nothing to do with rock. The principles that the terms encompass fit the record-making project very well, but in order to adapt such words to a usage outside the traditions in which they have come to be understood, their potential to "creep into the cellar like a horde of mice and undermine the groundwork"—as Erwin Panofsky says history ignored is liable to do—needs to be neutralized.[30]

Without wishing to commingle their histories, aesthetic orientations, or the beliefs of practitioners and audiences, I think it is fair to say that record making actually *is* similar in some ways to the making of musical scores. Compositional decisions are based on or influenced by a similar set of factors, which include technical competence, aesthetic belief, the needs of personal expression, a sense of style and language, a feeling for form and dramatic narrative, familiarity with other works, and so on. In addition, there is a functional similarity between rock composition and score-based composition that lies in their common focus on poiesis. Though they differ, both practically and conceptually, in their respective means of materializing the musical work, they share the aim of giving permanent, objectified form to musical relationships.

There are other areas of overlap as well, having to do with the experiences that participants bring to the project. Rock has always drawn from other musical idioms, and many rock recordists have experience with some aspect of written musical culture. Any young person who takes piano lessons, plays in a school band, or sings in a chorus absorbs something of the written musical tradition. Many young people also play in rock bands at some point and may go on to make records. Moreover, rock records are part of the larger phenomenon of sound recording, and many of the engineers and producers who work on rock recordings record classical compositions as well. Their overall musical sensibility is informed by the entire pool of their musical experience, which might also include jazz, varieties of "world music," or as in George Martin's case, comedy. In addition, records themselves remove many of the cultural barriers that traditionally were defined by such things as access to performance venues or one's ability to play an instrument. They level the field, allowing almost anyone to access almost any music. As such, they have had a great deal to say about reorienting relationships among musical idioms, and the weight of their influence has gone generally toward increasing, rather than limiting, interchanges.

In order to deal with many of the compositional issues posed by tracks—such things as thematic development and narrative structure—it will be useful to situate record making as a compositional project within a larger historical framework of music composition, at least in terms of the principles involved. Although using sound to compose musical works only became possible within the last century, the work concept is much older and derives originally from the very different technology of musical notation. The idea that musical composition is an activity by which "labor is converted into a durable product" was apparently recorded first by the music theorist Nikolaus Listennius in the sixteenth century in Germany.[31] Lydia Goehr has argued that the work concept began to be "regulative" at the beginning of the nineteenth century—also in Germany. "[C]omposers began to individuate works as embodied expressions and products of their activities," to see them "as ends in themselves."[32] At the same time, commentators voiced a deepening belief in the unmatched power of music—as embodied in works—to express the ineffable in human experience. As writer and composer E. T. A. Hoffman put it in 1813, music "is the most romantic of all the arts—one might almost say, the only genuinely romantic one—for its sole subject is the infinite."[33] In this ideological climate the idea developed that a musical composition was an autonomous entity whose meaning was contained entirely within itself. The notion of purely musical meaning was advanced in particular to advocate for the value of instrumental music. The work of "absolute music," as it came to be called, was made up of a set of relationships among constituents in a musical system cast in a unique form by its composer and preserved in a musical score, which was, in effect, a text.

Speculation about the nature of the work's content took various forms in the course of the nineteenth century. The romantic aesthetic articulated by Hoffman implied an emotional content. About the "completely romantic composer," Beethoven, and more specifically his fifth symphony, Hoffman wrote: "Beethoven's music sets in motion the lever of fear, of awe, of horror, of suffering, and wakens just that infinite longing which is the essence of romanticism."[34] G. W. F. Hegel pointed to various aspects of musical content and commented that above all, for music to "rise to the level of true art," it must have "spiritual content"; only then can it accomplish its "true task," which "is to bring that content to life in the listener's *subjective inner consciousness.*"[35] The prominent music critic Eduard Hanslick, fed up with what he regarded as the persistent "mixing up of the concepts of content, subject, and material," insisted in 1854 that in the context of such a conflation, music is "contentless." Only if we take "content in its original and proper sense" to mean "what a thing holds, what it includes within itself," can we make sense of the concept. And if we do this, we are left only with "the tones out of which a piece of music is made," which "have no other content than themselves."[36] In recent times, of course, there has been a great deal of interest in the semiotic content of musical works, the properties and functions of musical symbolism—notions that probably would have rankled Hanslick. These diverse and sometimes contradictory conceptions of musical content are tied to particular aesthetic stances and historical contexts, yet they share a common premise: however it is construed or interpreted by critic, historian, or audience, a work's content is the result of a composer's labor in the cultural field, which is recorded for all time in musical notation.

As Carl Dahlhaus reminds us, "the new insight that Beethoven thrust upon the aesthetic consciousness of his age was that a musical text, like a literary or a philosophical text, harbors a meaning which is made manifest but not entirely subsumed in its acoustic presentation—that a musical creation can exist as an 'art work of ideas' transcending its various interpretations."[37] Dahlhaus goes on to say that although this idea emerged within a particular historical context, it "is now taken for granted among the artistically well educated."[38] Indeed, it crops up in an assortment of divergent contexts. Its resonance can be felt, for example, in such famous aesthetic dualisms as Arnold Schoenberg's "style and idea" and Charles Ives's "manner and substance," as well as musings on the nature of the work/performance relationship that have long occupied philosophers.[39] Just as Beethoven refused to have his musical ideas limited by the practical limitations of Ignaz Schuppanzigh's "wretched fiddle," so Ives chafed at the confinement imposed by sound upon music: "Why can't music go out the same way it comes into a man, without having to crawl over a fence of sounds, thoraxes, catguts, wire, wood, and brass? . . . That music must be heard is not essential—what it *sounds* like may not be what it *is*."[40]

Along these same lines, the composer and theorist Benjamin Boretz has defined "the composition of works of art" as "the definition and creation of relational 'universes' of elements in whose interrelations are embedded hypothetical properties of relational behavior."[41] Because these "relational universes" can be represented in the form of musical notation, a work's essential identity lies in the visual yet silent realm of the musical score, in the pure realm of mind and idea, quite apart from the aural pleasure and sensual delight of musical performances. Of course, performers are liable to view this differently— indeed, the score/performance relationship presents a persistent complication—but the dominant trends in musical analysis in the twentieth century bear witness to the widespread influence of the notion.[42] As Boretz insists, "Sounds . . . are not part of music, however essential they are to its transmission."[43]

The persistence of such thinking is borne out by remarks made by Roger Reynolds during and after a talk called "Thoughts on What a Record Records," given at a conference in 1977. Reynolds sounded "a note of caution" about sound recording's "rigidity," its lack of "neutrality," and its ability to "elevate the unreal at the expense of the real." Even a composer of electroacoustic music, it seems, has a difficult time granting *sound* a place in the musical essence. In the exchange that followed the talk, Reynolds offered the opinion that the "generality and power of a score . . . refer to the notion that a model of music, of a class of musical experience, exists, and that this is a Western richness" that is "challenged in profound ways by recording, particularly by singular recordings of works." And following a longstanding ideological tradition, Reynolds made a distinction between the "visceral impact" of musical sound and "the work itself."[44]

If, as this sampling of comments suggests, the primacy of the silent musical text is taken for granted, it is inevitable that many of the principal elements of rock records and the record-making process will simply be overlooked, or at least undervalued—and the "artistically well educated" will have demonstrated the limits of their education. For a rock recording is not an "acoustic presentation" of a written text. It is itself a text, a sonic one; "what it *sounds* like" is precisely "what it *is*." It too "harbors a meaning," but in this case, the work exists as a particular manifestation. And therein lies an important difference. Records, like scores, can be said to have relational, emotional, metaphysical, or semiotic content. Indeed, such observations, all of which entail some sort of interpretation, are commonly made. What must not be overlooked, however, is that records, unlike scores, also have *material* content. That is, in addition to whatever we make them to be, they insist as well on being exactly what they are:

sound, directly experienced. Interpretation that fails to take this into account will inevitably distort the picture in some way.

Commenting on a cultural survey taken of college students, Milton Babbitt characterized the results in the "favorite composer" category as "a confusion." The top two composers named by the respondents were Bob Dylan and John Lennon. Babbitt claimed that his concern was not with "their tastes," but with the respondents' confusion of "composer" with "songwriter."[45] Babbitt is both, and the distinction that he makes would be reasonable enough except that it loses sight of the fact that these students did not know Dylan or Lennon by their songs alone; they knew them by their records. The important functional difference between a popular song and a classical work lies not so much in aesthetic or stylistic matters but in relative degrees of specification. A song has a built-in fluidity. It is "ontologically thin," as Gracyk puts it. Performances of most concert music, on the other hand, must hew to a more detailed prescriptive musical score. This higher degree of specification requires a different, more detail-oriented poetic process by which the composer's decisions gradually narrow the possible choices, until finally a particular set of musical relationships stands to represent the work. With the idea that scores themselves are primary sites of musical meaning and identity, classical compositions of the nineteenth and twentieth centuries have generally tended toward increasingly detailed written specifications, which attempt to define a work's parameters with ever greater precision.

The songwriter/composer distinction can thus be made on purely functional grounds; the two simply do not share the same aims. But rock songs—unlike, say, those of Tin Pan Alley—enter the culture in the first instance as recordings, which, like scores, are detailed and fixed representations of musical thought. To this extent, rock records already bear signs associated historically with musical works. They are, in Goehr's terms, "complete and discrete, original and fixed, personally owned units."[46] But they also expand the work concept, for as Richard Middleton points out, it is "recordings rather than scores which represent an extreme form of reified abstraction."[47] This is because unlike scripted works, records represent more than musical thought. They also encompass musical utterances and sonic relationships—material—whose particularity is immutable and thus essential to the work's identity. While it is clear that records are musical works and that they are created through a compositional process, the traditional meanings of these terms must be expanded if they are to be understood in this context.

As soon as we expand the work concept to include sound and utterance, the concept—as well as the nature of text, musical idea, creative process, and musical style—begins to take in elements and experiences that were previously not directly associated with the compositional process. The "relational universe" now involves many more kinds of connections. As regards the nature of musical ideas, for instance, record making represents "out loud" musical thinking. Ideas are not merely *expressed* in sound; rather, ideas *become* sound. Thus, concept and performance enter into an integral relationship that we perceive as a whole. And this is true not only for musical ideas, but also for ideas expressed in words. As Simon Frith has pointed out, "song words are always spoken out—we always hear them in somebody's voice."[48] As a result, their linguistic meaning is associated with the affective sense of the performance that embodies them—its timbre, intonation, and expressive qualities. In addition, the particular sonic configuration and expressive shape of the performance are influenced by such things as the choice of recording tools, the space in which the recording takes place, and the dynamics of the interaction among the members of the recording team. And this applies not only to the song but to all of a track's musical parts, for all of them are "spoken out" in particular performances.

What makes the Kingsmen's "Louie Louie" a good record? Neither lyrics nor melodic design, harmonic motion, rhythmic groove, or instrumental arrangement—all of which can be represented in some fashion apart from the record (though the lyrics would be at best an approximation)—hold the key to the answer. The record's power is in its sound, which represents multiple elements, processes, and voices—song, arrangement, sounds, techniques of sound recording and processing, musical performances, and all the particular ephemeral nuances that attend the moment of inscription. What is, from a certain perspective, mind-numbingly simple is in fact a complex network of phenomenal elements that we perceive as a whole. A record is, above all, a richly textured surface, which we apprehend only as a sensory, temporal, and complete experience. All of its parts must be present in order to grasp it. As soon as we section off some part of it—the lyrics, the chord changes—we are no longer dealing with the record. Such reductions may be useful for a particular analytic project, but their limitations must be kept in mind. In order to engage with records as they are, we must focus on the elements of which they are actually formed.

Susan Sontag, in her essay "Against Interpretation," criticized "the odd vision by which something we have learned to call 'form' is separated off from something we have learned to call 'content.' "[49] Interestingly, the statement echoes the concerns voiced by Hanslick, a critic "who can still be read as a spokesman for values that tacitly determine our use of language in the description of music."[50] The problem for Sontag, as for Hanslick, lay in what she saw as the persistent equating of content with subject matter, the notion that "a work of art by definition says something." She argued that the critical urge to interpret what was being said amounted, in modern times, to "an overt contempt for appearances," a never-ending excavation "to find a sub-text, which is the true one." As we have seen, Hanslick's answer to the hermeneutic impulse was to say that as regards subject matter, music is "contentless"; it is about nothing but itself. As for the separation of form and content:

> When we talk about the content of a work of art, we can really only make sense if we attach a form to it. The concepts of content and form mutually determine and complement each other. Where in thought a form does not seem separable from a content, there exists in fact no independent content. But in music we see content and form, material and configuration, image and idea, fused in an obscure, inseparable unity. . . . In music there is no content as opposed to form, because music has no form other than the content.[51]

Hanslick's use of the word "form" is, as he acknowledges, different from conventional usage in musical discourse, which takes it to "mean the architectonic of the combined components and groups of notes out of which the piece is made." His meaning, on the other hand, has to do with musical substance at the level of a work's "ultimate, aesthetically not further reducible, nucleus," which is its theme (*Motiv*). In a musical theme, as Hanslick saw it, form and content are fused in an actual presentation. "Thus the content of a musical work can be grasped only musically, never graphically: i.e., as that which is actually sounding in each piece."[52] It is in "tonally moving forms" that music reveals itself.[53] To "preserve music's substance," we must deny it "any other kind of 'content.' "[54]

In Sontag's argument, what Hanslick calls "the musically beautiful" is embodied in the principle of "transparence," which means "experiencing the luminousness of the thing in itself, of things being what they are." In our time, in Sontag's view, transparence "is the highest, most liberating value in art"; for we are so bombarded with sensory overload that our sensory faculties have become dulled, and what is needed is an awakening to what is actually before us. "We must learn to *see* more, to *hear* more, to *feel* more [emphasis in original]." Interpretation, however, sets up a "shadow world of 'meanings,' " impoverished, redundant duplicates that seek to "tame the work of art," with a loss in the process of both "energy and sensual capability." But by engaging in "a really accurate, sharp, loving description of the appearance of a work of art," the critic may "reveal the sensuous surface of art without mucking about in it." To do this, "what is needed is a vocabulary—a descriptive, rather than prescriptive, vocabulary—for forms. The best criticism . . . is of this sort that dissolves considerations of content into those of form."

In her advocacy for the direct apprehension of the artistic surface, Sontag points to several examples of films—Truffaut's *Shoot the Piano Player,* Godard's *Breathless*—"whose surface is so unified and clean, whose momentum is so rapid, whose address is so direct that the work can be . . . just what it is." Film was the obvious medium for Sontag to turn to as a young intellectual arguing passionately in the early 1960s that "in place of a hermeneutics we need an erotics of art." Rock, though a fundamentally sensory art form, was not yet on the critical map. It was not until it took on a subject matter deemed worthy of interpretation—in mid-decade with Bob Dylan and the Beatles—that intellectuals would begin gradually to engage rock as art. But if one approaches a record as it presents itself, without reducing it to this or that subset of content—that is, if one takes Sontag's advice—one encounters in tracks from Fats Domino, Eddie Cochran, the Drifters, the Marvelettes, Ronnie Spector, Buddy Holly, Sam Cooke, and dozens more an undeniably rich and complex sensory experience. It is the sonic presence of such records that has made them endure and, together, to develop into a network of influence and inspiration for succeeding generations of artists.

So where has this discussion brought us? Simply to an acknowledgment, again, of a history that, though it has nothing directly to do with rock, helps us to grasp what it is that rock records offer us. Although they were writing more than a century apart, for different audiences and about different things, Sontag and Hanslick both argued against the kind of interpretation that imputes metaphorical meaning to artworks at the expense of a true appreciation of what is actually present. Their common assertion that such critical practice devalues the work applies clearly to rock criticism, which for decades has simply omitted any detailed engagement with records' actual form. This is not to be taken as an argument for some kind of sonic formalism—still less, for idealistic autonomy—but rather as a conviction that criticism should engage things as they are. I am not at all against interpretation, as becomes clear in the next chapter. For that matter, neither is Sontag nor Hanslick, who is often charged erroneously with being a dogmatic formalist.[55] They are simply delimiting things in order to make the point clearly and forcefully that works of art as we encounter them are first of all about themselves. All interpretation proceeds from there. I, likewise, am advocating the primacy of a record's material form, rather than its subject matter. Not an evaluative primacy, but a logical one: the former embodies the latter. Without a record's material form there simply is no content. In a recording studio we can see the form of records develop as lips and fingers and arms move in musical time. These are the acts whose form the medium captures. Thus, the syntax and structural shape of songs and arrangements are absorbed in their material form, that is, in their utterance and its sonic presentation as it appears in our loudspeakers and headphones. This is Hanslick's "inseparable unity." Composing tracks involves making, capturing, and shaping sound. A track's formative elements include such things as actual timbres and textures, specific musical performances, and sonic images of ambient spaces. Its compositional procedures include such things as spatial arrangement, timbral manipulation, assembly of diverse "ear points"[56] into a composite acoustic image, and management of relationships among the various areas of the frequency spectrum, as well as producing (by whatever means) performances that, for the work at hand, are definitive. All of this can be apprehended only by hearing. Recordists work to a sonic canvas, which their audience experiences directly, unmediated except for vagaries of reproduction equipment. From both the poetic and the aesthetic sides, this sort of musical work demands, and repays, a full engagement with what Sontag calls the "sensory experience of the work of art." Let us turn now to an exploration of the nature of rock's sensory forms.

3

Sound as Form

And then there's the general quality that people never talk
about; it's called sonority, and that is the way the sound
leaps off the record and goes into your ear.

Jerry Wexler

Bob Dylan's original recording of "All Along the Watchtower," like
the rest of *John Wesley Harding* (1967), is an austere affair. Against the
contemporary trends in recording, which tended in varying degrees
towards the sonic opulence exemplified by *Sgt. Pepper's*, and in contrast even to the "thin wild mercury sound" of Dylan's own *Blonde on
Blonde* album, it strips things down to an elemental level—bass,
drums, acoustic guitar, voice, harmonica, three chords, and no obvious sonic manipulations. In this unadorned state the song's themes
of alienation and dread come across with an air of stark resignation.[1]

By contrast, Jimi Hendrix's recording of the song presents, from
its powerful opening flourish, a dramatic narrative that imparts a
very different meaning. Hendrix's rendition has a heroic defiance
about it. If the two approaching riders in the song's lyrics represent
uncertainty, if the wind and the wildcat represent danger, if the businessmen are the world's agents of betrayal, and if claustrophobic
confusion threatens to undermine the will of the protagonist, in
this version of the song he is willing to pit his musical power against
it all.

Hendrix uses various kinds of dramatic strategies in the course of
the track to accomplish his transformation of Dylan's song. In the
series of guitar solos that come with each refrain, for example, he
superimposes a long-range musical line—which unfolds in a steady
ascent across the span of the entire piece—on top of the relentlessly
repeating three-chord cycle. He also sharpens the narrative delin-
eation of the track by way of extreme textural contrasts between
verses and refrains. The significance of these gestures emerges over

the course of the track. But at the beginning it is the sheer *sound*, the way it "leaps off the record and goes into your ear," that lets us know we are in for something altogether different from the original version.

While the two tracks share the same song, their material elements are developed in quite different ways. In Hendrix's version both the instrumental and the vocal performances have an intense urgency about them in their aggressive articulation and rhythmic drive. Throughout the track the timbres are more varied in color and affective significance and fill far more of the frequency spectrum than in Dylan's version. From the highs of the cymbals and tambourines to the lows of the bass guitar and bass drum, the frequency space is put in play in a way that both animates the musical surface and delineates the track's structural design. The Hendrix track also presents the ear with striking uses of echo and ambience, which play on our sonic consciousness like impressionistic reflections of the song's lyrics. The echoes that trail behind their sources as they move across the stereo space resonate with the swirling confusion and untamed defiance of the song's protagonist. And among the track's many ambient images, that of the wood block stands out immediately; it casts a prominent shadow that disappears into the depths of the track, a sonic allusion to the "cold distance" from which the two mysterious riders approach. These are among the elements woven together to form the textural tapestry whose interaction with the song imparts the full sense of Hendrix's recomposition.

The elements that I've sketched out fall into five broad categories that represent all of the sound phenomena found on records: 1) musical performance, 2) timbre, 3) echo, 4) ambience (reverberation), and 5) texture. It is the configuration of relationships among these elements that gives the Hendrix track, or any other track, its full meaning and its unique identity. In addition to their phenomenal aspect, these categories include the activities and processes that shape the sounds. Timbre, for example, may be affected by electronic processes such as filtering and compression. Ambient images may be tailored using a variety of ambience simulation techniques. Although these five categories are interdependent, in this chapter each will be explored as a discrete aspect of the compositional project. While this is partly for the sake of analytic discussion, it also reflects something of the compositional process. For in practice the compositional focus continually shifts between isolated elements, various groupings of elements, and the piece as a whole.

MUSICAL PERFORMANCE

Sound recording has brought a new kind of consciousness to musical performance. Removing the dynamic energy and spectacle of the performer's presence and subjecting the performance to the scrutiny of repeated listenings presents a formidable challenge as well as new opportunities to musicians of all sorts. Because much of what impresses a concert audience is absent, musicians must rely far more upon purely sonic means to make their impression. Perhaps the most difficult challenge facing musicians when they record is somehow to leave in their performance an invitation to the listener to return again and again to the exact same set of expressive gestures—a project that seems to run counter to the very nature of musical performance. Historically, because they cannot be notated adequately nor ever repeated exactly, the expressive nuances of particular performances have been considered matters of performance practice, not composition. They are the variables that distinguish different performances of the same piece, tune, or song. They give the live performance its sense of unique moment and mark it as the performer's personal musical expression. While the work being played is represented by some set of more or less fixed relationships, the variables of performance bring out different aspects of its character. Recording, on the other hand, transforms the particularities of performance from ephemera to fixed concrete elements that are repeated precisely each time the work is heard. The state of fixedness that they impose on music is, for some, unnatural. As "we become aware of the fact of literal repetition, of mechanical reproduction . . . [music] ceases to be alive," writes Roger Sessions, and "in the most real sense . . . it ceases to be music."[2] In order to rationalize such a seemingly unmusical state of affairs, many regard recordings as reproductions or representative snapshots of music making that properly belongs to a specific time and place. For to think of records otherwise is to decontextualize the musical moment and set it adrift in an electronic void.

But it takes only a shift in one's point of view to regard the repeatability of recorded performances as a central factor in their transformation from activities to embodied characters. It takes only a willingness on the part of recordists and audiences to accept that the recording has its own aura and that its time and place as an authentic musical moment is each time that its sounds emanate from a loudspeaker. For if a performance can be repeated without the performer present, its record takes on an identity of its own, which it asserts with each repeated playing. Not surprisingly, effecting such a transformation—what I called in chapter 1 a transferal of aura—involves a process quite different from live music making. Recording musicians are well aware that as they sing and play they also perform acts of inscription, they leave something behind. Or better, they pass something on. Although their performances originate as activities, they become textual content. Performing in the recording studio is not an end in itself, but rather, a means of producing a track's constituent parts, of developing and executing specific musical utterances aimed at defining the character and identity of the record. The recording musician's task is to pass on his or her musical persona, and whether this involves a series of painstaking steps or a first-take spontaneity, the moment of performance is not the ultimate point of the process. There is an ever-present concern for how the performance will hold up over time, how well it will travel. For in the form of the work the performative moment is transformed into an enduring aesthetic object.

The performances that we hear on records present a complex collection of elements. Musical syntactic elements such as pitches and rhythms are augmented by specific inflections and articulations, which include particularities of timbre, phrasing, intonation, and so forth. Furthermore, the inscription process captures the traces of emotion, psyche, and life experience expressed by performers. That is, the *passion* of the musical utterance is yet another element of a record's identity. Stax trumpeter Wayne Jackson said of Wilson Pickett that he had "that ability to transfer a slice of his soul to tape."[3] It is this ability that the successful recording musician brings to the process. And the individuality inherent in each musician's performance means that different records of the same song will represent distinct works, rather than simply rearrangements. Think of Otis Redding's and Aretha Franklin's versions of "Respect," the Paragons' and Blondie's versions of "The Tide Is High," the Supremes' and Soft Cell's versions of "Where Did Our Love Go?" Differences of not only arrangement and sound but of gender, race, and cultural milieu are all etched into the records' grooves. It is common for specific musicians to be invited to participate in a project so that their personal musical sensibility and perspective can be incorporated into the overall work. Drummers such as Manu Katché, Kenny Aronoff, and Larry Mullen Jr., for example, make many guest appearances on a variety of different artists' records, always appearing as themselves. That is, they are not called upon to alter their styles in a chameleonic way, as professional studio musicians often are. And once again, it is not only their playing style but their recording style that they are known for: a combination of performance elements—rhythmic feel, tone quality, and so forth—and the actual sounds that contribute to the "voice" of a record. Experienced recording musicians actually play *to* the medium. As producer Rob Stevens puts it, "A good player like Jim Keltner knows how to hit the drums so they sound great on tape."[4]

The set of qualities that define a musician's recorded persona are immediately evoked by the lexicon of commonly understood musician references, such as the "Duane Eddy guitar sound," or the "John Bonham drum sound." Each of these refers first of all to a combination of a performance style and a recorded sound, and secondly, is a reference to a group of specific works and a broader musical style. Even expressions like "Everly-style harmonies" or "Dylanesque phrasing" allude to more than a particular harmonic configuration or a style of vocalizing. In the recording culture musicians' styles take on a symbolic quality, signifying a particular set of associations. This is still another element in the rhetoric of record making. When Mark Knopfler wanted to emulate ZZ Top on the Dire Straits single "Money for Nothing," (1985) he knew that a referential blues riff alone wouldn't do it. He phoned Billy Gibbons to ask how he got his distinctive guitar sound. Gibbons wouldn't say, and in the end Knopfler managed only a very rough imitation. Even so, the listener knows that this is not Knopfler's usual combination of guitar sound and playing style, which is itself quite distinctive. He has stepped out of his familiar character and put on a sonic mask.[5]

The symbolic attributes of performance styles can function in different ways, sometimes simultaneously. For example, an unlikely meeting of recorded personas on a given record may have the potential both to pose an intriguing interpretive problem and to sell to a wider audience. A famous such example is Eddie Van Halen's appearance on Michael Jackson's "Beat It" (1982). Van Halen represents not only himself but heavy metal in general, an overwhelmingly white rock style. Jackson, on the other hand, with his Motown background, represents a particular African-American pop tradition. The two styles are not blended in any way; one is simply superimposed on the other. They are meant to be intersecting entities, and as they cross one another's path their meeting enriches the track. At the same time, Van Halen's presence helped to gain airplay for the single on rock radio stations that would otherwise not have programmed it.

There are also collective performance styles associated with groups of records and historical periods—the Motown sound, the Muscle Shoals sound, the Stax sound, the Wrecking Crew sound. Each of these is made up of a more or less regular group of session musicians who contribute a characteristic group sound to the work of different songwriters, vocalists, and producers. The contributions of these musicians include, of course, their qualities as an ensemble, such as interactive rhythm and intonation. But in addition, they are often called upon to invent the musical parts that they play. Jon Fitzgerald reminds us that contrary to the common criticism of Motown as "an assembly line of interchangeable parts," under the tight control of producers such as Brian Holland, Lamont Dozier, and Mickey Stevenson, the recording process was in fact interactive. It was "likely to be a very dynamic and communal process" in which the players were given minimal direction—"about five chords and a feel" as pianist Earl Van Dyke put it—and were expected to provide their own parts. "Yes, they'd give you a chord sheet and say, 'You're on your own,' " recalled bassist James Jamerson, one of the Funk Brothers without whom, Dozier acknowledged, "a lot of the ideas wouldn't have been possible."[6]

The interactive nature of ensemble playing adds its own particular quality to a recording in the form of the energy passing among the players. During recording for Emmylou Harris's *Wrecking Ball* (1995), for example, a premium was placed on the interactions among musicians playing together in the studio. Overdubs were used sparingly in an attempt to capture a particular kind of musical atmosphere. Harris recalls:

> We would sit really close together with no separation, and work up the arrangements and go for a performance, with a live vocal and

minimal amount of overdubs. Bleeding into the microphones was kind of encouraged on this record. With that, I think you get another *participant* on the track, which is the room and the energy and the performance. It's an ambience that you can only get going with that live situation.[7]

On the other hand, the recording process includes performance techniques that are entirely different in concept and practice from any live situation. Overdubbing requires the performer to summon up inspired performances in the absence of not only an audience but other musicians. What in a live situation is an interactive interchange among players—a kind of musical breathing together—becomes a one-way responsive relationship between the musician and a fixed, unchanging musical partner, the track. Furthermore, the context and the musical clues that it provides may be limited. That is, if the track is built gradually, then there may be very little on tape for the overdubbing musician to respond to. Part of what makes overdubbing such a different, and difficult, kind of music making is the element of conjuring that it involves, the degree to which the musician's imagination must replace the missing elements of conventional musical performance.

Overdubs may be mere fragments of music, perhaps just a few notes to add a particular color or affective flavor to a track. Hence, while they may require concentrated imagination, technical proficiency is not always necessary. Musicians can bring their musical sensibilities to instruments other than their primary one, which can lead to some fresh and interesting approaches as they are forced to abandon long-established habits and patterns and focus primarily upon using their powers of sheer musical expression to create a musical statement that while technically simple, is flushed with expressive depth. "If things start sounding too commonplace on people's normal instruments, then I just ask them to play another instrument, just to come up with things from a more unusual or stranger angle," says Daniel Lanois, who produced *Wrecking Ball*. "In my experience, artists will create with almost any tool you present them with. It can be fascinating if you have your hands on something that you normally don't play, the idea being that the artist in you . . . should be able to make something out of anything. Musicians of that caliber can usually come up with something interesting with any instrument."[8] Mitchell Froom also finds this approach to be useful: "By having a lot of unusual instruments laying around in the studio, you can create an atmosphere where someone who barely knows how to play can find an unconventional, often naive approach to an instrument that really works."[9]

Performances may also be assembled by splicing together pieces of different takes. Although this may involve literal tape splicing, it can also include techniques such as recording many complete performances of a given part on separate tracks and then assembling a composite performance, or "punching in," that is, recording part of a performance (as little as a single note) within an existing one. Whatever form it takes, this practice represents the intrusion of analytic consideration into the midst of the musical performance. Peter Gabriel's vocal on "Love to be Loved," for example, was recorded some forty times, and David Bottrill recalls "probably" using "bits from each performance"[10] to construct the one that appears on the album (*Us*, 1992). In other words, the vocal "performance" on the recording, seamless though it may appear, was literally edited into existence. That is, it was composed.

Another practice that has become common since the advent of digital sampling is after-the-fact alteration of a performer's sound. This is especially widespread with drum parts, where the rhythm data is retained but the sounds are replaced or supplemented. Sound quality is an essential aspect of any performer's technique and expressive style; the act of performing involves continual responses to the sound being produced. The dynamic shape of a phrase, the specific articulation of a rhythm, or the improvisation of a fill, for instance, are always connected to what the performer hears. Indeed, *all* aspects of a performance are in some way interdependent. When a performance shaped in terms of one set of sounds is adapted to a completely different set, the relationships among the various performance parameters are the results not of a performative act but of analytic deliberation. Responsibility for reassembling and reordering the relationships may remain with the performer, or may pass to the producer or engineer, but in any case, the performance is transformed from an integrated, real-time process to a composed structure consisting of discrete elements.[11]

The performance practices sampled here are carried out within the individual performance; but the concept of performance-building extends to ensembles as well. With overdubbing, various components of a track can be recorded at different times. In its extreme form this leads to situations where a band can record an entire album yet never see one another in the recording studio, and living performers can "perform" with dead ones.[12] It also makes it possible to move master tapes around the world, recording different musicians in different places at different times, and creating collages of musical cultures and recording places. Roy Halee, who has worked with Paul Simon off and on as engineer and producer since Simon and Garfunkel's *Wednesday Morning 3 A.M.* (1964), offers the following account of the making of "Proof" from *The Rhythm of the Saints* (1991):

> It's like the U. N. We cut the track in Paris because the Cameroonian rhythm section live in Paris. That was two guitars, bass, keyboards and a drummer playing foot pedal and a high hat for time. Then we brought in "legit" horn players from Paris. We came back to New York and put a South African bass player on it [Bakhiti Kumahlo], an American drummer [Steve Gadd], and an accordionist from New Orleans [C. J. Chenier]. . . . Then we took it down to Brazil . . . where we put on all kinds of added percussion. Then we brought it back to New York and added on female singers from Cameroon and a shaker player from New York, Ya Yo. And then after all that, Paul put his vocals on.[13]

Unity of time and place, a given in live performances, is here replaced by a new dynamic, that of the virtual ensemble for which the recording is the only incarnation. In this setting the ensemble "performance" is in fact a composite assemblage—again, a composition. Relationships within the "ensemble" are developed through the course of multiple takes. In addition to providing greater control over sound quality and technical execution, recording performances separately offers the opportunity for a single performer to play multiple parts, fashioning each layer of the composite according to a single vision of the whole. Following the example of Les Paul, artists such as Todd Rundgren, Prince, Paul McCartney, Stevie Wonder, and Karl Wallinger have all, at one time or another, used multitracking in this way to create records embodying a virtual ensemble made up of the multiple talents of a solitary musical personality.

Perhaps most importantly, however, from the standpoint of compositional process, overdubbing can be used to influence musicians' responses, which in turn affects the form of the work. Through the ordering of events in the recording process, a performer's attention can be aimed in a specific direction and his or her performance cast as a specific kind of musical dialogue that might take place only in the studio. The primary reference point for a percussion performance, for example, might be a vocal, rather than, more typically, other groove instruments. Indeed, during recording, *any* kind of ensemble can be created via the headphone mix and used temporarily to influence the character of a given performance. These temporary combos serve a range of both pragmatic and expressive functions.

Lou Reed used this evolving ensemble technique in making *Mistrial* (1986), which at the time he called his "perfect" record, in that it turned out "just the way it's supposed to be." Although his preference had been to capture something of the feeling of musicians interacting in real time by recording basic tracks live, he had repeatedly been dissatisfied with the results. For Reed, the guitar and the voice are a record's central characters, around which the rest of the band should be oriented. Due to sheer studio logistics, however, he felt that the guitar on many earlier albums had been lacking in some way. On repeated occasions he had been forced to play while standing at a distance from his amplifier, resulting in what he felt was a loss of control over his sound. With the other band members "playing to that guitar," a kind of domino effect set in and the overall performance suffered. His solution, suggested to him by Ric Ocasek, was to record the guitar parts accompanied only by a drum machine and a guide bass track. When the guitar performance was shaped to his satisfaction, the real bass and drum parts were recorded. The multitrack process thus provided optimum logistical conditions for the creation of the instrumental track's central character, which in turn influenced the subsequent performances in a positive way.[14]

In accord with Emmylou Harris's statement about the energy of ensemble playing in the studio, there are many performers who refuse to split up their performances. They may feel that their identity is so tied to their live performance style that even in the studio they must retain the energy of ensemble interaction to capture an authentic representation. Or they may feel that the overdubbing process is too artificial and is thus antithetical to the intuitive spark of live music making. Or they may simply be inexperienced at recording, finding it difficult both technically and expressively to give a good performance under such conditions. For recording can become numbing in its painstaking detail and myriad considerations, which performers do not have to deal with when they perform live. In any case, studio resources allow producers and engineers to get the most out of performers by acceding to their technical and aesthetic preferences and habits, yet reserving for themselves the ability to shape a performance that "sounds like a record." Consider Butch Vig's account of recording Nirvana's *Nevermind* (1991): "The band is really into spontaneity and first takes, and they weren't very good at doing things over and over again. So every time they were warming up, I'd be recording. After I felt they had some good performances, I'd use an Akai sampler to take things and move them around."[15]

In these sessions, Vig, who is a drummer as well as an engineer and producer, managed to navigate between the musicians' sensibilities and the needs of the project. He notes that "alternative bands are more suspicious of technology than other bands"—an aesthetic viewpoint that he respects as a "purist thing." The bands do not want to "feel like [the music] has been heavily manipulated." Nevertheless, it fell to him to make the performance work as a record, whatever that might entail. And although the raw intensity of a live punk performance served as a referential frame, the process of making the record remained a deliberate one where the producer used the band's performances in whatever way was necessary to accomplish the task. Aware of the band's needs, Vig simply went about his business in an unobtrusive way.

Phil Spector's methods of working with his ensembles were anything but unobtrusive. Spector wanted to capture the feel and energy of live playing; he hired some of the best studio musicians in Los Angeles, including many fine jazz players. Although performances were usually recorded in complete takes, the process of honing the image of the track prior to recording was a tedious one for the performers. Spector built his instrumental accompaniments by experimenting with mixes and balances of sonorities as the studio musicians played their parts over and over again in an hours-long process that was a combination of arranging, rehearsal, and mixing. He continually made adjustments—in microphone placement, balance, arrangement, ambient processing, and so forth—until he heard the sound he was after. He used the performers to fuel his creative process, directing their skills to provide himself with a living sound canvas upon which he could work out his musical ideas. Bassist Ray

Pohlman recalls that Spector "always seemed to have an idea of what he was after, but I don't know if he could always *express* it. He would let it happen with the band and let it evolve."[16]

Jazz guitarist Howard Roberts contrasted a typical session for Nelson Riddle with one for Spector: "With other producers, there would be some little fine adjustments here and there, and you'd do four sides in three hours and leave. With Nelson Riddle, it sounds great. But with Spector, we'd sit there for hours on end on one tune, strumming these three chords."[17] The difference is clear. A typical Riddle arrangement is completely scripted; the recording session is dedicated simply to capturing a clear and transparent representation of a performance of the script. Spector, on the other hand, was seeking a sonic image that could not be represented in musical notation. Its only existence prior to recording was in his imagination. As the musicians repeated their parts again and again, they provided for Spector the material he needed "to get his piece figured out," as Roberts put it.[18] Billy Preston, who played the organ on Spector's production of George Harrison's *All Things Must Pass* (1970), recalls that the process "was monotonous as hell. But he was making it the Phil Spector sound."[19]

Removing musical performance from its traditional contexts and functions and turning it into material creates a variety of risks and problems. Although a record may be put together deliberately in a series of steps, it remains a real-time musical experience for the listener. It is perceived not as an analytic construct but as a musical performance and must, therefore, convey a believable expressive feel. In the artificial atmosphere of the recording studio, however, the human emotion embodied by musical expression is easily lost. The clinical scrutiny of every detail, the ever-present option to redo, the extensive editing possibilities—all of these are potentially stifling. As engineer Ed Cherney puts it, "If you have the time and money, you can play around with it forever and go past the moment where that 'Indefinable Thing' happens. Sometimes if you put just a little more tweaking in, you may start diminishing the emotional content."[20]

Cherney is speaking here not of musicians' performances but of his own as sound mixer. Perhaps because respect for the intuitive soul of the process is the responsibility of all the participants in a project, references to some kind of "Indefinable Thing" turn up again and again in interviews. "One of the great things Dan Lanois intro-

duced me to," says Peter Gabriel, "was this idea that when something special is happening, take two tracks and grab it. I mean whenever magic appears in the studio grab it, because it is your most
valuable commodity."[21] It is also a fragile one. As producer Russ
Titelman reminds us, "you have to be careful about not taking the
feeling out of a vocal performance by trying to get it too perfect. As
far as vocals go, you're always looking for the thing that gets you in
the heart."[22] In discussing studio performances recordists refer
repeatedly to the search for—and the ability to recognize and to capture—some ephemeral "magic" in a performance, even if it is only a
moment awaiting concatenation with other such moments. The most
often-cited criterion is "feel." In an environment where technological
manipulation and analytical parsing might threaten to drain the
expressive content from any project, musicianly intuition remains
both rudder and compass.

TIMBRE

Listeners to rock are commonly engaged in the first instance by a
sonic color. "Scan across radio stations," writes Robert Walser, "and
a fraction of a second will be sufficient time to identify the musical
genre of each. Before any lyrics can be comprehended, before harmonic or rhythmic patterns are established, timbre instantly signals
genre and affect."[23] Walser is speaking about the generic timbral
qualities associated with various styles of rock, but the principle
applies equally to individual bands and to individual tracks. Think
of the chiming electric twelve-string guitar sound that represents the
central instrumental character in the Byrds' first hit single, "Mr.
Tambourine Man" (1965), the out-of-tune acoustic twelve-string guitar that begins the Rolling Stones' "As Tears Go By" (1965), or the
ominous sound of Garth Hudson's organ introduction on The Band's
"Chest Fever" (1968). In each of these, a striking sonic character adds
a further dimension of sensory meaning to the pitch and rhythmic
elements of the musical part, creating a comprehensive formulation
of musical substance.

The instruments in these examples have in common a sonic distinctiveness that places them in a thematic role within the track. They
function differently, however, suggesting a range of significance that
specific sounds can have with regard to their place in a band's sonic

history and in rock generally. The guitar sound in "As Tears Go By" is unique to that track and functions, therefore, as an exclusive identifying element. That particular tuning is not characteristic of the Rolling Stones' sound; it happened on a particular occasion, was captured on tape, and was deemed acceptable upon playback. It has probably never been duplicated exactly. Another such example is the Velvet Underground's "Heroin," where the tuning of the guitars perfectly sets the mood of funky euphoria and then resonates with the protagonist's musings on narcotic transcendence. Timbral qualities associated with a particular tuning are often important affective features of a track, especially on older records. "One thing I strongly believe," says John Leckie, "is that two of the worst things invented in the last ten years are the electronic guitar tuner and the metronome click track. . . . Since the guitar tuner was invented, I've found the timbral quality of the music to be different, sometimes blander to my ears."[24] Indeed, the standardization these tools impose removes—for better or for worse—some aspects of a track's unique character.

Unlike the track-specific nature of a particular guitar tuning, the organ sound on "Chest Fever" highlights one of the perennial timbral characters that make up the sonic identity of The Band. The sound is certainly striking. With its distortion and ambience it fills the speakers with a menacing crunch as Hudson plays a somewhat unearthly fantasy that begins with an allusion to Bach's famous D Minor organ toccata. Standing alone without accompaniment, it provides a moment of high drama not only for this track but for the album as a whole. Hudson was famous for coaxing unusual sounds out of his keyboards, and a listener might expect to hear something quite similar, at least in effect, at a live performance. In other words, although the sound is a thematic element specific to "Chest Fever," it derives from a more general part of The Band's sonic palette.[25]

The Rickenbacker electric twelve-string of "Mr. Tambourine Man" has the most general significance of the three examples, representing not just a particular moment or a certain band member, but a constellation of associations that has continued to grow with time. Initially the sound may have been a "historically pivotal . . . reveille for a brand new rock and roll day,"[26] but it was also a central timbral element on most of the Byrds' subsequent recordings. As such it came to be associated with the musical style that they exemplified: a ringing, amplified mixture of urban folk elements with a rock beat often referred to as "folk rock" but perhaps better thought of as "Byrds rock." Given the prominence of the twelve-string on a number of popular and influential Byrds records, any later use of the instrument can hardly avoid calling those records to mind.

The different kinds of significance that these examples represent hint at the broad range of functions that timbre may have. For recordists, however, the many possible forms that timbre may take fall into two general categories: the physical and the rhetorical. The physical properties of sounds have to do with such things as frequency content, relations of loudness among overtones, and envelope configuration. These make up the timbral signature of an instrument. The rhetorical aspect of timbre involves the conventional associations that sounds have, which allow them to stand as symbols suggesting dialogues and resonances beyond the boundaries of the track. As Luciano Berio has expressed it, "When instruments like the trumpet, the harpsichord, the string quartet, the recorder are used with electric guitars (or in place of them) . . . they seem to assume the estranged character of quotations of themselves."[27] In what he terms an "obvious reference to surrealism," Berio finds that "[recorded] pieces by the Rolling Stones, the [Four] Tops, the Mothers of Invention, the Grateful Dead, and above all the Beatles" move beyond the "idea of *song* and develop into a sort of sound drama . . . in the form of a *collage*." In these dramatic collages, "the 'extra' instruments are adopted like polished objects from a far-off world."[28]

Certainly the Beatles were important figures in broadening the available palette of rock timbres. When George Martin suggested strings to Paul McCartney for the "Yesterday" arrangement, McCartney was leery of the associations this called to mind. "He hated syrup," Martin recalls, "or anything that was even a suggestion of MOR."[29] A ballad arranged for swelling strings seemed altogether too soft for the Beatles image at the time, and McCartney became interested in the idea only when Martin suggested a string quartet—no longer an association with "MOR," but rather the more exotic "far-off world" of classical music. Still, it was an unprecedented move for the Beatles. As Martin commented, "in the pop world of those days, [it] was quite a step to take"[30]—so much so that the track was not released as a single in the U. K., though it became a number one hit in the United States, a position it held for four weeks. Its success, along with the Beatles' widespread influence throughout rock culture, assured that the string quartet became an accepted element in the rock palette at large. Later that same year the Rolling Stones—with a much tougher rock and roll image than the Beatles—used a string quartet in "As Tears Go By." And, of course, Martin's fine double quartet arrangement is the sole accompaniment for the vocals in "Eleanor Rigby," completely displacing the standard rock instrumental timbres of guitars, bass, and drums. Throughout their careers, the Beatles steadily expanded their timbral palette and in the process changed the nature of conventional expectation for the entire rock idiom. Another example is the track for "Love You To," also from *Revolver,* which is built on a sonic foundation of sitar and tabla timbres. In a very short time rock's stylistic possibilities took on a very different appearance from the one presented by its original instrumental lineup of guitar, bass, and drums.

Timbre is the parameter that allows for the greatest range of experimentation in rock music. While highly chromatic melodies and irregular meters are unusual, the range of sound colors encountered on records is vast and ever increasing. Among these one might list the sounds of musical instruments of all sorts, sound effects, synthesized sounds, and simulated ambient images, any of which can be shaped with various electronic processors. As George Martin puts it, "In pop music . . . the sky's the limit. . . . We have an infinite palette of musical colours."[31] Bruce Swedien, who began recording in the late 1940s and has participated in what he calls a "transformation" in the techniques and aesthetics of record production, wrote in 1991 that "In modern music production, the only limit to our sonic palette is our imagination. . . . [W]e are now free to create a sonic canvas with our creativity as the sole limiting factor."[32] To be sure, "modern music production" has benefited from technological developments that have provided ever greater resources for sound shaping. But the impulse to thematize recorded sound and to use it as a formal element rather than a documentary representation is apparent on records from rock's earliest days. Subsequent developments have simply continued and expanded the practice—a continuation of aesthetic that connects recording practices in all of rock's varied styles and genres in a multifaceted tradition of record making. In other words, the "infinite palette" is not simply the playground of individuals' imaginations but a product of historical accumulation. The rhetorical sense of sounds develops through the process of cultural practice.

The symbolism attached to sounds in rock is a source of identity for tracks, artists, styles, and audiences. It can be a powerful force. When Bob Dylan switched from acoustic to electric guitar in 1965, there was an uproar from those who saw it as a move against the presumed authenticity associated with the urban folk style of the early sixties, of which Dylan had been the leading light. The symbolic significance of the sound obscured for a great many listeners any other sense of the music. Yet rock artists and audiences are so finely attuned to timbre as a stylistic element that categorical distinctions are far more precise than simply electric guitar versus acoustic guitar. Sounds carry with them entire stylistic legacies, and as rock has developed, the nuances of the stylistic language have become ever more refined. No one would confuse the bright, ringing guitar sound of "Mr. Tambourine Man" with the heavy, distorted guitar sound that opens Led Zeppelin's "Whole Lotta Love" (1969). But to rock fans there is an equally obvious difference between the distortion of "Whole Lotta Love" and that of Jimi Hendrix's "Purple Haze" (1967). And the distinction carries over to the performers—Roger McGuinn, Jimmy Page, and Hendrix. The timbral differences become associated with perceived differences in overall artistic persona that include both off- and onstage images projected by the artists, as well as playing styles and repertoires.

Electric guitar distortion is common to many rock styles. It is one reason why many call the Delta Rhythm Kings' "Rocket '88,' " recorded by Sam Phillips in 1951, the "first rock and roll record." It gives Link Wray's "Rumble" (1958) its reason for being. And it is the sound that put the Rolling Stones at the top of the pops for good, in the form of the riff that announced "(I Can't Get No) Satisfaction" (1965). But this generalization does not begin to tell the story of the conflicting stances associated with different *kinds* of distortion. The distorted guitar sound on Def Leppard's *Pyromania* (1983), produced by Robert "Mutt" Lange, for instance, is highly refined, clean and smooth, like large slabs of polished marble; on Nirvana's *Nevermind* it is ragged, edgy, and searing. They each project different images, representing different musical styles and aesthetic attitudes. Lange is known for spending a great deal of time in the studio carefully crafting sounds, and the Def Leppard sound is intentionally controlled, made safe for mainstream pop consumption. Like cinematic special effects that thrill but are never mistaken for reality, it is prized mainly for its larger-than-life quality. For Rick Savage, the band's bassist, "the whole idea of Def Leppard is escapism." Lead vocalist, Joe Elliot concurs: "It's all wine, women, and song. Nothing annoys me more than records about politics this, Greenpeace that. . . . All we are is total escapism."[33]

Nirvana's Kurt Cobain, on the other hand, alludes to the kind of distortion heard on punk rock recordings dating back to the Velvet Underground's *White Light/White Heat* (1968). The guitar tracks on *Nevermind* are as raw as the vocals, which, rather than "escapism," are more like a total immersion in Cobain's world. Here, distortion is part of an intensely personal expression, a sonic assault on the mainstream shot straight from the soul of the outsider. In addition to its own sonic energy, it draws symbolic power from its association with precursors like the Stooges and the Sex Pistols. The guitar here is meant to sound like a spontaneous eruption of maverick psychic energy manifested in musical expression, and while the symbolic image may be at odds with the actual process—remember Vig's after-the-fact manipulations of Nirvana performances—invoking the symbol convincingly is part of the record-making craft.

These thoughts about the symbolic character of sounds lead us back to their physical properties. There are material reasons why sounds strike us as they do. The mental images conjured by adjectives such as "dark," "bright," "muffled," or "edgy" have what we might call spectrographic translations. That is, they refer to a particular configuration of physical characteristics. Recordists manipulate these characteristics as they create their sonic tapestry. They do not simply *record* sounds; in common parlance, they "get" sounds. That is, they tailor the sound image in some way using the tools and techniques at their disposal. Recording inevitably changes a sound's character in some way. Merely aiming a microphone involves sorting through many options, to say nothing of choosing a microphone, a preamp, and a recording medium, setting levels, or applying equalization (EQ) or compression. Skillful manipulation may be required even if the aim is to make it seem as though the recording is a transparent portrait. But one of the most pervasive practices in rock recording is the search for some distinctive sonic quality—distinctive, that is, in relation to conventional associations. As they go about getting sounds, often in adventurous ways, rock recordists' search for distinctive colors may lead them far from acoustical reality and deeper into a sound world born of the imagination.

Again, the Beatles provide a rich trove of examples. Acoustic guitars, unlike electric ones, are usually not treated with distortion, but for the Beatles the sound became a favorite. Paul McCartney remembers that the trick "was to over-record an acoustic guitar, so you'd swing the needle into the red and it'd be there, hard, every time you'd played it." As a result, "the acoustic would come back like an electric, it wouldn't distort too much, it would just mess around with that original sound. It'd make it *hot*."[34] McCartney cites "Ob La Di, Ob La Da" as a track where this was done, but the guitar is masked somewhat by the piano. A more dramatic example of the technique can be heard on "I'm Only Sleeping," from *Revolver*.

Once they gained their creative freedom in the studio, radical sonic manipulation became an integral part of the Beatles' creative process. Altered tape speed, backward tape effects, and unusual electronic processing were added to their already extensive timbral palette. In rock after the mid-sixties, no sound was unthinkable. As engineer Eddie Offord remembers, "If you thought of something and could figure out a way of how to do it, then you were on your way." Working with Yes in the early 1970s, Offord presided over many sessions where unusual sounds were created through a combination of technical know-how and imaginative fancy. Recalling one of the tracks from Yes's *Close to the Edge* (1972), he illustrates the sort of lengths that the team went to in search of fresh sounds:

> For the guitar solo on a song called "Siberian Khatru" I had two mics, one a regular close-up and the other on a twenty-foot cord which I had the assistant swing in a circle around the studio. It was going close to Steve's [Howe] amp on every cycle, and that gave it a real kind of Doppler effect as it went by.[35]

Variations on the Doppler effect, most famously associated with the rotating speaker sound of the Leslie cabinet, designed by Don Leslie for use with Hammond organs, are common on rock records. When the Beatles discovered that they could put virtually any sound through a Leslie, they did so, at least as an experiment. Working with Roxy Music, Chris Thomas, in an unlikely move aimed at finding a sonic character "that was different," put Paul Thompson's snare drum sound through a Leslie on the track, "Love Is the Drug," from the *Siren* album (1975).[36] But as Offord indicates, the effect can be produced in different ways, each with their own sonic nuance. Engineer Joe Hardy tells of creating the effect by "putting two wireless SM58 microphones on a ceiling fan" and using them to record an acoustic guitar. This unusual technique was the solution to a specific problem:

> I wanted this acoustic guitar to sound sort of like a Leslie, but the problem is that when you run an acoustic guitar through a Leslie cabinet, it sort of destroys the acoustic-ness of it—once you amplify the guitar, then it's no longer an acoustic instrument. It may be a cool sound, but it's a different thing.[37]

Such anecdotes are literally innumerable. Recordists tell of vocals pumped through wah-wah pedals, bass drums filled with volcanic rock, microphones placed inside paper towel tubes, loudspeakers wired to work as microphones, electric guitars strummed with an airbrush—nothing seems to be out of the question in the pursuit of distinctive, that is, "cool," sounds. In the words of engineer Joe Chiccarelli, rather than "the standard hi-fi model of getting everything to sound good," the aim is "to push the limits in search of the unique."[38]

Ultimately the physical and the rhetorical aspects of sounds merge. That is, they serve different functions at the same time. For example, from a physical standpoint a glockenspiel's function is to add high frequency information to the overall frequency structure of a track. In a setting such as Bruce Springsteen's "Born to Run" (1975), it provides an etched quality to the melodies it doubles, helping them to stand out from the thick surrounding texture. However, it also makes a clear reference to Phil Spector, who used the glockenspiel similarly in many of his "wall of sound" productions.[39] Thus, as the glockenspiel fulfills its orchestrational function it also makes specific connections to an artist, a style, a body of work, and an era, all of which factor into the sense that we make both of the sound and of its context, the track.

Like any other formal element, timbre can also play a significant thematic role—both physically and rhetorically—in a track's structural design. U2's "Zoo Station" (1991), for example, from *Achtung Baby*, uses two general types of timbres in a way that delineates son-

ically the track's overall narrative. At the same time, the timbral juxtaposition reaches beyond the song to make a symbolic statement
about the band's history. As the track begins we hear a collage of distorted guitar sounds. Although U2's guitarist, Edge, was known for
creative experimentation with guitar sounds and effects, these are
unlike anything heard previously on a U2 record. In fact, U2's preceding sessions in the studio had produced *Rattle and Hum* (1988), a
paean to the roots of American rock and roll. At the end of a New
Year's Eve concert in Dublin on the last night of 1989, Bono told the
crowd that U2 had to go away for awhile and "dream it all up again."
The result of their retreat of eighteen months was *Achtung Baby,* and
the album's opening track, "Zoo Station," stands as an announcement that U2 had changed. If the strangeness of the guitar timbres
posed an immediate interpretive problem, the entrance of the snare
drum did little to orient the U2 fan. Its low frequencies are sharply
attenuated and it has a cold, processed sound, something like beating
on a tin can. The physical relationship between the snare and the primary guitar riff (see figure 1) is complementary. The guitar is thick,
drenched with a submerged kind of ambience, and occupies a lower
part of the track's overall frequency spectrum, while the snare sound
is thin, quite dry, and pitched higher. The rhetorical sense, in which all
participants to this point are unified, points to the highly processed,
mechanized sound of the techno/industrial genre. The sonic allusion
is to a futuristic, machine-ruled world—an image quite at odds with
the passionate humanism that U2 had been known for. Before any
words are sung, the sounds alone alert the listener that the band has
moved into new expressive territory.

While the first few seconds of the introduction set up an intellec-
tually puzzling atmosphere, the bass entrance provides a visceral
presence that goes straight to the body, enveloping the listener in
pulsing, vibrating energy. It also brings in a contrasting character, one
that fulfills expectations both in terms of rock recordings at large and
U2's own catalog. At the first vocal entrance in the introduction—
structurally analogous to the song's chorus—the murky industrial
sounds give way to the relative clarity of the soaring natural voice.
This is the Bono that we know. Simultaneously, the anchoring bass
riff releases, providing a further sense of lift. As the song moves on
to the first verse, the mechanized atmosphere of the introduction

Figure 1

returns, joined now by a strange, robotlike vocal sound—Bono's industrial double. Throughout the track the strange tension of the verses is followed by the soaring release of the choruses, and each time the change is signaled by vocal timbre as well as the harmonic release of the bass. The contrasting interplay between sounds that are familiar and sounds that are highly processed and thus disorient the listener's expectations of genre and artist identity creates a sound drama whose structure roughly mirrors that of the song; at the same time, it makes a historical statement about the band's evolving identity. The sense I get is of U2 alternately looking backward and forward within the same track.[40]

Brian Eno was one of the producers of *Achtung Baby*. Previously, Eno had produced U2's *The Unforgettable Fire* (1984) and *The Joshua Tree* (1987), and though he was not part of the creative team when the sessions for *Achtung Baby* began, he was brought in as they foundered. The move made sense because of the prior successful collaborations. But more importantly, U2 was attempting, uncertainly, to expand its sonic identity, and Eno, with his long and varied experience as an artist for whom the most subtle sonic nuance may hold a profound significance, provided a steadying and confident influence. Eric Tamm has written about Eno's own so-called ambient music: "Much of the meaning . . . hinges on very subtle factors having to do with the vertical spectrum of tone color; the exact hues of a sound, down to almost imperceptible shifts in overtone structure, are for Eno the substance of the music itself."[41] Furthermore, "If in the classical work the timbre may be said to adorn the structure, then in the ambient work the structure adorns the timbre."[42] This is an interesting twist that seeks to rearrange some conventional music theoretical priorities, and it is a useful move for shaking up some well-worn attitudes toward musical analysis. The example of "Zoo Station," however, presents yet another way of looking at (or hearing) the issue. Here, neither timbre nor structure are adornments; rather, each complements the other, intensifying the overall effect of the narrative as the tension and release of the song structure is mirrored by the changes in timbre.

ECHO

Echo is simply the replication of a sound. It is produced by recording a sound on tape or in computer memory and playing back the recording immediately following the original sound. The word is often used interchangeably with ambience, or "reverb"—as in "echo chamber," which is in fact an ambient chamber—but the two are quite different in both nature and function. The difference was brought home to executives at RCA when they heard the first recordings Elvis Presley made after he had come to the label from Sun Records. Discrete echo is an integral part of the distinctive sound of Presley's early records. The RCA engineers, apparently unaware of Sam Phillips's technique, sought to replicate the effect using added ambience, but the cavernous quality of the ambient atmosphere on "Heartbreak Hotel" is altogether different from the nervous rhythmic shake that propelled so many of the Sun sides. The change in sound was at least partly responsible for the initial corporate consternation at RCA, with executives wondering, as they watched Carl Perkins's crisply echoing "Blue Suede Shoes" climb the charts, whether perhaps the wrong artist had been signed.[43]

Echo has proven to be extremely versatile as a compositional resource in rock. It provides recordists with an array of timbral, textural, rhythmic, and atmospheric possibilities, depending on the configuration of the relationship between the source sound and its replica. The elements of this relationship include: 1) temporal separation (delay time), 2) relative amplitudes, 3) numbers of repeats, 4) possible spatial separation (on a stereo or surround sound recording), and 5) potential processing of the echo independently of its source. Because it is a post factum imitation of an initial sound, echo is often referred to as "delay," and its use, as a "time-domain" process. The way the delayed sound is treated and set in relation to its source determines the type of effect it produces and the function that it has in the track. For example, a low-amplitude single echo with a very short delay time—below 25 milliseconds—may act simply as a textural thickener, adding weight and presence to the source sound but having no distinct identity of its own. Such short delays are commonly used for subtle enhancements that are inaudible as discrete sonic entities yet provide an extra layer of sonic complexity and interest.

Raising the echo's volume to a level roughly equal to that of its source produces a distinctive timbral effect often referred to as automatic double tracking (ADT). As the name implies, the effect approximates the sound of a doubled performance produced by overdubbing. With ADT, although the delay time is still too short for the echo to be perceived as an independent image, the timbral effect is marked. Listen, for example, to John Lennon's vocal on "I'm Only Sleeping." Because he didn't like the sound of his natural voice on tape, Lennon had been in the habit of doubling his lead vocals. The process was tedious, and around the time of the *Revolver* sessions (1966), Ken Townsend, who was working as a technician at Abbey Road Studios, devised a means for producing a similar effect electronically. Lennon's voice was sent to a second tape recorder whose motor was controlled by a variable speed oscillator. Because tape echo is produced by the time gap corresponding to the distance between record and playback heads, varying the speed at which the tape covers that distance allows the echo's delay time to be tailored to create the desired effect. The sound can be heard throughout *Revolver*, especially on tracks where Lennon or George Harrison takes the lead.

Short delay times can be used to create a range of timbral effects. Feeding a controlled amount of delayed sound back into the input of the second tape recorder (thus producing several repeats of the echo) and varying the tape speed within a narrow range (thus causing a continual modulation in the source/echo time relationship) produces the effect that came to be known as flanging. On George Harrison's "Blue Jay Way" (1967), a track filled with imaginative timbral treatments, the flanging effect on the vocal and the snare is particularly striking. To an exotic-sounding melody that features major third, minor third, and raised fourth scale degrees, a processed voice sings, "There's a fog upon the lake / And my friends have lost their way." The timbral treatment resonates perfectly with the song's lyrics, melodic configuration, and languid vocal style. It is an element of the track's overall thematic flow, and as such, it changes as the track progresses. In the choruses the dramatic sense of the treated voice is intensified as its choked sound, squeezed now through a rotating Leslie speaker, pleads, "Please don't be long / Please don't you be very long." Because Townsend's invention allowed for the speed of the tape machine producing the echo to be varied in real time using the oscillator, the Beatles used it as they would a musical instrument. Engineer Geoff Emerick recalls, "John—or George if it was his song—used to sit in the control room on mixes and actually play the oscillator."[44] Timbral extensions of a sound produced by flanging, phasing, chorusing, and so forth are all echo-based, each representing a type of sonic treatment associated with dynamic modulation of the source/echo time relationship.

As the source sound and its echo become more widely separated in time, the latter takes on more of an individual presence, which again can produce a range of effects. The famous echo that Sam Phillips used on many of his Sun Records sides was also produced by a second tape recorder, but in this case with something like a 70-millisecond delay between source and echo. In this application the temporal relationship is fixed, producing not a timbral effect but a constant close-range mimicry. Known as slapback, this configuration provides a distinctive rhythmic feel to a track, an urgency. On Elvis Presley's "Blue Moon of Kentucky" recording of July 1954, the voice's echo adds a quality of nervous energy to the words and a rhythmic density to the overall texture of the track. The effect is influenced by tempo, performance style, lyrics, amplitude, and timbre. The quick tempo insures that the voice continually crowds the echo—a breathless effect that is further heightened by the rushed vocal phrasing. Presley's clipped delivery is filled with incisive attacks, emphasizing the hard consonants in the lyrics. The resulting percussive quality is passed on to the echo, so that even though it's kept well in the background in terms of loudness, the hard quality of the echo's attacks imparts a pervasive rambunctiousness to the overall rhythmic fabric that emanates from a place somewhere within the track.

"Blue Moon of Kentucky" is a fairly typical example of the slapback effect. But Phillips also used tape echo for more than its rhythmic energy. Presley recorded the Rodgers and Hart song "Blue Moon" some six weeks later, and on this track Phillips used the doubled voice to create an entirely different effect. At this track's slower tempo the undulating echoes are felt not so much as rhythmic pulses but as ghostly shadows. Indeed, the sustained notes during the falsetto section and on some of the words—like "moon"—obscure the echo's attacks altogether, creating instead a timbral effect, a kind of hollow phasing sound. For the words that are not sustained, the track's slow tempo allows space for the echo to sound more distinctly, as does the echo's relative amplitude, which is louder than on "Blue Moon of Kentucky." All in all, the echo's individual prominence contributes to the track's haunted feeling.

Because of its association with a particular musical style, slapback echo is often invoked as an associative reference. Bruce Springsteen, for example, emulates the effect on tracks such as "She's the One" (1975) and "Working on the Highway" (1984), though in each case the emulation is of a different order. On "She's the One" the slapback is incorporated into a larger vocal texture thickened by doubling and harmonization—more Spector than rockabilly. Thus, while the slapback serves as an allusive reference, the overall texture combines several stylistic elements. In "Working on the Highway," on the other hand, the slapback is closer to a direct stylistic quotation. It produces the same sort of tremulous shake as Presley's "Baby, Let's Play House" (1955).

In the development of a music so stylistically dependent upon machinery, the history of technology and the history of musical style are linked.[45] The slapback effect was a result of technological possibilities of the 1950s, with which it remains associated. In the 1960s and 1970s, echo's rhythmic possibilities were expanded through the use of tape loops employing either tape machines or a dedicated device such as the Echoplex, which was essentially a tape loop in a box. Recordists sometimes went to great lengths to create the desired rhythm. Roy Thomas Baker tells of one tape loop used for the vocal introduction to Queen's "Now I'm Here" (1975), where two tape machines were placed about ten feet apart to produce a two-beat delay and a sort of auto-antiphonal effect with multiple Freddie Mercurys.[46] In the 1980s, when computer-based digital delay units—which allow delay times to be set in millisecond increments—became widely available in studios, such rhythmic effects became common. Making it possible to set delay times that coincide with a track's metric subdivisions at the touch of a button, digital delay brought unprecedented flexibility and control to the source/echo relationship, and echo became a standard element in the mechanized groove. Listen, for example, to Nile Rodgers' production of David Bowie's "Let's Dance" (1983), with its groove-synchronized echoes of synthesizer stabs and temple blocks bouncing across the stereo spectrum; or Tom Petty's "Don't Come Around Here No More" (1985), whose groove, under the influence of coproducer Dave Stewart (Eurhythmics), is the product of sixteenth-note echoes rolling off of the tom-toms and snare. The latter was a popular technique of the time, a sort of 1980s version of slapback controlled now with digital precision. Paul Young's recording of "Everytime You Go Away" (1985) uses it on the kick, snare, and cow bell as a pronounced afterbeat. Oftentimes, this effect is used only for the snare, and at low volume, creating more of a broad shadow for the backbeat than a clearly articulated attack. In "Everytime You Go Away," however, the rhythmic stutter is quite distinct. It is removed during the guitar solo, reinstated during the final pre-chorus, removed again for the final choruses, and brought back once more for the coda. Thus, echo joins the rest of the instruments in the percussion ensemble with its own part in the musical arrangement.

"Everytime You Go Away" also illustrates some popular contemporary uses of time-based timbral processing in which the bass and some synthesizer and guitar sounds are treated with various chorusing effects. In addition to its rhythmic influence, digital delay brought about the widespread use of echo's timbral effects, for it provided precise control over numbers of repeats (feedback) and modulation of the time relationship between source and echo. Instead of "playing the oscillator," the recordist could now program the rate and degree of change in the relationship to produce an extensive palette of timbral effects that can be called up instantly. Guitarists like James Honeyman Scott (the Pretenders), Edge, and Andy Summers (the Police) incorporated such processing into the fabric of their styles. Likewise, keyboardists, bass players, drummers, and vocalists all took a new interest in the palette of sonic effects that could now be produced so easily. Treatments that once were available only in recording studios, and even then only with some effort, now became common in live performances.

It is important to remember that echo, though initiated by a source, is a separate sound and can therefore be treated independently. That is, it can have a different timbre, stereo placement, or ambient image from its source. Many of the tracks on *Revolver*, for example, have the vocal and its ADT-replicated echo set on opposite sides of the stereo spectrum. Although the delay time is very short, the spatial separation creates a vocal image that is spread out across the stereo field, the voice and its counterpoised double framing the dimensions of the stereo space. As with temporal separation, spatial separation gives the echo a more individual presence. It becomes a distinct character in the sound drama. Peter Gabriel's vocal on "Love to Be Loved" begins with a combination of both temporal and spatial separation between source and echo, creating an atmospheric effect that emphasizes the introspection of the lyrics. Through the first half of the song the voice is echoed with a short but noticeable delay time. The replica is panned to the left of its source and set at a lower relative volume, in effect casting a shadow that sweeps rapidly from right to left across the stereo space with each phrase. Gabriel begins the song quietly. As he measures each halting phrase, the focus on his voice is diffused as it repeatedly disappears into its own shadow. The sense of sonic mystery is both sensually pleasing and affectively resonant with the singer's tone of voice. Indeed, when at the line "In this moment" the tone of voice intensifies and takes on a new urgency, the echo disappears momentarily, leaving the voice suddenly exposed. It returns immediately, but not as a directional shadow. It is now balanced on either side of the voice.

In the second half of the song—beginning with the suspension of meter and the line "This old familiar craving"—the echo recedes, bringing the vocal forward, increasing its presence and altering its affective character. The sense is of coming out of shadow into light. The change underscores the pleading quality of the vocal at this point. Thus throughout this track the vocal echo is used dynamically to guide the focus of the listener's attention in ways that correspond to the affective sense of the vocal performance, changing the listener's perspective and intensifying the dramatic progression in the song.

In 1976, when David Bowie asked Tony Visconti to work with him on the sessions that would produce *Low*, Visconti mentioned that he had acquired a new piece of gear, "the second Eventide Harmonizer [a delay-based processor] in the U. K.," whose "virtues" he had been exploring. "When asked what the Harmonizer did," recalls Visconti, "I replied, 'It f— with the fabric of time,' to which Bowie responded, 'Holy shit! Bring it with you.' "[47] Recordists have long had a fascination with echo, and new tools and applications continue to develop. It has been a rich source of distinctive sonic treatments. But the fascination also stems from the integration of mechanical time and musical time. Echo, unlike ambience, is not produced acoustically. Its creation and manipulation always involves some kind of machine. The machine-made replica calls forth a metaphoric aura encompassing such images as mirror, memory, shadow, doppelganger, color, mask, ghost, projection, hallucination, hiccup, ricochet, quiver, and pulse. Using echo as a compositional resource represents a willing invitation held out by recordists to their machines to join in the creative process. Moreover, the use of echo is a vestige of rock and roll's initial preoccupation with record making. An echo is a recorded sound, and using it as a formative element foregrounds the essential power of sound recording to capture and control moments of time represented in sound and to transform those moments into material strands of the musical work.

AMBIENCE

Multiple echoes produced by sound reflecting randomly off of surfaces in an enclosed space accumulate to form an aural image known as ambience, or reverb. While echo is a literal replication, ambience is the acoustic context of a sound. It reveals itself as the sound calls forth the immanent properties of the surrounding air and the surfaces that enclose it. Recording microphones hear source sounds and the resulting ambience as a composite sonic image, which can be shaped by microphone choice and placement, as well as by processing techniques such as equalization and compression.[48] Because the ambience imparted by a recording space is integral to a sound's aural identity, the relationship between the two is a central concern for recordists. Is the sound of the room to be minimized by close miking and/or damping? Or should its presence be emphasized? Does its frequency content need to be filtered in some way? Will it be used for a special textural effect? And the sound of the recording space is only the first of what may be many ambient images to be considered. The myriad possibilities offered by various ambience simulators are also among the compositional choices to be made. For sound that is produced at a particular location can effectively be "placed" somewhere else through various techniques of ambience generation, such as an "echo chamber," a vibrating steel plate, or computer software. The last has given recordists for the last twenty years an unprecedented array of possible ambient configurations, that is, any sound can be placed anywhere. The image of a cathedral, a concert hall, or a cavern can be drawn by sound that is actually produced in a small room. Furthermore, the programmability of separate reverberation parameters—pre-delay, decay time, and so on—allows for the creation of any number of virtual acoustic spaces that have no physical equivalent. Ambience is a mediating force that gives form and character to the sound world of the recording. Like the mirror in Jean Cocteau's *Orphée*—which serves as a doorway between two dimensions—it draws the listener into an aural world whose shape, dimensions, lighting, and perspective it helps to define. Because we associate ambience with space, it provides the illusion that the recording exists in some unique place, the true world of the disembodied voice.

Like echo, ambience can take on a presence of its own, independent of the sound that called it forth. It can be separated from the sound in space and time; it can be processed separately; or the sound can be removed from the mix altogether, leaving only its ghostlike ambient image. And, of course, it can be made as loud as desired. It can be cast as a problematized central character, rather than a supporting one. In short, shaping the ambient image is a matter of expressive intent, and the range of possibility is vast. However the phenomenon is employed, it always involves a relationship between a sound and its consequent reverberation, and the myriad ways of shaping and manipulating this relationship involve choices that carry considerable affective significance.

No rock recordist has had a greater love of ambience than Phil Spector. It was one of his favorite devices, and it figured prominently in his "wall of sound." At Spector's recording sessions at Gold Star Studios in Los Angeles, where most of his sessions between 1958 and 1966 took place, parts were commonly doubled and tripled, the large group of musicians overwhelming the relatively small recording space with a wash of reverberant sound. According to Jack Nitzsche, who worked as an arranger for Spector, a typical rhythm section included "four keyboards . . . a grand piano, a Wurlitzer electric piano, a tack piano, and a harpsichord . . . three acoustic guitars, three basses (acoustic, electric, and a six-string Danelectro bass), electric guitar, three or four percussionists, [and] a drummer."[49] What was a kind of musical soup in the studio, with sounds both blending together in space and bleeding into one another's microphones, could be controlled by the use of multiple microphone inputs in the control room. The ambience of the room could thus be tailored and shaped by experimenting with different microphone placements and balances. The entire mix was then fed to a loudspeaker in one of Gold Star's ambient chambers, located in a converted bathroom. This sound, with its own set of ambient characteristics, was picked up by a microphone and mixed back in with the rest of the track, creating yet another textural resource.

Marshall Lieb, who as a member of Spector's first band, the Teddy Bears, participated in the early recording projects, recalls that they were "working on the transparency of music." The idea was to have "a lot of air moving around, notes being played in the air but not directly into the mikes." For the Teddy Bears, this involved overdubbing with the sound of previously recorded tracks playing through loudspeakers, rather than headphones, back into the recording space to be picked up once again by the recording microphone. "Then," says Lieb, "when we sent it all into the chamber, this air effect is what was heard—all the notes jumbled and fuzzy. This is what we recorded—not the notes. The chamber."[50]

In 1964, jazz guitarist Barney Kessel, playing his first recording date for Spector, who was producing the Righteous Brothers' "You've Lost that Lovin' Feelin'," had much the same impression:

> [T]here was a lot of weight on each part. . . . The three pianos were different, one electric, one not, one harpsichord, and they would all play the same thing and it would all be swimming around like it was all down a well. Musically, it was terribly simple, but the way he recorded and miked it, they'd diffuse it so that you couldn't pick any one instrument out. Techniques like distortion and echo were not new, but Phil came along and took these to make sounds that had not been used in the past. I thought it was ingenious.[51]

The extravagant use of ambience was a prominent stylistic feature on record after record that Spector produced in the late 1950s and early 1960s. As the records became hits, their sound became part of rock's recording lexicon. Paul McCartney recalled an instance where exaggerated ambience was used to solve a specific problem with the mix for the coda of the Beatles' "Hello, Goodbye" (1967). With all other musical and sonic components in place, it was the addition of large amounts of ambience on the drums that finally brought things together. "We had those words and we had this whole thing recorded but it didn't sound quite right, and I remember asking Geoff Emerick if we could *really* whack up the echo on the tom-toms. And we put this echo full up on the tom-toms and it just came *alive*."[52] Acknowledging the inspiration for the move and the reference thus invoked, McCartney added, "We Phil Spector'd it."[53]

Exaggerated drum ambience was introduced to the rock mainstream by the success of Peter Gabriel's third album. Steve Lillywhite and Hugh Padgham, who had been experimenting with reverberant drum sounds in a stone-lined room at the Townhouse studios in London, were enlisted in 1980 as producer and engineer, respectively, for the Gabriel project. Padgham remembers that while he had "wanted to hear drums sounding more wide open and trashy"—against the carefully damped drum sounds that were so prevalent through the 1970s—this was "the first time that big drum sound appeared in an overblown way."[54] And responding to a question in a 1986 interview, Lillywhite remarked, "I suppose it was thought of as quite a milestone in sound, especially the drum sound we got."[55] Of course, "wide open and trashy" drum sounds recorded in reverberant rooms had been a characteristic feature of Led Zeppelin records since the 1960s, but there had been a widespread attraction to varying degrees of a drier drum sound throughout the 1970s on hit records representing different styles and recording scenes—London, New York, Los Angeles. Think, for instance, of Pink Floyd's *Dark Side of the Moon* (London, 1973), the Eagles' *Hotel California* (Los Angeles, 1976), Fleetwood Mac's *Rumours* (Los Angeles, 1977), or Steely Dan's *Aja* (New York, 1977). The radical processing technique used on the drum sounds for Gabriel's album was indeed remarkable, and with the album's success, its influence proved immense in the 1980s across rock's styles and genres. Phil Collins, who played drums on the album, was so impressed with the sound that he enlisted Padgham to engineer and coproduce his own *Face Value* a few months after the Gabriel sessions. Like Gabriel's album, *Face Value* was a hit. The dramatic drum entrance on "In the Air Tonight," the album's first hit single, assured that recordists everywhere would take notice and that many would seek to emulate what was known at the time as "the Phil Collins drum sound."

Gabriel's album opens with "The Intruder," a song about home invasion, and from the outset there is a palpable sense of the affective power of the drums' ambience. Playing alone for the first two bars, they present a forceful image of control that both fits the song's theme and ushers the listener into the record. We are immediately taken from the acoustic world as we know it into a strange soundscape of unknown dimensions where sounds behave in unfamiliar ways and the air itself is controlled by machines. The conceptual principle is the same as in the Spector recordings. Ambience is used in fashioning a unique sound world set apart from our experience of acoustic reality, but in this case the ambient air is imploded into a small space and then cut into pieces.

The first step for Lillywhite and Padgham in creating the sound was to record the drums in a large, reverberant barn. The repeating rhythmic pattern that Collins plays on the snare and kick drums is both stark and brutal. His playing is heavy and machinelike, and without the high frequency sheen of high hat or cymbal. Microphones were placed out in the room, away from the drums, so as to capture a maximum amount of room sound. Once the ambience was recorded, it was subjected to a processing technique using compressors and gates. First the dynamic range of the ambience was highly compressed, in effect squeezing its energy into a tighter space and thus increasing its explosive character and elongating the sustain of its decay. Then the sound was put through a gate, a device that can be programmed to alter a sound's envelope. In this case, the gate was used to truncate the decay, which the compression had intensified. As a result, the natural tailing away of sound that we associate with ambience was cut off abruptly. This much of the production story is available in various accounts. Listening to the track, we can further make out a difference between the kick and the snare. The ambience on the kick drum has about a quarter note's worth of sustain, giving it something of a cavernous quality and a slight hint of decay. The gate on the snare ambience creates an abrupt cutoff after about an eighth note's duration—while the compressed ambience is still in its explosive phase.

In contrast to Spector's hazy wash of ambient texture, the effect in this case is one of textural clarity. Within the sonic complex of the track as a whole, all of its constituents hold a tightly prescribed place. The gated ambience on the drums resolves a physical contradiction:

it evokes the sense of size associated with large, open ambient spaces while at the same time confining the sound to a clearly delineated place in the track. Limiting each eruption of sonic intensity to a short burst solves the problem of preserving textural clarity without diminishing the ambient drums' visceral power. But conceptually the sound is richly problematic: Where is this place that the ambience evokes? It is completely unfamiliar. With the ambient decay continually truncated, there is a sense of things being always interrupted, of their natural course being curtailed and controlled by a dominating force. And the strange behavior of sound in this atmosphere dictates the terms of our acoustic perception. Because it makes no sense in terms of our experience of the natural sound world, rather than perceiving the ambience as space, we are reoriented to hearing it simply as an extension of the drums' timbre, whose strangeness underscores the dramatic sense of the song's creepy lyric.

While the drum ambience on "The Intruder," as well as on the following track, "No Self Control," seems to have a thematic connection to the lyrics, as the effect moved into the sonic mainstream it was used on all kinds of songs regardless of their meaning or style. It simply became part of the sonic vocabulary. Indeed, some configuration of the effect became a preset on stock digital reverb units and drum machines. Rather than resonance with the song's lyrics, then, the use of ambience in problematic ways may simply be a matter of sonic architecture, as is the case with Buddy Holly's "Peggy Sue" (1957), where the drum part alternates between wet and dry as the sound of an ambient chamber is alternately switched on and off. The juxtaposition of two different sound spaces throughout the course of the track causes changes in sonic perspective that influence both dynamics and texture. The relationship between the two kinds of drum sounds is treated to its own development as the track unfolds. In the introduction, the contrast between the two appears as simply a novel sonic effect. As the track progresses, however, each takes on a specific association: the ambient drums are associated with the voice and the lyrics, the dry ones with the instrumental sections of the arrangement. Furthermore, rather than simply mirroring the song's form, the interplay between the two drum sounds follows its own course, its own rhythm. In the first verse the ambient drums play throughout; in later verses the dry drums often intrude between vocal phrases, interrupting the sonic cohesion of the voice's accompaniment and introducing a secondary level of articulation into the track's narrative structure.

Multiple sound spaces may also coexist synchronically within a track. For example, on Bruce Springsteen's "Atlantic City" (1982), a second voice sings along with the lead vocal, but at some apparent distance from it. The second voice has a lower volume level in the mix, but more importantly, and unlike the lead vocal, it is drenched in ambience. At times, it's a distant cry, floating freely behind the phrases of the main vocal. In the choruses, however, it joins the lead in rhythmic unison to sing the lyrics in harmony. Still, it remains in its own distant place, increasing both the spatial and expressive dimensions of the track. Rather than the simple reinforcement of the lead vocal that a backing vocal usually provides, here the second voice is a dramatic foil. One cannot help wondering why it sounds like this. Turning to the song for clues, we find a man in the midst of a fatalistic premonition, "tired of comin' out on the losin' end" and with "debts no honest man can pay," on his way to "do a little favor" for some apparent underworld figure. As he invites his sweetheart to meet him in Atlantic City with the phrase "Everything dies, baby that's a fact," the eeriness of the distant cries is suggestive. Are they from beyond? Is the distant voice the protagonist's own spirit-self beckoning or joining in conjuring the fateful vision? Perhaps. In any case, the superposition of the two ambient images makes us wonder, even as it strikes us physically with a poignant sensual quality.

Spector's 1962 production of "Zip-A-Dee-Doo-Dah," sung by Bobby Sheen and released in 1963 under the name of Bob B. Soxx and the Blue Jeans, is another track that presents us with an impression of music happening in two different places. But the effect here is more subtle, and perhaps even more mysterious. Arriving at the desired balance for this track was especially difficult. Three hours into the session, engineer Larry Levine suddenly brought down all of the faders. In trying to accommodate drums, percussion, acoustic bass, two electric basses, two electric guitars, piano four hands, and tenor and baritone saxophones, as well as the added ambience from the chamber, in the proportions that Spector was calling for, the levels had simply become too high for the recording to be anything but a distorted mess. Levine began again to build the mix, keeping a careful eye on the VU meters while Spector listened intently to the sound coming from the control room monitors. At a certain point, he commanded Levine to hit "record." Levine protested that he had not yet turned on electric guitarist Billy Strange's microphone. The guitar's sound was bleeding into other instruments' microphones, but it had no focused presence of its own. Spector, however, insisted: this was to be the sound of "Zip-A-Dee-Doo-Dah." For it was at this moment that the complex of relationships among all the layers and aspects of the sonic texture came together to bring the desired image into focus.

As long as Strange's unmiked guitar plugs away as one of the layered timbral characters that make up the track's rhythmic groove, it is simply one strand among many in a texture whose timbres sound more like impressionistic allusions to instruments than representations. But the guitar has a latency about it, a potential. Because it has no microphone of its own, it effectively inhabits a different ambient space from the rest of the track. As it chugs along in its accompanying role, it forms a connection with a parallel sound world of which we are, for the moment, unaware. Indeed, we would never know of the secondary ambient layer were it not for the fact that this guitar is the one that takes the solo. As it steps out of the groove texture and asserts its individuality, a doorway opens to an entirely other place in the track. It becomes quite clear that this guitar inhabits a world all its own, which has been before us from the beginning yet has somehow gone unnoticed. We are drawn in, shown around briefly, and then returned to the more familiar: Mr. Bluebird on our shoulder, a wonderful feeling on a wonderful day. Yes, the strange metallic timbre of this guitar is one of the cool sounds of rock. But to me, the really exciting thing about this moment is the sudden shift of aural place—and unlike in "Atlantic City," for no apparent reason. It brings home quite clearly that when we enter into the sound world of the record, the terms of our perception are controlled by the whim and fancy of the record makers.

With the proliferation of ambience-simulation devices, such combinations of multiple simultaneous ambient images have become quite common. Indeed, every musical part in the mix may have its own ambient image. The introduction to "The Intruder," for instance, has four levels of ambience that create a set of planes whose arrangement defines the perspective and depth of the sound stage. Besides the drums, there is a spiky sound effect that is quite dry, with very little air around it. Its lack of ambience brings it to the front of the sound stage and heightens its eerie effect. The rhythmic stabs—

either processed guitar or synthesizer—have an ambience with hardly any decay. The ambience is prominent enough to impart a sense of air to the sound, but is given no breathing room of its own. The artificial cutoff places the rhythmic stabs in some sort of conceptual proximity to the drums. That is, we cannot tell what the ambient information is conveying with respect to "place," so we hear it mainly as a timbral hue. Finally, the piano is "down a well." As with the second voice in the Springsteen example, it seems to be in a completely different place from the rest of the instruments.

In the development of a track's texture and expressive atmosphere, lack of ambience can be just as effective as its presence. Ambience causes a sound to linger, while dry sounds, lacking the sustenance of the surrounding air, come and go more quickly. Sly Stone's *There's a Riot Goin' On* (1971) and *Fresh* (1973), for example, are both unusually dry-sounding records, which contributes to their intriguing starkness. On the one hand, the dryness leaves plenty of space for complex rhythmic interactions to speak through clearly. At the same time, the spare sonic quality matches the music's mood, which is so much harder than the optimistic and far more ambient anthems of earlier Family Stone records. It is surely one of the reasons that *Riot* is characterized as having a "darkly understated sound" in *The Rolling Stone Encyclopedia of Rock & Roll.*[56] As the presence of ambience creates a distancing effect between the natural sound world and that of the recording, so its absence moves the recording "closer" to the listener. The effect can be unsettling. At the beginning of the Red Hot Chili Peppers' "Under the Bridge," a track on *Blood Sugar Sex Magik,* both guitarist John Frusciante and singer Anthony Kiedis seem to be standing in the same room as the listener. Rather than drawing the listener into the record, they seem to come forth from the loudspeakers, entering the listener's personal space. The singer demands an intimate hearing. Is he here to share a secret? Will we have to get involved? The song turns out to be a confession of loneliness, and ultimately, a haunted memory of the singer's mortal confrontation with drug addiction. The lack of ambient distance gives the track a gritty, *vérité* quality that lends a stark edge to the confessional tale. The "realness" associated with such a lack of ambience is a general characteristic of vocals on rap records, whose sonic ethos originated in "a very poor place," as Kris Parker (a.k.a. KRS-One) puts it.[57] "Under the Bridge," though not rap, is certainly a tale from a "very poor place"—the junkie's streets—and its dryness seems altogether appropriate to its mood. But the sparing use of added ambience throughout *Blood Sugar Sex Magik* also reflects a more general aesthetic stance. As drummer Chad Smith tells us, "There's no shit on the tracks, not a lot of modern technology, tweaks and reverbs. It's straight in your face, loud, raw—just like we played it."[58] Producer Rick Rubin, who began as a rap producer, states simply, "I don't like reverb, and on the Chili Peppers record we didn't use any."[59]

TEXTURE

> I had just finished mixing *Under the Red Sky* and I was
> happy with it. But [Dylan] came in, listened to it, and said,
> "Eaahh, it's screwed up. The mix is screwed up. I can hear
> everything." That was the first time I had that complaint.
> But you know, he was right. I went back and made it
> murkier, which is what old-time blues and rock 'n' roll
> records were about. They were a little dark, maybe a little
> ambiguous in terms of who was playing what. The mix was
> much better that way. Bob knows.
>
> Ed Cherney

In music, the meaning of the term "texture" is usually delimited by a descriptive adjective such as "homophonic," "polyphonic," "rhythmic," "instrumental," and so forth. My references to "ambient texture" and "vocal texture" are just such cases. But now I would like to use the term in a more inclusive way: to characterize that quality of composite sound images created by the interaction of diverse elements. "Texture," as Robert Erickson has put it, "always denotes some overall quality, the feel of surfaces, the weave of fabrics, the look of things."[60] On records, this "overall quality" involves timbre, relative amplitudes, rhythm, ambience, frequency range, chord voicings, spatial configuration, and so forth. Creating and molding textures entails bringing all of a track's elements into a desired balance that involves a complex set of proportions and angles of intersection. Dylan's complaint about Cherney's mix was simply that although the constituent parts of the track were clearly audible, the feel of the textural balance was off. That is, the parts were right, but the relationships among them were not. The ensuing remix speaks to the importance placed upon textural feel in the record-making process. For as a determinant of a record's character, texture is as fundamental as song. It is the way that everything, including song, fits together—the way that the record presents itself.

The aural images that records place before us have a detailed sonic intricacy about them, a sensory richness that invites us to listen to them again and again. I have often found careful listening to be repaid with delight even when the song and the performances are not to my taste. I also find that the harder I listen, the more I am aware of how much there is to hear and how much the record artfully withholds from me. For on many records textural depth is provided by instruments that are barely heard, or often not consciously heard at all. Like the invisible undercoats that build up the surfaces of paintings, sounds and musical parts may lose their individual identities and become inaudible as distinct characters, yet their presence is felt in the overall sound and affective sense of the texture. On Phil Spector's production of George Harrison's "Isn't It a Pity" (1970), for example, there is an underlayer of acoustic guitars on the right side of the stereo field that reflects the song's melancholic mood with a steady pulsing articulation of the repeating harmonic cycle. After the first verse, the guitars recede behind the high hat and tambourine. No longer heard as strumming guitars, they are "felt rather than perceived," as Richard Williams has observed.[61] Their function from this point is to provide an inscrutable depth to the track, a textural thickness that is also a manifestation of the track's affective character emanating from within. As such, they amount to an almost subliminal expression of the rhythms, harmonies, and mood that are evident on the track's surface.

The effect created by these guitars relies on two basic arranging techniques: doubling and layering. Doubling provides a basic thickness, a sense of size and enhanced presence, as in the case of a string section or the five rhythm guitars Spector called for on John Lennon's "Happy Xmas (War Is Over)" (1971) or the common practice of double-tracking. In each case, a single musical part gains a textural density both by way of instrumental mass and by the slight variations in tuning, timing, dynamics, articulation, and so forth that result from multiple performances. Of course, the part can also be played by any combination of timbres, and on "Isn't It a Pity" the guitars are doubled prominently by piano. Layering, on the other hand, involves

combining strata of different musical parts and managing relationships of balance among them. In this case, textural density is controlled by the amount of varying sensory information packed into a
given time frame. On "Isn't It a Pity," in addition to the guitar and
piano doubling, there are other, less prominent guitars playing
slightly different rhythmic parts in different areas of the stereo
soundstage, as well as strings, voice, and eventually, the percussion
instruments. All except the strings and the voice share in the same
general rhythmic gesture—a deliberate duple articulation of the
pulse. But because each plays a slightly different part, the ear is presented with a multiplicity of rhythmic and timbral events. As the
change in balance from the first verse to the second illustrates, such
textural relationships are dynamic, open to reconfiguration, as new
instruments come to prominence while others recede. While each
layer by itself is quite simple, in combination they create the enveloping sensation of a multidimensional sonic space that provides depth
and breadth to the track. The associations of size and distance that
textural balances can impart are in some ways similar to ambience;
with texture, however, these associations do not refer to acoustic
spaces, but rather, to the dimensions of the track itself.

Like the rest of a track's elements, its textures have little to do with
acoustic reality. They are shaped electronically by combining layers
of electronically processed sound—miked, amplified, recorded, filtered, compressed, synthesized, and so on—with the aim of developing a unique sonic presence for the work at hand. A single texture,
for example, might combine the quality of attack achieved by a
sharply struck snare drum with the breathy quality of a soft, low
flute sound that contains, apparently within itself, the shimmering
harmonic and lightly percussive sound of a strumming acoustic steel
string guitar with most of its low frequency identity removed. The
process of creating this composite texture would require at least a
precise proportioning of amplitudes; a careful, complementary shaping of the overtone content in each sound through equalization; a
determination of what sort of rhythm the guitar should play; and
decisions about how much to separate the sounds in the stereo spectrum (the more they are separated, the more distinct their individual
identities). These relationships can then be frozen and the texture
used as a strand in a larger textural configuration, where another set
of such relationships would come into play.

As individual parts are woven into the larger fabric, the fabric itself assumes authority. One strand or another may momentarily arrest attention, but in general, the parts are subordinated to the whole. And while its constituent timbres may be more or less generic, a track's textures exist as unique composite images. Spector recordings offer one example after another of this principle. Indeed, the "wall of sound" is one thick textural mass, many of whose constituent parts are indistinct to the ear. Spector's love of the impressionistic effect created by the overall sonic tapestry was one of the reasons he insisted that monaural records were superior to stereo. With no spatial separation between the sounds on the record, they all merged into one massive, opulent texture from which only the vocals and the most salient musical gestures stood out. This is perhaps a vestige of Spector's admiration for Fats Domino records, many of which were made at Cosimo Matassa's studio in New Orleans, where the sounds of Dave Bartholomew's bottom-heavy arrangements reverberating in the small room tended to create a textural wash behind the vocal.

Brian Wilson was a great admirer of Spector. He worked in the same studios in and around Los Angeles during the same period of time, using many of the same musicians. When Spector released "Be My Baby" in 1963, Wilson "immediately bought ten copies . . . and played them incessantly," learning "every note, every sound, the pulse of every groove."[62] From Spector's recordings—and by occasionally observing his sessions—Wilson "learned . . . to think in terms of production, rather than songwriting."[63] In other words, to think like a composer of records.[64] The influence of Spector and the Beatles, as well as his own competitive nature, drove Wilson to successive creative peaks in the recording studio, culminating in 1966 with *Pet Sounds*—itself one of the most influential albums in rock history—and the subsequent single, "Good Vibrations."[65] Among *Pet Sounds'* many gorgeous textures—all mono—are those on the track "God Only Knows," an arrangement for twenty-three musicians playing together in the studio, "the different sounds bleeding into one another, producing a rich, heavenly blanket of music."[66] The basic rhythmic feel for the track is provided by repeating staccato quarter-note chords whose texture at various points in the course of the track is made up of organ, harpsichord, piano with slapback echo, sleigh bells, and pizzicato strings. With the exception of the bells, none of these draws attention to itself individually; they are balanced in such a way that they create a single, richly textured instrumental character whose constituent elements are much less apparent than its overall quality. Complementing the rhythmic figure are whole-note chords played by a group of instruments whose blend, again, removes much of their individual character. After careful listening to the finished track as well as a working version without vocals, one can say with some certainty that the whole-note texture in the introduction is composed of strings and accordion, with the long notes of the French horn melody joining in.[67] With a great deal less certainty one might assume that the flute and bass clarinet, which play the four-note lead-in to the first verse, are also part of the mix, but there is no purely aural way to be sure. In any case, our attention is fixed on the composite, which, of course, includes all of the particular ephemera—such as ambience and amplitudinal balance—that are captured on tape. Each of these two textural subsets, one mainly rhythmic, the other harmonic, serves a very simple and straightforward musical gesture, yet their textural depth imparts an exotic quality to the track. In each case, familiar instrumental colors are largely absorbed into a textural mass that is itself a color—a new one. And this new color is to be found in only one place: here in the sound world of "God Only Knows."

Karl Wallinger's "Way Down Now" (1990) is an example of a different type of textural treatment that nonetheless serves a similar aim to that in "God Only Knows," namely, enriching simple musical gestures with elaborate textural play. In this case, however, rather than densely stacked mono textures playing in rhythmic unison, we have a chaotic parade of varying interpretations of the basic musical gestures—a repeated rhythm (see figure 2) and a shifting chord sequence (V, IV, I in the verse; I, V, IV in the chorus)—spread out across the stereo soundstage. The chord sequence is played by two electric guitars, organ, bass, and piano. One guitar is panned to the left and heavily distorted, the other to the right and cleaner; the organ and bass are in the center; and the piano—playing with a hammered, percussive quality, yet held down in volume so it is placed well "behind" the other instruments—seems to be on both sides but not in the middle. Each of these instruments articulates the chord sequence with its own voicings, rhythms, and melodic figuration. The rhythmic figure is carried by two bass drums—one panned left,

Figure 2

Figure 3

one right—bass, and piano. Again, the specific rhythms played by each instrument are free variations on the basic pattern. The instrumental vamp in the introduction and between verses adds a third basic gesture to the mix: a melodic fragment that is, once again, articulated differently by the two guitars and the organ (see figure 3).

Wallinger has made an atypical stereo mix here, placing most of the elements on one side or the other with only the bass, organ, and the coda guitar solo in the middle of the soundstage. In addition to the left/right guitars, each side has its own complete drum kit and voice. The balanced distribution of similar sounds playing similar gestures on either side of the soundstage creates a sense of expanse that from one perspective, subsumes their rhythmic, melodic, and timbral variances in an overall gestalt. However, if we journey deeper into the track, we find a wealth of detail that illustrates how various parameters work interactively to form the track's textural image. Putting it as simply as possible, textural depth is developed by any combination of elements that differ from one another in some way. Such differences increase the density of sonic information, which, in turn, places greater perceptual demands upon the listener—hence the impression of "depth." That is, one is forced to enter more deeply into the track's aural space in order to make out what is happening. The differences may be of timbre and loudness, as is mostly the case in "God Only Knows," but they may also occur in the realms of stereo placement, rhythm, melodic articulation, chord voicing, and so forth. In "Way Down Now" the apparent balance implied by the distribution of similar sounds on either side of the stereo spectrum is offset by differences in loudness and sound quality that create multiple textural levels within instrumental sections. That is, each section—gui-

tars, vocals, drums—has differences among its constituents that create a more or less complex textural subset of the overall track. For
example, with regard to loudness there is a general side-to-side textural depth created by the uneven prominence of the right bass drum
over the left, the left voice over the right, and the right guitar over the
left. Furthermore, the sonic characters of each of these pairs is quite
different—hence the side-to-side image includes a multi-timbral
interplay as an aspect of the textural spread.

The percussion section on "Way Down Now" has several types
and degrees of variance that contribute to its textural configuration.
The two snare drum parts are separated in space but are almost iden-
tical in rhythm, sonority, and amplitude. The rhythmic variations
between them are slight enough that they can almost be taken as a
single part that has been routed to different places in the stereo spectrum. The tambourine (left) and shaker (right) are likewise symmet-
rically balanced in amplitude, placement, and rhythm in a steady
sixteenth-note pulsation, but they are different sounds. Thus they
exhibit a difference in sonority that the snares do not. The bass
drums—the other prominent members of the percussion ensemble—
though placed in a similar left/right counterpoise, have a more complex relationship. To begin with, their amplitudes are unbalanced.
Indeed, the only section of the song where the relationship between
the two drums can be heard clearly is the bridge, where the overall
texture of the track thins out considerably. The bridge also clearly
exposes the different sonorities of the two drums. Furthermore, their
rhythmic parts are quite different. Although they obviously share the
same groove, they are not synchronized with anything like the precision of the snare drums. The plurality of attacks, sonorities, and
dynamics creates a thick bed of kinetic activity in the track's low end,
the nature of which is, again, "felt rather than perceived."

Clearly, among the many interactive elements that shape the textural image of this track, one of the most important is rhythm. The
various articulations of the arrangement's essential gestures yield a
random multiplicity of attacks that gives the track its infectiously
rambunctious character. Rhythmic interplay also figures prominently in the textural configuration of John Hiatt's "Through Your
Hands" (1992), where it is used, however, in a quite different way. A
rhythm obliquely at odds with the prevailing groove is folded into
the timbre of a single instrument by way of the rhythmic pulsations

of the tremolo effect. The resulting rhythmic conflict animates the textural weave and gives the introduction, first verse, and first chorus a feeling of quivering suspension that seems to complement the song's lyrics. Electronic tremolo is produced by an oscillation in amplitude whose speed and intensity can be controlled to create the desired effect, perceived as a timbral alteration of the original sound. But because the effect is created by a rhythmic oscillation, it is possible to set up a specific rhythmic relationship between the timbre and the basic pulse of the track, and in "Through Your Hands" this is exactly what occurs.

Beginning with the introduction, two electric guitars, panned left and right, play variations on the same figure (see figure 4). The guitar on the left side has the tremolo effect, which at this speed creates a triplet rhythm in relation to the track's underlying pulse. By itself, then, this guitar part contains a degree of rhythmic ambivalence, for as its attacks subdivide the basic pulse with duple rhythms they continually break up the regular oscillations of the tremolo, creating a sort of rhythmic wash from the layering of duple and triple subdivisions. On the surface, this rhythmic conflict, together with the guitar's prominent presence, appears to be the sole source of the suspended effect. But the guitar on the right side participates in a subtle yet crucial way by adding to the rhythmic gesture a textural one that deepens the aural image, at once increasing the conflict, anticipating the rhythmic direction that is to come, and contributing to a sense of restless movement in the stereo space. As with the two bass drums in "Way Down Now," the nature of the effect is veiled by the relative loudness of the two parts. That is, the degree of rhythmic tension between the two guitars is controlled by the balance of amplitudes between them. The guitar on the right is much quieter, its subdivisions practically indistinguishable. Yet from its submerged place in the track it firmly articulates—along with the small flourishes of the shaker and finger cymbals—the rhythmic groove that will eventually take over the track.[68]

After the first chorus, an acoustic guitar enters on the right side and clearly foregrounds sixteenth-note subdivisions in its strumming pattern, asserting both place and rhythm. For the first time we hear a clear duple groove articulated from a previously obscure place in the track (the right-hand side), though it still struggles to establish itself against the ambiguity of the tremolo. Shortly thereafter, however, at

Figure 4

the beginning of the second verse, another acoustic guitar playing a similar part appears on the left side, balancing and reinforcing the first. At the same time, the drums enter, providing a solid rhythmic foundation. The tremolo guitar now recedes into a texture that, while still awash in pulsing oscillations, is firmly rooted in a duple rhythmic feel. This guitar has gone from being the dominant textural presence, in terms of both rhythm and timbre, to being simply a component timbre in a larger texture. And the rhythm articulated by the tremolo guitar's counterpart—the barely audible guitar on the right-hand side—emerges now as the track's central groove, its function transformed by the textural shift. With the emergence of the groove, the feeling of the entire track changes. Even the rhythmic articulation of Hiatt's vocal becomes more incisive in the second verse. Furthermore, the stereo space, so animated to this point, now becomes a more stable canvas. As it moves from its suspended setting and settles into the rhythmic flow, the song appears retrospectively to have floated down through the air and landed finally on the ground.

Such textural gestures play an important part in delineating a track's narrative structure. Verses and choruses, for example, are often given quite different textural treatments. In the early 1990s, juxtaposition of radically different textures between verse and chorus became a stylistic hallmark of so-called alternative rock, though the principle is time-honored.[69] But while such changes of texture often simply mirror song structure, they can also provide the track with a narrative layer that is more through-composed in conception, spanning the song's usually sectional and strophic form with an overarching gesture. In "Through Your Hands" the initial textural gesture unfolds across four structural subdivisions—introduction, first verse, first chorus, and interlude. For most of that time, it seems to parallel the progression of both the harmony and the lyrics, whose initial goals—the V-I cadence and the line "through your hands"—are reached at the end of the first three subdivisions, that is, at the end of the chorus. The tremolo texture, however, carries on a bit further, which allows the suspended effect to cross-fade with the emergent groove. Moving at its own pace, the textural modulation introduces a secondary layer of narrative rhythm that further enriches the track's unfolding.

As is often the case with such textural moves, the progression seems to reflect a change in the tone of the song's lyrics. The first verse tells of a dream of faith in which the dreamer, reaching "past the scientific darkness," is wrapped in the coat of an angel. In the second verse, as the texture loses its rhythmic ambiguity, the lyrics move from dream to worldly skepticism. "You wouldn't know a burning bush," Hiatt sings, "if it blew up in your face." Heard in this light, the textural gesture takes on significance as a programmatic enhancement of the ideas and sentiments expressed in the song.

On the other hand, a textural sequence may unfold independently as an impressionistic underscore having no apparent correspondence with the song's lyrics. Moreover, it need not mirror any of the song's points of formal articulation. It might instead proceed at its own pace, providing the track with another level of gestural rhythm in its overall design. The textural transformation in Harrison's "Isn't It a Pity"—whereby the rhythmic, timbral, and harmonic functions of the strumming guitars are gradually absorbed by tambourine, high hat, shaker, and piano—takes place across the length of the song's first one and a half verses. The guitars recede to their ultimate place in the track's texture by subtle degrees, and while the entrances of the percussion instruments follow the phrase layout of the song, the overall gestural move has its own temporal disposition.

Daniel Lanois's production of "Amazing Grace" (1989) uses a textural gesture that divides the track's duration into roughly two large halves and serves as a primary agent in the track's dramatic unfolding. The effect is achieved in a way somewhat similar to that in "Zip-A-Dee-Doo-Dah" and "Through Your Hands," in the sense that there is a character present from the beginning whose features are difficult to discern but which holds a latent power. At a certain point the mysterious character reveals itself in a textural shift that feels like an arrival from some distant place.

In this case, the distance is created, and then bridged, by differences of loudness. The track begins with an atmosphere that imparts to the familiar song an altogether unfamiliar, mood-stricken quality: It is in the minor mode; its traditional harmonic scheme is gone; its melody is sung in a highly ornamented way by Aaron Neville, mirrored in a rough kind of gestalt by a synthesized pan flute melody playing a third lower. The synthesized bass, doubled by a weird, cricketlike sound, repeatedly intones the tonic note with a mantralike insistence. It is reinforced by a bass drum, and both share a steady groove with sixteenth-note inflections. By contrast, the vocal and flute parts appear to float in a state of meterless suspension. In addition, other solitary timbres—pulseless sound-objects, with no sense of melodic or harmonic progression—gradually drift into the soundscape one by one, each in its own distinct space, yet all coalescing into a haunting, otherworldly sound collage.

In the background is a very faint strumming guitar texture spread across the middle of the track, a glimmering backdrop on which the other sounds are placed. The guitars are strumming sixteenth notes and articulating chords, both of which prefigure the climactic gesture that will follow the second verse. But at this point they are perceived mainly as a distant textural haze. There appears to be a harmonic move from I to III at the words "was blind, but now I see." However, while the character of the E in the flute sound is clearly transformed from that of a fifth above the tonic A to that of a major third, it's hard to make out why this is so. The track seems simply to emanate a change of harmony somehow. There is only a vague shift in the background texture of the strumming guitars—whose identity is still barely perceptible—as the tonic bass riff momentarily drops out. And if the harmonic impression of the guitars is subtle, the rhythm is practically inaudible, a mere shimmer. At this point, the relationship of these guitars to the foreground of the track is one of enigmatic distance. Their presence is perceptible, but their features are unknowable.

The significance of what hovers hidden in the background of the track is revealed after the song's second chorus. As if from nowhere, guitars strumming sixteenth-note chords emerge into the foreground, falling into the rhythmic flow of the bass and kick drum, and lift the veil from the track. In a subtle touch, the meterless guitar on the left side of the soundstage that has aimlessly uttered two notes repeatedly throughout the second verse and ensuing chorus finally reveals its purpose as it appears to give birth to the strumming guitar on the right. Up to this point the guitar on the left has repeatedly risen from B to C in a seemingly static gesture. Suddenly it proves to have been working all along to deliver the most dynamic moment in the track to this point. It finally moves past the C, rising from D to E, and as it reaches the upper note the strumming guitar breaks into the foreground as though delivered through the effort of the guitar on the left.

In quick succession, the second rhythm guitar enters on the left side of the soundstage, and the track's harmonic stasis is broken by a harmonic progression. Now the harmonic and rhythmic elements of the background have moved to the front in a textural shift that propels the piece into a new section where harmonic and rhythmic motion become the main focus. What had been a static soundscape of more or less suspended objects is transformed into an image of rushing, forward motion. Furthermore, the sense of distance is bridged. Even the characters that had been in the foreground become louder now. Among them, the voice moves forward into a strong, clear light as it delivers the song's final refrain: "I once was lost, but now I'm found / Was blind, but now I see."

These analytic sketches provide a glimpse of how recordists approach textural composition, how they combine the track's formative elements to create both its fabric and its sonic narrative. Any track can be approached in this way, no matter how simple or complex. By listening carefully to what a track presents, we gather testimony about its compositional process, even as we gain a deeper awareness of its richness. This is the sort of testimony that Frank Zappa points to when he writes in his autobiography:

> On a record, the overall timbre of the piece (determined by equalization of individual parts and their proportions in the mix) tells you, in a subtle way, *WHAT* the song is about. The orchestration provides *important information* about what the composition *IS* and, in some instances, assumes a greater importance than *the composition itself.*[70]

What Zappa calls the "overall timbre" or "orchestration" is made up of the elements that I have outlined in this chapter, the particular recorded manifestations of the musical parts and sounds that render "the composition itself." In his characterization of the interface between sounds and song, Zappa is emphatic about their interdependence. It is the record's sound that tells us "what the composition is." When we approach records as complex sensory surfaces whose sound-form is also their content, we not only hear them in a deeper way but also increase our appreciation for recordists' compositional concerns and the wealth of meaning that the sounds hold.

4

Places and Tools

The title of George Martin's memoir, *All You Need Is Ears*, at once makes reference to his long association with the Beatles and calls attention to a basic principle of record production: making records is an empirical process guided and informed by physical perception. Compositional decisions are based on responses to specific aural images, and ears are the windows through which all evaluations are made. This chapter explores the factors that influence the sound image, the impression the sound makes on the recordist, and the decisions that result.

All recorded sound has an aesthetic dimension to it. It is shaped by choices made according to the recordists' musical sensibilities about the relationships among source sound, room acoustics, the various elements of the signal path, and the recording medium. Because sound and aural perception in the studio are always influenced by electronic components and architectural design, there are many apparently nonmusical issues that fall within the framework of compositional practice. Recordists must take these issues into account in both the planning and the production stages of recording projects. While there are many conventional recording techniques and practices, recordists also develop personal approaches to integrating these various mediating influences into an overall musical style. Thus, there is often little separating the practical and the creative applications to which tools and rooms are put; there is a continual interchange between the two.

This is why, for example, Lou Reed, songwriter and musician, spent two and a half years "gearing up" for his *Set the Twilight Reeling* album (1996) by seeking advice from various technical specialists and experimenting with a range of equipment to find the pieces that best suited his sonic conception of the project. And all of this was undertaken and completed before the songs for the album were written.[1] Steve Ripley—songwriter, engineer, and band member in the

Tractors—puts it this way: "The creative process isn't just the three-minute song. It's literally making the cords you're going to use on the microphones and deciding what microphone and amp you're going to use. It's all part of the process down to that final moment where I have to turn it loose and send it off to the manufacturing process."[2]

The number of possible choices among tools and recording places is huge. Decisions on how to proceed are made according to a varying set of criteria, which include availability, cost, musical style, and personal preference. While the technical characteristics of recording tools can be measured according to abstract standards tabulated in a list of numerical specifications, their value as artistic implements is a matter of subjective judgment. Rooms and tools have their own "personalities" that impart varying degrees and types of coloration to recorded sound, and although one might imagine that recordists would prefer to have the most current top-of-the-line equipment at all times, budget permitting, this is not always the case. The home-made demos that Los Lobos members David Hidalgo and Louie Perez made in pre-production for *Kiko*, for example, were technically very primitive. Yet precisely because of their technical limitations, they provided "quite a few clues" as to the direction the project should take. According to the producer, Mitchell Froom, they were "the best demos you would ever hear in terms of character." They had been recorded on a four-track tape machine that "had so much distortion and compression on things that it gave us the idea of how the percussion should sound."[3] Because the atmosphere of the demos seemed so right to all the members of the composition team, Froom and engineer Tchad Blake sought, improbably, to emulate the effect of the demos' technical limitations once formal recording began. In search of "grungy, dirty, squashed sounds," as Blake puts it, the drums were "mainly recorded . . . in a little vocal booth, sometimes just using a Calrec [stereo microphone] through some really rotten compressors."[4] These unconventional recording techniques were complemented with unusual instrumentations and arrangements to give *Kiko* some strikingly original textures. The overall result is an album that stands out not for its "grungy" or "rotten" sound—in point of fact, it sounds beautifully crafted—but for its originality.[5] The conventional practices of using good quality compressors and recording drums with multiple microphones in a large room were set aside for the sake of an artistic vision. Similarly, Tom Dowd recalls that Phil Spector, while working at Atlantic in the early '60s, chose to stick with the two- and three-track formats he had been successful with, even though Dowd was cutting other Atlantic sessions on the eight-track: "He had better ways available to him, but if it impaired or impeded or made him insecure, technology means nothing. . . . You don't make a Phil Spector a victim of technology."[6]

Because the character of a piece of equipment contributes to a record's unique sonic patination, equipment is often chosen more for its perceived aesthetic properties, its "musicality," than its technical specifications. The use of tube-based sound processing, for example—an old and for some time practically discontinued technology—has had a great resurgence in recent years. As Paul McCartney observed, "valve [tube] equipment . . . gives you a record-y type sound."[7] The "record-y" coloration consists of an apparent sonic warmth—a pleasant sonic distortion that has become part of the aural tradition in rock. Such "vintage" technology is used widely to mask the stark clarity of digital recording, as well as to evoke associations with recording styles of the past. The degree and nature of the residue left on a record's sound by the circumstances of its production vary a great deal. But whether they are the result of conscious choice, accident, or logistical contingency, the mediating factors of production become part of a record's history and, potentially, traits of its stylistic character and identity.

PLACES

Because the acoustical properties and behavior exhibited by architectural spaces and construction materials have various coloring effects on sound, their effects are among the first things that recordists must consider (unless, of course, a sound source—a synthesizer, say—is routed directly to the recording device via "direct injection"). "Listening . . . in the [recording] room is very important," says Bob Norberg, a veteran Capitol Records engineer. "I wouldn't try recording anything without first understanding what the whole package was saying."[8] In other words, to strike the desired proportional balance between the sound itself and the coloration imparted by the room, one must understand the relationship between the two.

The nature of this relationship will suggest to the recordist ideas about microphone choice and placement as well as possibilities for further sound processing such as equalization or compression.

There are many studios whose distinctive sound is forever linked with the recordings made in them. Phil Spector, for instance, returned to Gold Star Studios in Hollywood again and again to capture the sound of its spaces and incorporate them into his tracks, each time tapping into a sonic resource with which the public had become familiar through its appearance on past Spector hits. According to Larry Levine, who engineered many of Spector's sessions, "the Wall of Sound was indigenous to Gold Star, to the studio, the chambers, the walls."[9] Most of Spector's hits were produced there, and Levine maintains that when Spector finally moved on, in 1966, he "was out of that old thing. Once he left Gold Star it was over."[10] That is, the change of recording venue, which also meant change of a compositional resource, was accompanied by a change in style. In a case like this, a room's ambient signature plays such a prominent part on a record that it becomes a stylistic hallmark, taking its own place in the lexicon of recording practice. On Public Image Limited's *Album* (1986), producer Bill Laswell wanted to evoke John Bonham's drum sound as recorded on Led Zeppelin's fourth album (1971), a sound that bore the signature of Headley Grange, the large English country house where most of the album was recorded.[11] In an effort to capture a similar ambience, drummers Ginger Baker and Tony Williams played inside an elevator shaft at New York's Power Station Studios with microphones suspended inside the shaft. "Basically, we were trying to replicate the length and depth of a stone hall to get that great bass drum sound that John Bonham got," says engineer Jason Corsaro, adding, "Of course, the Bonham sound is pretty much just Bonham."[12] Indeed, all three drummers have distinctly different sounds. The intent was not to have Williams and Baker alter their own style to emulate Bonham, but rather, to allude only to the ambient texture that the recordists associated with Bonham's sound on a specific record—an allusion, as it were, to Headley Grange.

Before the various types of ambience synthesis were developed, all reverb was produced either by the room in which the recording was made or by some other architectural space where sound was reproduced by a loudspeaker and the resulting ambience captured by a microphone. The ambient sound was then combined with the original sound during either recording or mixing. Thus, in addition to the acoustic character imparted by a studio's recording space, the studio's "echo chamber" added a particular sonic atmosphere to the recording. Just as the chambers at Gold Star were a major element in Spector's recordings, so the sound of Buddy Holly's 1956–58 recordings made at Norman Petty's studio in Clovis, New Mexico, is in part a result of the acoustic characteristics of the room above Petty's father's gas station, which served as the studio's ambient chamber. Beginning in 1947, Bill Putnam, one of the first to use added ambience extensively, used "the ladies washroom" adjacent to the penthouse space in the Chicago Civic Opera building that served as the studio for Universal Recording.[13] When Elvis Presley first recorded for RCA in Nashville, added ambience was provided by a stairwell in the building. But because the stairwell was also used for other purposes, ambience was not its only contribution. According to Presley biographer Jerry Hopkins, "whenever anyone pulled a Coke from the soft drink machine at the foot of the stairs, that sound was included on the recording."[14] Ambience simulators were common when the Ramones recorded their *Rocket to Russia* (1978) album, but none were yet available at the newly opened Power Station in New York, where the album was mixed. Again, a stairwell was enlisted. Engineer Ed Stasium pumped the recorded tracks, including the memorable "Teenage Lobotomy," into the open space and mixed the ambient sound in with the recorded tracks. "On that vocal," according to Stasium, "you could really hear the stairwell because it's so open and the drums are so dry."[15]

In a track's web of particularity, studios and ambient chambers contribute a particularity of place. "Create a unique environment for each record wherever possible," says Daniel Lanois, who has often recorded in unusual locations—an Irish castle for U2's *The Unforgettable Fire* (1984), an old New Orleans apartment house in the Neville Brothers' neighborhood for their *Yellow Moon* (1989).[16] The peripatetic Lanois has set up his own studio in a number of places—a thirty-room house built soon after the Civil War on the edge of the French Quarter in New Orleans, a house built into the side of a mountain overlooking the Sea of Cortez in Mexico, an old movie theater on the Pacific Coast Highway in Oxnard, California. "I like the strange rooms that you find in old houses and buildings," he says. "You get a sound that's unique to that record, a sonic signature, if you like."[17] Similarly, producer Brian Ahern avoids conventional studios—which he calls "sterile and generic"—almost altogether. For the past twenty-five years he has worked out of a mobile studio—his own Enactron Truck—moving from place to place, using whatever recording space he feels is most appropriate for a given project.[18]

The criteria for effective recording spaces—unlike mixing rooms—vary enormously. Creative recordists take advantage of room peculiarities and work around acoustic deficiencies. Tracks have been recorded in all sorts of spaces exhibiting all sorts of acoustic behavior, and notable aspects of a track may be linked to some specific set of acoustic circumstances. At the Record Plant studios in New York, for example, engineer David Thoener "used to stick drums in this first-floor back area behind Studio A, where they used to put the garbage." Although it was "a real drag for the drummers, because they'd have to stay out there eight hours a day drumming with garbage around them . . . everyone agreed it was a killer sound because there was a lot of marble around and cement walls,"[19] which provided a bright and highly reverberant sound. Conversely, characteristics of a room *designed* for recording may occasionally present a problem whose solution itself contributes to the uniqueness of the track. The small size of Norman Petty's studio, for example, made it impossible to record drums on Buddy Holly's "Not Fade Away" (1957) without drowning out the rest of the band. According to Petty's associate Jerry Fischer, drummer Jerry Allison was moved out of the studio and into a foyer, but the sound was still unmanageable. Finally, a cardboard box was substituted for the drums. The box's light, popping sound seems odd for the driving Bo Diddley-style beat, but the sound's unusual character is in keeping with rock recordists' pursuit of unusual sonic treatments, and it makes a good counterpart to the backing vocals. In this case, then, a distinctive aspect of the musical work resulted not from compositional design but from logistical contingency.[20]

There are, of course, many ways other than ambience in which a studio leaves its mark on a recording. These can range from the impressionistic—the feel of a place—to the concrete. "The way we made records kind of coincided with the studio," recalls Sam Phillips of his Sun Records days. "There was something about the looseness that rubbed off on the recordings."[21] The Stax studio, on the other hand, contributed something more substantive to recordings made there. Housed in a building that had once been a movie theater, the studio was very large, and the musicians, who for the purposes of sound separation were forced to stand quite far apart, played together without headphones. The regular Stax musicians—Booker T. Jones (keyboards), Steve Cropper (guitar), Al Jackson (drums), and Donald "Duck" Dunn (bass)—were accustomed to the resulting time delay, and they used visual cues to compensate and to keep a tight sense of ensemble. But their pulse was just slightly behind that of the singers. "It became a very delayed thing by the time Al heard the singers singing, by the time he hit it and we hit it," recalled Steve Cropper. However, when the band "hit it, there wasn't this big splatter. There was this very tight backbeat."[22] The delay between vocalists and band caused by the studio layout became a stylistic feature of records made there. Comparing Wilson Pickett recordings made at Stax in 1965 (e.g., "In the Midnight Hour," "Don't Fight It") with those made the following year at Fame Studios in Florence, Alabama (e.g., "Land of 1000 Dances," "Mustang Sally"), the effect of the Stax studio's room delay is quite apparent. On the Stax recordings Pickett is consistently slightly ahead of the band, which imparts a certain rhythmic fluidity to the tracks. On the Fame recordings, Pickett's vocals are laid right in the pocket of a tight, solid groove.

Jerry Wexler, who produced these Pickett sessions, had his own reasons for choosing the studios. Through the 1960s and 1970s, he traveled regularly from his home in New York to Alabama to produce records. In part, this was to take advantage of the skills and sensibilities of the musicians clustered around the Muscle Shoals area,[23] but it also suited his desire for a sequestered working environment, away from the daily concerns of business and home. In these surroundings, he felt "concentrated and relaxed at the same time." He likened these trips to retreats "in the Catholic sense"[24]—quasi-monastic experiences focused entirely on the recording project. His success in Alabama became legendary—especially the records he produced with Aretha Franklin—which, in turn, led him back again and again. "People criticized me for staying at Muscle Shoals for too long. Maybe they're right, maybe they're wrong. I don't know. But I got very comfortable there. It's what's coming through to you in the control room. Where you start feeling it the best is where you want to go."[25]

The associations between records and the places where they are made may lead recordists to employ a particular studio in search of not only a sound but a resonant connection to a particular record or style, the significance of which may be apparent only to the artists themselves. In 1979, George Clinton, who was working at United Sound in Detroit, told an interviewer, "All we got to do is lay the rhythm tracks here at United Sound, and I can record the other tracks anywhere in the world. Because this particular room has that sound that hits you right *on* your primal button. And people be thinking, 'What does that remind me of?' and they don't connect that subliminally they're hearing that old Motown sound on the bottom in this room."[26] Clinton's purpose in using the studio is both sonic and psychological. On the more objective side, he is interested in the room's influence on the low end of the frequency spectrum. But his personal sense of connection with Motown, kindled by working in this studio, is itself something of an influence on the recording process. As he says, listeners would be hard pressed to identify the connection. Indeed, great numbers of Motown records came out of the far more famous Hitsville U.S.A. studio, also in Detroit, which ran nearly around the clock. As the company outgrew Hitsville, Motown artists began using other Detroit recording venues, but none is identified as having an exclusive Motown signature sound. In this case, then, the choice of studio is a response to some personal experience. For reasons known best to Clinton, United Sound provided both a preferred acoustic environment and an intentional personal connection to a particular strand of the record-making tradition.

On the other side of the glass, in the control room, too, the quality of the sound image presented by the monitor loudspeakers is affected by the acoustical character of the space. The acoustical requirements here, however, are quite different. Just as the recording space affects the sound of a musical performance, the control room's acoustical character impinges on the perceptions upon which compositional decisions are based. But while a recording space's unique "sonic signature" may add a desirable distinctive personality to the performances recorded in it, mixing requires an acoustic environment whose character is as neutral as possible. "Acoustically, a control room should do nothing at all."[27] It should act as "a very accurate acoustic microscope,"[28] providing "a laboratory environment for the monitor speakers and the mixer."[29] Control rooms, then, are subject to a different acoustic standard, functioning as a sort of "everyroom" in which recordists can make decisions that will hold up in myriad listening environments. For if the configuration of a control room adds further coloration to the sound that is being monitored through the loudspeakers, it is impossible to make informed decisions that will hold up when listening circumstances change. It's like painting in poor light: the artist is continually reacting to false cues. For example, equalization applied to filter out an overly resonant frequency will prove inappropriate if the resonance is simply the result of control room coloration. When the recording is played in a different space, the frequency in question will simply be diminished, perhaps affecting the overall timbral balance of the mix. Since the goal is to create a track that can be more or less faithfully reproduced under a variety of listening conditions, control room designers are always in search of better ways to provide recordists with an acoustic environment that is as objective as possible.

Sometimes recordists opt for a non-studio location. While such special circumstances can be needlessly expensive indulgences, they can also provide an atmosphere conducive to music making and creative experimentation, lending the project "a sense of focus," as Daniel Lanois puts it. The Red Hot Chili Peppers' *Blood Sugar Sex Magik* was recorded in an old mansion in Laurel Canyon outside of Los Angeles. Most of the band stayed together in the house during recording, literally living with the project. All the members agreed it was the best recording experience they had ever had, avoiding what Anthony Kiedis calls "the impersonal, anal-retentive, tight-ass quality that studios have."[30] Bassist Flea recalls that the casual atmosphere was "stimulating for our creativity." Drummer Chad Smith, the only band member who did not sleep at the house, summarizes the general feeling among the group, including producer Rick Rubin and engineer Brendan O'Brien: "It was so relaxed, as opposed to the atmosphere of most recording studios. It gave the music real character. And we could record anywhere in the house. You don't need an *exactomundo* environment. A room and mics, and you make the noise."[31]

One of the most famous rock recordings, The Band's eponymously titled second album (1969), is an extremely successful example of location recording. The recording site was a pool house on a Los Angeles estate that had formerly belonged to Sammy Davis Jr. In 1967, the members of The Band established a creative headquarters in a house known as Big Pink in West Saugerties, near Woodstock,

New York, where they lived, wrote, and recorded demos for two years.[32] Within a year, the atmosphere of communal creativity that surrounded Big Pink produced The Band's first album, *Music from Big Pink* (1968). But the album was in fact not recorded there. Conditions were simply too primitive, and when it came time to make the record, formal recording sessions were held at A&R Studios in New York, as well as Capitol and Gold Star in Los Angeles. As artistically successful as *Music from Big Pink* was, the group felt that the sound they were after was somehow compromised by a state-of-the-art studio environment and its attendant aesthetic of polished, high-tech refinement. They were looking for an unvarnished "woody, thuddy sound"—as guitarist and songwriter Robbie Robertson characterized it—that would better resonate with their music and lyrics, an earthy and eclectic stylistic mixture that included allusions to many older non-rock musical styles.[33] "We'd be thinking Harvey-burgers and they'd be thinking caviar," recalled bassist Rick Danko about their work with some of the more commercially successful engineers of the time.[34] The Band was determined to create a different kind of working environment for their second album, something more like Big Pink.

The Los Angeles house was large enough to accommodate all band and crew members, and once the pool house had been given a bit of acoustic treatment and a rented console had been installed, recording began in March of 1969. Most of the songs had been written previously. The task now was for the musicians and their producer, John Simon, to "discover the sound of the band," as Robertson put it.[35] First the instrumentation for a particular song was arrived at through collaborative experimentation, the musicians freely switching instruments in search of a unique overall sound. Then they worked out the details of the arrangement. Finally, when the arrangement and performance had settled, the track was recorded, usually in the morning—everyone playing together in the pool house, which doubled as both studio and control room. Overdubbing was limited to adding extra instruments to the basic track. Living and working together in relative seclusion, the group recaptured the spirit of their highly creative Woodstock period. "It was very cozy on our own with nobody there looking over your shoulder and making you stick to schedules,"[36] recalled Robertson. As with the Chili Peppers, the importance of location for the project lay in the atmosphere it provided for the musicians. The Band's years together on the road and the members' complementary roles made them unusually democratic collaborators. In the pool house they were able to practice the kind of communal give-and-take music making and improvisational creativity to which they were accustomed. The setting they chose for the album fostered the working methods they were most comfortable with and helped them to reach what many have felt was a creative peak.

TOOLS

In the process of recording and mixing, sound changes from acoustical to electrical energy and back again, traveling through various electronic devices along what is commonly known as the signal path. In recording, a microphone transforms sound waves into electrical impulses; a cable carries the electrical signal to a microphone preamplifier and on to a recording device; the signal may also pass through a compressor, an equalizer, or a console, each of which adds its own coloration to the sound. Mixing involves an even more complex signal path that includes the console, amplifier, and monitor loudspeakers, as well as any number of sound processing tools accessed at a central patch bay. In a complex mix, electrical signals move through a dense web of wiring before finally emerging from the loudspeakers as sound once again.

Influenced by logistical concerns, personal preferences, and the aesthetic stance of the project at hand, recordists employ a wide range of tools and techniques to capture, shape, and combine sounds. Equalizers manipulate timbre; digital delays produce echo and provide the means for producing echo-based timbral effects such as chorusing and flanging; reverb simulators provide ambience; textural composites are assembled at the mixing console; and, of course, musical performances are captured by microphones. Some recordists prefer as much transparency as possible. In this view, proper microphone selection and placement, together with a good performance on a good sounding instrument, should obviate, or at least minimize the need for equalization, compression, or other processing. On the other hand, some recordists subject virtually every sound to more or less elaborate treatments. Tom Lord-Alge, for example, has called himself "one of a new breed of engineers" who are "not afraid to use

EQ . . . not afraid to use compression," who will "do whatever it takes to make it sound different, less predictable."[37]

Also, because musicians react instinctively to the sounds they hear, electronic mediation may influence musical performances. "I'd much rather spend three hours messing around with a guitar sound when it's getting recorded, than just sticking something down and then trying to tackle it (in the mix)," says Robin Guthrie of the Cocteau Twins. " 'Cause the sound that we make, that's the sound that sort of inspires the notes that we play."[38] Tony Visconti tells a story of such a collaboration between musician and machine, each reacting to one another, in Bowie's *Low* sessions (1977). On the track "Speed of Life," drummer Dennis Davis asked for the effect Visconti had placed on the snare to be run through Davis's headphones. The sound was the result of feeding the snare sound through Visconti's new Eventide Harmonizer, which was set to lower the snare's pitch and to add feedback. The precise way in which the Harmonizer reacted to the incoming signal, however, depended on the intensity of the signal at its input. When Davis "could hear the effect as he played, he was able to control the sound by how hard he hit his snare."[39] Thus, the snare drum sound took on a range of timbral variation reflecting the interactive performance of drummer and machine.

MICROPHONES

The first step in the signal path is the microphone. In many ways microphones are the technological soul of any recording project; the effectiveness of all other tools and techniques depends upon the quality of the image that the microphone is able to deliver. It is often noted that what Roland Barthes calls the "grain of the voice"—"the body in the voice as it sings"—is at least as essential to a rock song's meaning as the words or melody.[40] That is, the sound of a particular voice in a particular performance carries a sort of phenomenal meaning that completes the sense of the song. Microphones not only capture this "grain"; to an extent they participate in creating it. The microphone serves as an alchemic doorway between performance and text. Sound enters the doorway as fleeting variations in air pressure and is instantly transformed—or, more precisely, transduced—into a corresponding electrical signal that can be printed on some form of recording medium. But the process inevitably changes the

original sound in some way. Thus, the coloring effects of the microphone itself, along with those of its placement, must be appropriately
matched with both the source material and the stylistic and expressive intentions of the project—a task requiring aesthetic judgment in
addition to technical expertise. Decisions about microphone choice
and orientation in relation to the room and the sound source depend
on a feel for the affective character of the sound in question and a
sense of its role in the track. To be sure, the basic characteristics of
microphone design offer some practical guidelines as to applications,
and there are conventional procedures that are considered normative. But aesthetically speaking, as one writer puts it, "there is no
'correct' microphone for any application."[41]

The process of "hearing" sound and then converting it to an electrical signal is subject to a number of variables that account for the
coloring characteristics of particular microphones. The basic microphone types are condenser and dynamic, the latter having two sub-
types: moving coil and ribbon. The differences in their design and
operating principles make for characteristics that recommend one or
another in certain situations. Condensers, for example, respond very
quickly to transients (rapid changes in sound pressure) and have a
very wide frequency response, producing a detailed sonic image.
They are commonly used for recording the rapid transients of certain
percussion instruments (e.g., cymbals, acoustic guitars) and for capturing the fine details of vocal performances. Moving-coil dynamic
microphones, on the other hand, have slower response times but are
capable of handling very high sound pressure levels. They are often
used in live performance and for recording such things as electric
guitars—especially heavily distorted ones—and snare drums. Also,
their slower response times can effectively smooth out the kind of
piercing attacks that might be encountered with brass instruments.

Within these basic microphone types there are many variations
among components that account for the sonic personalities of particular models and even of individual microphones. Renowned microphone restorer and builder Stephen Paul refers to the configurations
of elements that can make a microphone completely unique as
"alchemical formulas." "There was a feeling that in this thing was
magic," he says of the Neumann and AKG mikes of the 1940s. "There
was something that transcended its technology, something that transcended the limitations of the time in which it was made. . . . [T]he

whole microphone has the aura of a Stradivarius. It's like a musical instrument, and it has a sound of its own."[42] In his modifications of both new and vintage microphones, Paul balances experience and science with an appreciation for the chaotic unpredictability of our "vibratory universe." Believing that "the phenomenon of acoustics is so complex that no math can truly do it justice," he appeals repeatedly to enchantment, "an essential part of the formula," in discussing his work: "Sometimes I sit for hours staring at a piece of my work—a wiring harness, or a circuit board I've built by hand, and I realize after a while that what I'm doing is spending a lot of time imbuing it with energy, putting a spell on it."[43]

The subtle art of microphone placement is nearly as important a factor in the rendering of the sonic image as microphone design, and recordists continually refine and expand their technique through experimentation. The placement determines the degree and type of coloration and defines the relationship between source sound and room sound. Considerations include not only the microphone's orientation to the sound source—as defined by distance and angle—and the acoustic characteristics of the room, but also the microphone's sound-gathering properties. Microphones hear sound differently according to their directional, or polar, pattern, which determines the way in which a microphone responds to sound reaching it from different directions. The three basic polar patterns are: 1) unidirectional (subdivided into cardioid, supercardioid, and hypercardioid), 2) omnidirectional, and 3) bidirectional. A microphone configured in a cardioid pattern picks up sound that is directly in front of its diaphragm and slightly to either side and attenuates sound that arrives from any angle outside of this field, thus minimizing room reflections and leakage from other instruments. An omnidirectional pattern, on the other hand, picks up sound equally from all sides, and a bidirectional pattern responds to sound at its front and back, but not at its sides.

A microphone's polar pattern, frequency response characteristics, and placement are all factors in its timbral effect. For example, one characteristic of a unidirectional or bidirectional configuration, known as the proximity effect, is a marked boost in bass frequencies when the microphone is placed very near the sound source. It is a kind of distortion, and it can create a muffled boominess that requires filtering. On the other hand, with controlled use it can be an expressive device, adding, for example, a warm intimacy to a vocal performance. Steve Albini has used the effect to create some very large recorded guitar sounds, notably for Kurt Cobain on *In Utero* (1993). He notes that the low-frequency information emanating from an electric guitar amplifier cabinet is in the nature of "cabinet resonance, rhythmic transients, and physical pumping of air."[44] This is not the pitch content of the guitar part, but rather, its supporting resonance. "Capturing it on tape can make the recording seem more physical," writes Albini, "and the careful use of proximity effect allows you to completely tailor the low end by moving the microphone, sometimes by fractions of an inch."[45] Albini's comment illustrates the degree of subtlety involved in microphone technique and brings up another interesting point: the master recordist uses microphones to capture not only sonic and musical elements, but also the weight of apparent physical presence.

Microphone choice also involves considerations of musical style, genre, and affect. Bruce Swedien speaks of using different microphones for Michael Jackson depending upon a song's tempo, groove, the theme of its lyrics, and so forth.[46] Because the choice is a matter of aesthetic intent, recordists may be guided in unconventional directions by their intuition. Although condenser microphones are the most common choice for recording vocals, Phil Collins's distinctive vocal presence on records such as *Face Value* (1981) and *No Jacket Required* (1985) was the result of using a dynamic moving-coil microphone. According to engineer Hugh Padgham, the setup he used to record Collins's vocals "is basically a cheap mic and a cheap compressor." The microphone he uses is a Beyer M88—the same one Collins uses in live performances—which "gives a nice rough edge to his voice." The signal is then passed through an Allen & Heath minilimiter. "It's a vicious limiter," says Padgham, but "it works well with Phil. . . . It gives that guttural sound to his voice."[47] Moreover, Collins "actually sings to the sound of his voice going through this setup." That is, the processed voice is present in his headphones as he sings, which in turn influences his performance. This unconventional configuration is uniquely suited to the particular timbral character of Collins's voice. "What sounds good on Phil doesn't necessarily sound good on other people," says Padgham. "I've tried this particular setup on Sting, and it doesn't sound good."

As Padgham explains, in Collins's case it is not only the microphone but the compressor too that shapes the vocal sound. Like so much else in the record-making process, the signal path is made up of complementary relationships, and managing these is an important part of rendering the recorded image of a musical performance. On *Oh Mercy* (1989) Daniel Lanois captured some of the most richly detailed vocals that Bob Dylan has ever recorded. Wishing to make a specific timbral association with a "vintage" type of sound, Lanois chose his tools accordingly: tube technology for microphone and compressor and a classic preamplifier/equalizer. "I went for the old sound in his voice and got a great, big, warm sound that also has a lot of presence," says Lanois. "[W]e used a Sony C-27 A, a valve [tube] mic, through an LA-2A tube compressor, with a Neve 4-band pre-amp, a 1976 model, I think."[48] Many modern recordings confine the voice to a space in the track that is tightly defined (i.e., by equalization, compression, amplitude, positioning, and ambience), producing a sharply focused image. This gives the vocal an incisiveness that allows it to project from the mix. Dylan's vocal on a track like "Man in the Long Black Coat," on the other hand, has a breadth and thickness that give it an altogether different affective sense—what Lanois refers to as "the old sound." The tools help to define the dimensions of the vocal—its physical size in the track, its relative "naturalness," its apparent proximity to the listener—and to highlight certain of its features in specific ways. In other words, in addition to their physical effect on sound, the microphone, preamp, equalizer, and compressor are active participants in the development of a dramatic character.

RECORDING FORMATS

Once sounds are converted to electrical signals, they are sent to a recording device for encoding and storage using one of two general types of technology: analog or digital. Analog recording uses magnetic tape to store the electrical signals from microphones or electronic instruments in the form of magnetic patterns that are analogous to the audio waveform. Upon replay, the patterns are reconverted into electrical signals and, at the loudspeaker stage, into a representation of the original waveform. With digital recording, on the other hand, the electrical signals are converted into streams of binary code that are then stored on tape or in computer memory.

The sonic differences between analog and digital recording are a source of some debate. Analog is more "active" than digital in adding its own set of characteristic features to the recorded sound. As anyone who has ever made an analog cassette knows, the recording machine and the choice of tape have a readily apparent effect on the sound being recorded. Even among high-end professional equipment, however, the characteristic qualities of particular recorders, alignment levels, types of noise reduction, tape stocks, and tape sizes and speeds differ. Choices are made according to subjective standards as well pragmatic concerns, such as reliability and cost. Daniel Lanois, for example, finds 2-inch twenty-four-track Ampex tape running at 15 inches per second with Dolby A noise reduction to be a "very musical" format.[49] Many of his contemporaries, on the other hand, would insist on 30 inches per second and Dolby SR, if they used analog at all. Still others find 2-inch sixteen-track machines to be the best analog has to offer. The most obviously apparent coloration with analog is the addition of tape hiss, which is generally viewed as something to be minimized. Over the years, a series of developments in the technology of noise reduction have been driven by recordists' desire to decrease the intrusion of tape hiss. On the other hand, the coloration introduced by tape compression—a presence-enhancing effect that occurs when recording at high levels—is for many a sought-after characteristic of analog recording. Says Lanois:

> I get better bass on analog. I suppose that when you saturate tape, you get a musical result. When you hit it hard, you get a "loudness" effect. . . . I think when you hit analog tape hard, the midrange collapses, therefore there is the impression of more top and bottom so you get the "loudness" curve effect, which is a musical curve.[50]

Bob Clearmountain, on the other hand, is "frustrated" by the fact that "the analog machine is changing the sound."[51] To his ears, digital sound is "just better" because it is a more transparent format than analog.[52] However, digital sound is often criticized for sounding "harsh," "brittle," or "cold." That is, its relative lack of the coloration to which recordists are accustomed is regarded as a kind of distortion in itself. "There's a certain kind of compression that you get from analog recording," says Don Dixon. "It takes away a lot of the transient peaks. For some kinds of pop recordings, softening up those transients just gives you a better sound—it's a sound we're used to anyway."[53] In other words, the characteristic sound quality of analog recording has set the frame of reference. As the "sound we're used to," it permeates rock history. For many recordists it is an essential aspect of any rock recording, especially for bass, drums, and guitars.

Although digital recording offers extreme flexibility in editing, very accurate sound reproduction, no tape hiss, no degradation of high frequencies with repeated playing, and a greater number of tracks available on a single machine, many recordists continue to resist it. "For years now," says Robbie Robertson, "I've had recording engineers, producers, musicians, people off the street say, 'Stay away from this digital stuff. It's not musical. It does weird things to your ears. It's like standing in front of a radar oven too long.' I've heard all these myths."[54] The digital/analog debate is, once again, a matter of aesthetics. Both formats have particular strengths, and at this point most recordists use both in the course of a project, depending on what is being recorded. Following a common practice, veteran engineer and producer Al Schmitt uses the sixteen-track analog format for rhythm tracks—to "get the warmth and punch"—and records vocals digitally, which allows composite vocal tracks to be constructed easily and with no loss of sound quality.[55] Bruce Swedien mixes some tracks to analog and others to digital simply, as he puts it, "because they affect me differently."[56]

Robertson points out that the analog machine is a kind of sound processor as well as a recording device, and "[i]f you want this effect that it gives you, you can go through this machine."[57] However, in deciding to use the digital format for his *Storyville* album (1991), he and engineer Steve Nye—previously a "die-hard analog fan"[58]—determined that the analog effect could be duplicated by adding "just a little bottom EQ and a little compression. It was virtually the same thing, but [we] had better control over it."[59] Tony Visconti, whose extensive engineering and production career began well before the proliferation of digital recording, praises the digital format for delivering, finally, the sounds as originally crafted by the recordist: "I came to accept that the public would never hear what we chosen few heard in the studio—until digital came along."[60] Like Clearmountain, he prefers a format that functions as a faithful replicator rather than as an effect. In his view, "Tape compression, although it is a reality that has become a romantic notion, is not an accurate means of equalization and is unpredictable. If I am compressing and equalizing a kick and a snare and I take a considerable amount of time doing that, I don't want the 'storage system' to change that hard work."[61] As for digital recording's lack of conventional coloration, Visconti believes that engineering technique and high quality tools can create the same effect with digital technology. "I can still make a recording with that 'classic' sound using modern equipment and modern digital tape—it doesn't depend on analog tape or equipment more than 30 years old."[62]

The ongoing analog/digital controversy calls to mind similar debates that have surfaced periodically throughout the history of recorded sound. In 1936, Cedric Wallis wrote the following in an article for *The Gramophone* entitled "The Future of Recorded Romanticism":

> In those days [of acoustic recording] battle raged between two schools of opinion, who called themselves, respectively, Realists and Romantics. The Realists stood out strongly for as accurate a reproduction as possible of the actual sounds recorded, but the Romantics held that a certain sacrifice of accuracy was permissible, nay, even desirable, if it induced a quality more pleasing to the ear. To a Romantic, realistic records were always 'shrill' or 'thin,' or both. To a Realist, a romantic record would appear "wooly" or "foggy."[63]

The similarity—even in the choice of adjectives—to the analog/digital debate is striking. Not only is the basic issue the same, but in both cases the terms of competition between the two technologies are, in the end, not technical specifications but aesthetic judgment.

MONITORS

Stored sound images remain in a silent world of iron oxide particles and digital data until they are reconfigured and delivered to the listener by the loudspeaker. Monitor speakers and the amplifiers that power them are the final link in the sound-reproduction chain, and all sonic decision-making in the recording studio is based on the information they provide. The wide variety of monitors preferred by different recordists is a telling sign of the problematic nature of assessing that information. There is no absolute standard for accuracy, and the sound of a recording can vary a great deal when played through different speakers. Since the aim is to create a sonic image capable of retaining its basic integrity in a variety of listening circumstances, recordists must be careful how they respond to the sounds their monitors present. Even a well-designed speaker with a wide and flat frequency response can tell only one story, and its very precision may prove misleading. For in the real world of rock reception, sound reproduction is subject to a vast range of technical and acoustical circumstances, most of which are less than optimal. In some cases, recordists have abandoned a personal favorite monitor because it was misleading as a reference; it "just sounded too good."[64]

Nowhere are the unrealistic conditions of studio listening more apparent than in the wall-sized "main" monitors. Although they are among the most striking visual elements in any control room and their sound is invariably impressive to clients of the studio, their use as a benchmark reference is usually confined to the extreme low end of the frequency range. "Usually, the only time they get used is when the band comes in and wants to listen," says engineer Terry Date. "They always want to turn up on the big speakers loud, and then I leave the room."[65] The essence of Date's comment is repeated again and again by recordists across the spectrum of rock styles, who prefer to use smaller "near-field" monitors to better approximate real-world listening conditions, as well as to minimize the influence of room acoustics. These monitors are usually of average quality, producing a sound that fairly represents a middle way in sound reproduction. The aim is to approximate as nearly as possible the widest range of listeners' reproduction systems. "Most of my records don't sound good in optimum conditions," says Brian Eno, "where there are very large speakers which are extremely well balanced and have lots of high and low frequencies. I mix, really, for what I imagine most people have—medium-priced hi-fi—and for the radio a bit as well."[66]

While recording technology has improved markedly, and many problems that in the past constantly threatened to diminish a recording's intended effect have been eliminated, the problem of monitoring remains pervasive. The experience of creating a mix that sounds great in the studio and terrible on all other systems is a common one for inexperienced recordists. A successful mix is one that travels well, rather than one that is perfectly tailored to a particular listening environment. Given that sonic particularity is one of the fundamental concepts of record production, this presents something of a paradox. But it also removes the idea of particularity from the realm of abstract theory and illustrates the practical limits of the concept. Recordists must continually face the challenge of making a very specifically configured work with the criterion that it have a general effectiveness in myriad circumstances.

As they strive to cultivate a perspective relative to possible reproduction scenarios, recordists reference their work on several monitors of differing size and quality and in different environments. John "Jellybean" Benitez, for example, mixes "on the Yamaha NS-10s and the E-V Sentry 100s [near-field monitors]—going back and forth between those two and whatever [other] monitors that are in the studio," listening for "different things on each speaker." When he finishes a mix, he also listens to it on the small built-in speaker on a Studer two-track tape recorder, believing that if the integrity of the mix holds up in such unflattering conditions, listeners will be able to "hear it on anything."[67] Perhaps the intended sonic image exists only in the mind of the mixer, but as a practical matter, he or she relies on some combination of place and loudspeaker for a familiar general reference that allows them to hear their own mix in relation to others they have come to know over time. Fittingly, for many rock recordists this most trusted listening environment is their car.

Although many engineers and producers take their own favorite near-field monitors with them as they travel from one studio to another, there has been something of a standard speaker in use since the early 1980s in studios throughout the world. Though it is not especially accurate—as evidenced by the once-ubiquitous "tissue paper mod," whereby the tweeters were covered with tissue paper to tone down the overly bright high end—the Yamaha NS-10 was accepted as a good average representation of real-world circumstances. Engineer Elliot Scheiner comments that NS-10s are "more realistic. It's not a great-sounding speaker . . . so you know that when you get a mix, or if you get anything sounding good on those, it's going to relate to the outside world."[68] Moreover, by using them as a common reference, recordists gain a common medium through which to compare their work with that of others.

THE CONSOLE

The console is the nerve center of the control room. A full-featured modern console, such as those manufactured by Solid State Logic,

Neve, or Euphonix, has a set of channel strips that allow computer-automated control over amplitude, equalization, compression, gating, and panning for every sound on the track. The console provides the means to develop amplitudinal, spatial, and frequency relationships among the track's many individual musical parts and sonic treatments. It also serves as the organizational center of the control room, directing the routing of all signals to and from the tape recorder and the studio's various sound processors, providing the ability to instantly isolate any signal or to group a subset of signals, and offering the flexibility to create different simultaneous mixes—a headphone mix for the recording musicians and a control room mix for the engineer and producer.

Unlike other recording tools, consoles are usually permanent installations, custom-configured for a given studio's needs. Indeed, until the early 1970s, consoles were individually designed and built, often by the studio's own engineers and technicians. Now there are many manufacturers of mass-produced consoles, offering various designs and features, and new control rooms are usually designed with a particular console in mind. As a matter of studio economics, consoles are designed to meet the needs of a wide range of potential clients. Flexibility, sonic transparency, and clarity are among their most valued features.

Like other tools of the recording trade, however, consoles have their own personalities, which manifest both in their sound and in their ergonomic design. In addition to a console's overall sound, the character of a certain manufacturer's equalization is often cited as a reason for preferring a particular console. Another important consideration is a console's design features. How well do they match the recordist's preferred working methods? How extensive are the console's capabilities and how flexible are its functions? How many inputs does it have? How straightforward is its operation? In short, can the console serve as a creative ally, helping to streamline the logistics of the process?

Prior to a project's final mixing stage, a console's sonic and functional capabilities are generally outweighed by considerations of studio acoustics and atmosphere. For recording, the console may even be bypassed altogether in order to maintain the shortest possible signal path, though once recorded, signals are routed through the console to create temporary working mixes—for the headphones of overdubbing musicians, for example. During final mixing, however, the situation changes. Now the console actively participates in assembling the sound of the finished work. Its equalization and automation functions may be especially important to the project's outcome. More inputs than were needed during recording may be required during mixing to accommodate all the musical parts and sound-processing schemes. Because recording and mixing require different things from a console, a project is often moved to a different studio for mixing— one whose console is better suited to the requirements of the mix or is simply the preferred "instrument" of the mix engineer.

SIGNAL PROCESSING

> Nearly all the processing equipment you find in a studio gives you a way of changing the sense of space that the music is happening in.
>
> Brian Eno

In developing a track's various elements, recordists make use of an array of sound processing devices that provide control over the elements' defining parameters. So-called time-domain processors have already been touched upon in the discussion of echo and ambience, but there are two other categories of processor to be considered: timbral processors (equalizers, pitch and amplitude modulators, and so-called psychoacoustic processors), which affect a sound's frequency content, and dynamics processors (compressors and gates), which affect its envelope. Equalizers, and often compressors and gates, are available on the console, but many times an outboard processor is preferred. As with microphones, all of these tools have a range of types and applications. There are standard practices, to be sure, but there are also innumerable techniques developed through creative experimentation or out of the need to meet the demands of a specific situation. Some processors have pronounced personalities and add their own distinctive flavor no matter how they are used. Others, more transparent in their operation, are chosen when subtle sonic refinements are required. In any case, sound shaping tools are used, as Eno says, to "change the sense of space" in which the music is happening, that is, to move the music from the natural sound world in which it originates into the sound world of the record.

Often several processors are linked in series, setting up more or less elaborate chains of interdependent processing. There are also devices that offer several functions in a single unit: a compressor/limiter/expander/gate, for example; or a processor that combines echo, ambience, and equalization. Additionally, many compressors and gates have a "side chain" function whereby they are controlled not by the signal they are processing but by some other source. For example, a gate on a snare drum microphone might be controlled by an equalized version of the snare signal. The gate opens not in response to what enters the microphone but to the presence of the side chain signal, which is "tuned" to attenuate areas of the frequency spectrum inhabited by unwanted sounds that might falsely trigger the gate. This technique yields a clean snare track with minimal leakage. Similarly, compressed room ambience can be made to add explosive power to a track's low end by keying the compressor to the bass drum, in which case the compressor will only allow the ambience to pass when the bass drum strikes. Using sound processors interactively in these ways extends the range of sound sculpting techniques by adding further layers to the relationships between a track's sounds and the forces that shape them.

TIMBRAL PROCESSING

Equalization involves the manipulation of particular areas of the frequency spectrum whereby bands of frequencies are selected and then incrementally boosted or cut in order to precisely tailor a sound's color, which, in turn, affects its place in the overall frequency structure of the track. In addition to the frequency range, the width of the selected frequency band can be defined by the user. Equalization can help to overcome a variety of sonic problems for individual sounds. George Massenburg began designing and building equalizers with precisely this aim in mind: "To get the 'boink' out of the snare drum. To reach for the frequency of the Helmholtz resonator of an acoustic guitar, which, when picked up with a cardioid mic, can be 'boomy,' and just take that much out."[69] Problems with sounds that are "dull," "harsh," "thin," and so forth, can be corrected by identifying the problematic frequency range and shaping it to achieve the desired result. In addition, equalization can be used to enhance a sound—restoring a polish, clarity, or presence that may have been lost in the process of recording, or imparting a quality that the sound never had in the first place. Engineer Tom Tucker, for example, uses an array of equalizers for additive processing (boosting selected frequencies) depending on musical and sonic context:

> If I want something to be crunchy, I use SSL EQs, like for drums.
> However, I use a couple of different EQs for the bottom. I will use
> the SSL EQ in the 80 to 150 Hz range, because it's kind of punchy,
> and then for the deeper stuff, where I really want the subs to be pure,
> I will go to an Avalon or Pultec. The API is very clean and pristine.
> It can get harsh, though. If something is already a little harsh, I might
> opt to add the Neve for the additive EQ, or a Pultec, which has a
> very soft top.[70]

Equalization is also useful for combining sounds into a complex texture. For while the timbral configuration of a sound heard by itself may be satisfactory, it may prove problematic when combined with other sounds. Hence equalization decisions involve not only timbral but also textural considerations, and manipulation of equalizer controls is ultimately guided according to how relationships among timbres account for the overall sonic image. Butch Vig describes his application of this principle on the first Garbage album, a record filled with multiple simultaneous drum parts, guitar overdubs (twenty or thirty on some tracks), and noise effects:

> We try to create little pockets or niches in the music by radically
> filtering sounds. . . . If you have a distorted guitar tone that is a wall
> of sound, it's hard to fit in a track that already has pumping bass, all
> these drums, and many other guitars. But if you filter the distorted
> guitar severely, you can find a spot for it to sit in. If you listen to it
> by itself, it sounds really shitty because there's no top or bottom end.
> But when you put it in the track—because there's so much body in
> the rest of the track—it's a full-sounding guitar.[71]

While many master recordists counsel conservative use of equalization, the application that Vig describes was suited to a particular problem associated with a very dense musical arrangement. Radical equalization is also used when the aesthetic aim is to alter a sound's basic character and so also its symbolic association. As noted in chapter 3, timbre functions in two primary ways: as physical entity and as symbol. In the case of the former, measured use of equalization shapes a timbre's physical characteristics from the "outside," as it were, leaving its essential character unaffected. When equalization is pushed to extremes, it works from the "inside" of a sound, transforming the sound's personality to the point that it is no longer in the same rhetorical category as it was originally. When played through a wah-wah pedal—a variable bandpass filter—for instance, a guitar may still be recognizable as such, but its timbre takes on a new set of associations. Likewise, a voice that is equalized to sound as though it is emanating from an old radio, a telephone, or a public address system—something like the verse sections of Björk's "The Hunter" (1997), say—makes an allusion to something beyond the track. And recall in chapter 3 the snare sound on U2's "Zoo Station," its tinny racket confronting the unsuspecting U2 fan with a bold new dare. Equalizers aside, all timbral processors tend to transform the symbolic quality of sounds. A tremolo, Leslie, or vocoder effect really amounts to a timbre in its own right. Rather than shaping sound in an unobtrusive way, it always leaves its own obvious traces and associations.

DYNAMICS PROCESSING

The two basic types of dynamics processing are gain (loudness) reduction and downward expansion. The devices that perform these functions are commonly, if somewhat crudely, referred to as "compressors" and "gates," respectively. Gain reduction is used to control the dynamic range of individual musical parts, as well as of the overall mix. Electronically limiting the degree of variation in dynamics effectively controls the loudest dynamic peaks and thus allows the overall average signal to be raised without causing distortion, increasing the presence of lower level sonic details. The recordist selects a threshold of volume above which a signal's intensity is reduced by a definable ratio. If a 4:1 ratio is selected, for example, a rise of 8 decibels above threshold will result in only a 2-decibel increase in actual loudness. The effect is similar to that produced by "riding" a fader—turning the gain up or down as the music goes along. Before versatile compressors became widely available, engineers used just such a technique to keep things under control. The compressor performs the task automatically and also provides control over attack and release times (of the compressor itself), in addition to threshold (the level at which it begins to work) and ratio (how much gain reduction it applies to the signal). In addition, so-called multiband compression allows different areas of the frequency range to be compressed in different ways. These controls make it possible to set the range of operation for the compressor from the practically inaudible to the dramatically obvious, depending upon the requirements of the particular situation.

The three basic types of gain reduction used in record production—compression, limiting, and leveling—in fact represent different configurations of the same basic phenomenon. Though there are units dedicated to one or another of these functions, a gain reduction device with controls for threshold, ratio, attack time, and release time can produce all three types, depending upon how the controls are set. At a ratio above 8:1, and with fast attack and release times, compression becomes limiting—an application that drastically attenuates signals above threshold. This is useful for controlling large transient peaks that would otherwise cause distortion. The combination of a high ratio, low threshold, medium attack time, and medium-to-slow release time constitutes leveling, a process whereby the signal's gain is constantly reduced—in effect smoothing out the program material. Perhaps because "compression," "limiting," and "leveling" denote such similar functions, the terms are often used imprecisely by recordists. However, when using sound-shaping tools, recordists follow their ears first of all; specific control settings and the accompanying terminology are regarded as only loose, basic guidelines. When engineer Shelley Yakus was asked how much compression he used, for example, he replied simply, " 'Til it sounds right." According to Jack Douglas, who worked for a time as his assistant, Yakus "would tape cards across the VU meters so he couldn't see them. He'd say, 'You'll know when it's wrong.' "[72]

While limiting dynamic range might be viewed as a constriction of musical expression, the net effect of compression is somewhat different. For one thing, the dynamics on a rock recording are ultimately controlled not by the musician but by the channel faders on the console. The dynamic structure of the track is achieved through a choreographed series of fader movements that take place as the multitrack tape is being mixed to stereo. Compression is applied not to limit the musical effect of dynamics but to provide a focusing mechanism to sharpen the sonic image in one way or another. Compression allows the recordist to fashion for the sound image a desired degree of resolution by tailoring the contour of its loudness and thereby shaping some aspect of its character. Even in the most transparent applications it can provide enhanced clarity, and this is perhaps its most valued function in rock recording. It allows each musical part to retain a focused presence wherever it is placed in the mix and however its actual volume is manipulated at the console. Moreover, it brings out the part's sonic nuances. Hence the most subtle sonic artifacts—the tailing away of a crash cymbal, the sound of a plectrum scraping across guitar strings, the nuances of vocal sounds—tend to hold their place in the mix and project from the loudspeaker. Recall Dylan's vocal on "Man in the Long Black Coat," noted earlier in this chapter. Compression is an important element in rendering its grainy detail, bringing out the weathered throat sounds, and allowing them to come close to our ear and linger in an intimate way.

On the other hand, the powerful punch of oversized drums and guitars and the physical presence of the bass are also direct results of compression. This is perhaps why Tony Visconti refers to compression as "the *sound* of rock."[73] Packing the sonic information into a tighter dynamic space can provide fullness and concentration of energy in a sound's attack, in effect intensifying it by amplifying its low-level sonic details while clamping down on its transient spike, whose dynamic intensity would otherwise cause distortion. The result is a louder overall experience whose visceral quality comes across at any listening level. The bass sound on Janet Jackson's "Control" (1986), for example—a digital sample of car horns that engineer Steve Hodge added "a bunch of low end" to and "compressed the living daylights out of"[74]—thrusts forth from the loudspeakers with an intensity at once aggressive and infectious. Hodge has emphasized the hard growl of the sound and highlighted its percussive aspect, which in combination with the compressed bass drum gives the track an irresistible punch in its low end, a stylistic essential of successful dance tracks. The bass line's sonic character also complements and intensifies its rhythmic momentum.

When compressors are pushed to extremes, they can produce marked timbral effects. The background texture for the track "Goodbye" from Emmylou Harris's *Wrecking Ball*, for instance, is impossible to identify, for its constituent timbres are melded into a haunting canopy of sound that surrounds the vocal and the fingerpicked acoustic guitar. Daniel Lanois discloses that the texture was created by radically compressing two instruments—a piano and an electric Vox mandoguitar—effectively fusing them into a single sonic entity. "We put a huge amount of compression on the piano and the mandoguitar, and it turned into this fantastic, chimey harmonic instrument," says Lanois. "We almost got the old Spector '60s sound, not by layering, but by really compressing what was already there between the melodic events happening between these two instruments."[75] The compression merged both the sounds and the musical material into a unique composite texture.

Compression, like all other sound processing, is often used behind the scenes to develop a track's texture in ways that are not readily evident. In a common practice known as multing, recordists manipulate duplicate signals in different ways. Typically, one signal is processed either slightly or not at all while the other is given a more or less intensive reshaping. The altered signal is then mixed in at a lower volume and perhaps at a different location in the stereo spectrum to create the desired effect. Douglas, for instance, uses an application that he calls "bussed limiting," where drum tracks are grouped together on a single bus of the console to which compression is applied. The result is a sharply focused mono image of the drums and drum ambience, which is then combined with the unprocessed stereo mix of the drums. Though the compressed mono image may itself be almost indistinguishable, it serves to tighten the overall drum sound and provides it with added projective punch. Similarly, engineer Michael Brauer uses the technique to enhance snare ambience by emphasizing the attack on one snare while eliminating it on the other. The compressor clamps down hard on the second snare signal, momentarily reducing its gain by 40 decibels, and then instantly releases it as soon as the attack has passed, leaving only the snare attack's ambient image as it echoes around the room. According to Brauer, by mixing these two snare sounds together "you can take a regular lousy snare drum and turn it into a John Bonham kind of snare."[76]

The other main type of dynamics processing—expansion—is the opposite of compression. Expansion *increases* dynamic range, typically in a downward direction, to silence unwanted sound. Controls are set so that as the volume of program material falls *below* threshold the expander engages at a definable rate to reduce the signal further. Using this technique, noise between vocal phrases, for example, can be eliminated unobtrusively. When the singer begins to sing again, the dynamic level rises above threshold and the device becomes inactive. Another common application is the tailoring of sounds to remove unwanted artifacts (e.g., room reflections, ringing, buzzes, rattles) that become obtrusive only after the major portion of the sound wave has passed; the expander in effect "chases" the desired sound's natural decay. Like compressors, expanders provide control over threshold, ratio, attack, and release times. The configuration of these controls determines whether the unit functions as an expander or a gate—something that gradually attenuates or something closer to an on/off switch. The term "gate" is commonly used to denote any use of the device. In addition to the aforementioned controls, many gates include frequency, bandwidth, and range controls. The first two allow the gate to be "tuned" so that it is triggered only by sounds falling within a specified frequency range. The last allows the user to set the lower limit of expansion.

The use of gates can add significantly to the clarity of a recording by eliminating extraneous sounds on a track and controlling microphone leakage. Such clarity is not a universally desired quality, but rather a stylistic option. Recall in chapter 3, for example, Emmylou Harris's comment about leakage being "encouraged" on the *Wrecking Ball* sessions. The random mixing of sound that occurs in such a scenario can add an impressionistic textural depth to the track. The tight, clean sound of many modern pop records, on the other hand, owes a great deal to the use of gates. The difference lies in the degree of precision with which sounds are separated. If the aim is tight control over every individual sound, gates can be very helpful. A separate gate on every drum microphone, for instance, helps to isolate each drum on its own track, effectively providing the recordist with the same kind of discrete control as a drum machine with separate outputs for each drum sound. The recordist can then deliberately fashion the drum image during the mix. If a natural randomness is desired—as on most punk recordings for example—microphones are gated more loosely or left ungated to pick up whatever they hear. In this case, the recorded impression is of a complex, interactive sonic play among the drums and the ambient images they evoke. The two techniques can also be used together, gating each drum while leaving a stereo pair of overhead microphones open to capture the overall sense of the drum kit/room ambience interaction.

With their ability to shape the envelope of a sound—to reshape a sound's temporal character—gates can also be used to create a variety of effects. Gabriel's "The Intruder" provides a dramatic example. Not only are the drums and the room ambience extremely compressed, the decay of the ambience is controlled by a gate. As the gate abruptly cuts off the natural decay, it creates a sense of space unique to the track. This kind of sculpting can be used on the attack portion of the envelope as well by using a gate in the manner of a volume pedal—setting a high threshold and slow attack time to remove a sound's initial transients and causing it to fade in rapidly. Because our ability to recognize timbre relies heavily on the information contained in the attack portion of a sound's envelope, altering this information creates an altogether different timbral character.

These are the basic tools with which recordists capture and shape sounds. As with any artistic tools, their use involves subjective and intuitive judgment, as well as technical ability and practical consideration. One hears time and again from recordists of all styles of rock from every historical period that in record making "there are no rules." The statement applies to the empirical nature of the recording process in rock, as well as the willingness to pursue untested paths, to extend creative imagination to the use of machines, and to resist the potential overshadowing of artistic aims by technological dogma. But while recordists are not bound by convention, they are certainly guided by it. Whatever combination of tool, technique, and recording space is employed, a successful result is one that meets the aesthetic aims of those involved in making the record. And inevitably, these aims are influenced by the participants' reservoir of listening experience. Most recordists have a wealth of anecdotes about how they have broken the rules of physics and thereby achieved a successful artistic result.[77] But however unconventional the technique and unusual the resulting sound, the shared history of recorded sound and musical style serves as the anchoring backdrop against which intuitive decisions are measured.

5

Tracking and Mixing

As multitrack recording gradually became standard practice in rock, the distinction between recording and mixing as separate stages of a project grew. It is not uncommon at the mixing stage to move a project to a different studio or to hand over recorded tracks to a new engineer. Though the two stages may be separated in time, however, they remain, as they were for early rock and roll recordists, interdependent stages in a single process. A track's final form is arrived at through a series of evolutionary steps that flow from recording, which generates material and brings the piece to a certain stage of completion, to mixing, which finishes the process. Thus, the work's specificity is developed by degrees. For example, because multiple recorded performances can be edited into a single composite, deciding on the ultimate take of a given part may not be a pressing issue during recording. For some artists, simply keeping the flow of music making going may be more important than analyzing each take immediately. In such cases, a preliminary mixing stage follows recording in order simply to complete the "performance." Moreover, sounds can be modified or replaced after they are recorded. Timbre, echo, and ambience can be altered or added at any time, changing the sound and perhaps the sense of what was originally committed to tape. The possibility of after-the-fact editing means that no recorded track is absolutely complete until the final mix.

"I record with the mix in mind," says Tom Lord-Alge.[1] That is, awareness of the connections between recording and mixing is part of the recordist's craft. Ideas and performances at the recording stage are assessed in terms of a work that is in the process of developing but whose ultimate form is, for the moment, only imaginary—"nothing more than an auditory concept that floats in the mind."[2] Decisions, for instance, about whether to "print" a timbral or ambient effect while recording a performance or to leave it until the mix, when more of the overall track is in place and the precise quality of the effect can perhaps be better determined, are based upon an idea of the final mix's configuration and also the recordist's preferred working method. If as the track develops the effect turns out to be inappropriate, the performance may be unusable. On the other hand, the recordist may have a clear enough sense of the intended mix that there is no real risk in committing the effect to tape. Committing to a particular sound will influence the assessment of subsequent sounds, in effect, building the mix as the recording process unfolds. For many, this is the preferred way to work. "I've learned that I hate mixing," remarked Karl Wallinger after completing his *Egyptology* album (1997). "My thinking these days is that if it's not sounding good the night you do it, then any amount of mixing isn't going to make it sound much better."[3] Similarly, for Tchad Blake "recording without knowing how things are gonna sound in the end" is unacceptable. During the recording for Pell Mell's *Star City* (1997), bassist Greg Freeman remembers that Blake had the project "in mix mode from square one, as if he were mixing from the very beginning."[4] In cases such as these, so-called monitor mixes—rough mixes made for reference purposes—sometimes end up being the final versions.

This is not to say, however, that the mixing stage for these projects was obviated altogether. While he may have grown tired of mixing himself, Wallinger nevertheless handed several of the tracks on *Egyptology* over to Steve Lillywhite for polishing. And on *Star City*, the mix was the point at which arrangements were finalized as Blake and the band (which includes two other professional engineers, Freeman and Steve Fisk) liberally employed a subtractive technique that Blake calls "mute-button arranging."[5] This involved selectively muting previously recorded tracks, altering an earlier conception of the arrangement. Still, these approaches are quite different from, for instance, the Def Leppard *Pyromania* sessions as described by engineer Mike Shipley: "I remember at the beginning of *Pyromania* there was no idea of how we were going to do the drums. All Mutt [Lange] was saying was that we'd have to figure out some way to do the drums in the end."[6] The structure of the album's songs and arrangements changed many times in the course of recording, which would have been impossible had the drum track been finalized at the outset. The drum sounds were finally supplied by a Fairlight sampler, "stacking up a bunch of snares and bass drums" to create sounds for the mix that the musicians never heard while cutting the tracks.

Clearly, as with most of the issues we have encountered, there is a wide range of possible approaches to the recording/mixing sequence. How the project proceeds depends on recordists' attitudes toward the process, which are, once again, informed by both practical requirements and aesthetic sensibilities. In any case, recording and mixing are dynamically interactive stages. While an idea of the final mix influences decisions during recording, that idea is itself subject to change as it moves toward realization through the recording process. Rough mixes are made along the way that develop, refine, or perhaps alter the original plan, like a series of developmental sketches.[7]

RECORDING

"The word 'record' is misleading," writes Evan Eisenberg in his illuminating and entertaining book, *The Recording Angel: Explorations in Phonography*. "Only live recordings record an event; studio recordings . . . record nothing. Pieced together from bits of actual events, they construct an ideal event."[8] Insofar as recordings of classical music are meant to be apparent renderings of "events"—that is, performances of scores—perhaps the various editing techniques to which they are subjected are at odds with a narrow definition of "recording." Eisenberg, however, does not limit his discussion to classical recordings; he presumably means his formulation of "phonography" to apply to "studio recordings" in general.

But for rock recording—multitracking especially—Eisenberg's observation is problematic because it approaches the issue from the wrong end of the compositional process. The often fragmentary instances of music making that are collected throughout the recording stage of a project are not "bits of actual events"—that is, they are not disassembled pieces of a virtual whole. Though they are not meant to stand alone, they are complete events in themselves, stages in a process. Their status as events, however, is only the beginning of their ontological journey, for such performances serve a larger purpose than either the moment of their performance or its remaining record. Once recorded, they become ingredients of a work in progress. Each overdub is a step in the making—indeed, the discovery—of a work that does not yet exist, and therefore the recorded moment cannot claim to represent even in part. Rather, each overdub is a generative act that moves the work a step closer to realization.

Because a rock record is not a constructed representation of an "ideal event," but is rather a musical work that comes into being through recording, its making casts musical performance in a new light and in some ways changes its very nature and function. As we have seen, musical performance in this context is an act of both utterance and inscription. Thus, recording is a process whereby events become works. This consciousness pervades the recording team; when playback begins, all ears focus on the disembodied voice.

Although recording is aimed at accumulating a work's constituent material, it is not simply a collection process. It is the setting down of ideas—some rough, others fully formed—so that they may be heard, that is, experienced and evaluated as manifestations. As ideas take on the material form of recorded performances they further the creative process, giving rise to other ideas and shedding new light on the developing work. Borrowing from Paul Berliner, we might call it "thinking in sound."[9] Or, as producer Chuck Plotkin puts it, "You listen to the music. The music speaks to you. . . . And if you listen hard enough, you can *hear* what you're doing. . . . That's the whole thing. That's what you do: You put some music down and you listen to it. . . . Listen hard."[10] As sound images are inscribed on the tape, layer upon layer, each step leads in some way to the next. Even the blind alleys contribute to the generative process. Karl Wallinger calls it "a learning process where we see what the songs become."[11] The "learning process" for his *Goodbye Jumbo* resulted in sixty hours of material, which was edited down to fifty-eight minutes.

This conception of recording is of course not limited to multi-tracking. Claiming that "even those recorded songs that exhibit a marked reliance on improvisation and expressive elaboration need to be evaluated ultimately as considered compositions,"[12] Paul Clarke points to Greil Marcus's assessment of Elvis Presley's earliest recording sessions. "Nearly every record Elvis made with Sam Phillips," wrote Marcus, "was carefully and laboriously constructed out of hits and misses, riffs and bits of phrasing held through dozens of bad takes. The songs grew slowly, over hours and hours, into a music that paradoxically sounded much fresher than all the poor tries that had come before."[13] This account is confirmed by Marion Keisker, office manager of Phillips's Memphis Recording Service, who recalls that "each record was sweated out with hours of do it again and hold onto that little thing there."[14]

Marcus's use of the term "constructed" rightly suggests that these recorded performances, though recorded as complete takes, without overdubbing or tape editing, are still the result of a building process. Simply capturing good performances does not make a *record*, and record making was Phillips's aim: "I wanted simplicity, where we could look at what we were hearing mentally and say, 'Man, this guy has just got it.' But I wanted some biting bullshit, too. Everything had to be a stinger. To me every one of those sessions was like I was filming *Gone With the Wind.*"[15] Phillips wanted the directness, the "simplicity," of a great live performance. But the added aim of making the record "a stinger," of imbuing it with its own sense of immediacy, involved a process wherein the work's aura was developed gradually through a series of recorded takes. Phillips speaks of going "into the studio to draw out a person's innate, possibly *unknown* talents,"[16] and of performers "*creat[ing]* in a studio" (emphasis added).[17] In other words, at its best the recording process can lead to heightened moments, which include not only performance parameters but also qualities of sound, the flow of energy among performers, the particular way in which things come together. At the outset of their adventure the recording team may be uncertain of the outcome. But with a keen ear out for the arrival of defining moments, the recording process itself can serve as a path of discovery. After leaving Sun and moving to RCA, Presley stuck with what he had learned from Phillips, developing the record's aura through multiple takes. The magnificent racket that is "Hound Dog," for instance, is the last in a series of thirty-one tries.

Long before they reach an audience, a track's various elements are subjected to innumerable listenings. Each performance and each sound is carefully assessed for the impression it makes as it plays through the loudspeakers. This requires a combination of listening perspectives. On the one hand, details are scrutinized with a dispassionate ear out for problems of intonation, distortion, unwanted noise, and the like. On the other hand, and more importantly, the overall image is evaluated according to the feeling it imparts. Does the electronic emanation seem to have a soul of its own, something that reaches out to the listener in some way? This assessment is intuitive, a function of the aesthetics of those involved. These two perspectives are also evident in the recording process itself as the recordists alternate between two kinds of awareness: spontaneous, intuitive expression—the moment of performance—and deliberate critical analysis. The makeup of the recording team suggests the designation of tasks and roles—for example, the musician records a take (expression), and the producer decides whether or not to keep it (criticism)—but in practice these overlap to a great extent, and any member of the team at one time or another may switch back and forth in his or her own mind between the two awarenesses. Peter Gabriel characterizes this duality as a "two-levels-of-energy system." One level, "energy 'Z' . . . is a sort of performance-inspired, red-light-on, pumping energy." It involves "feel-based" musical interpretation, improvisation, and spontaneous interactions, both among musicians playing together and between overdubbing musicians and the track. The results of "energy Z" are then examined in minute detail using "energy 'A,' which is analytical energy . . . where you are able to zoom into decisions . . . and really get involved in the microcosm."

Gabriel describes a hypothetical breakdown of performance parameters to illustrate how the "two-levels-of-energy system" can work in each step of track production:

> So let's say layer one is defining a melody. You're not worrying about the kind of sound you're using. You just turn the red light on and you're off. People are dancing around the studio. Then switch over to energy A and look at what you've done in order to figure out ways to improve it. . . . Layer two is when you choose your palette of sounds with some tool you've created, maybe a joystick or something. When the red light goes on you perform the tone color changes. When that's done, you switch to the analytical stuff and do the small detail work. Level three, say, is adding the nuance to your performance, using breath or a keyboard or whatever. This is the process. You go layer upon layer, each time you try to force yourself into this high-energy performance mode before you get lost in the forest of analysis.[18]

Gabriel is describing a process of building a synthesizer performance—where melody, tone color, and nuance can be edited separately—but the statement is representative of the recording process in general. As each layer of performance is recorded, the two levels alternate. The continual shifting from one kind of consciousness to another keeps the process balanced between technical craft and artistic intuition. And the "two-levels-of-energy system" applies to the entire recording team. Because musical magic may come in momentary flashes of inspiration, improvised musings, or happy accidents, the "energy A" control exerted by producers and engineers must be balanced by an "energy Z" willingness to allow the dynamics of the process itself to take over. Producers must strike a balance between unpredictability, which may yield something extraordinary, and control, which keeps the project focused and on budget. It is the engineer's responsibility to make sure that all musical magic is captured, even if it happens at an unexpected moment or has some technical shortcoming. Sensitive engineers roll tape whenever they sense something beginning to happen in the studio, even if the musicians are warming up or experimenting with a still-unformed idea. Some simply roll tape at all times. "Always have the machine in 'record,' " says Tom Lord-Alge. "Any time there are musicians in [the studio] screwing around, or singers warming up, or whatever, you should be recording."[19]

In exploring a record's creative history the inevitable question arises: Where does recording fit in the overall, multi-stranded creative process as outlined in chapter 2? Commonly, songwriting precedes recording, in which case a more or less finished song provides the initial direction for the track. But popular songs in general are variable musical entities, subject to interpretive treatment in most of their aspects. Rock songs in particular, apart from their recorded manifestations, can be very sketchy indeed. Are melody, chords, words, tempo, and arrangement set before recording begins? Have they been carefully worked out in pre-production rehearsals? Are they at least generally indicated by a demo tape? Or is the "song" just an outline, or perhaps merely a title that provides some guidelines as to mood and atmosphere?[20] As we have seen, some artists begin recording without songs, fully integrating the task of capturing sounds with that of musical invention. A groove, a sound, or a concept may serve as the point of departure. Brian Eno describes his recording method as "in-studio composition, where you no longer come to the studio with a conception of the finished piece. Instead, you come with actually rather a bare skeleton of the piece, or perhaps with nothing at all."[21] Pink Floyd's "Echoes" (1971)—originally entitled "Return of the Son of Nothing"—began as simply reserved time at EMI's Abbey Road Studios. "Anytime that anyone had any sort of rough idea, we'd put it down,"[22] recalled drummer Nick Mason. Eventually thirty-six different "bits and pieces" (working title: "Nothing, Parts 1–36") were brought together in a single twenty-three-minute piece.

Whatever the state of the songs and arrangements when formal recording sessions begin, the first parts to be recorded are usually those that make up the "backing track," or "basic track"—the foundation. This includes drums and bass, as well as chording instruments such as guitars or keyboards. Depending on the style of the music, the backing track may be built layer by layer right from the start, or it may begin with a more or less full musical performance that is subsequently enhanced with overdubs and sound processing. In styles that make extensive use of synthesized and sampled sounds—such as rap or techno—records are usually built gradually, beginning with nothing more than a tempo on a click track. Recordists, often working alone, record layer upon layer with a MIDI sequencer, tape recorder, digital audio software, or some combination thereof, crafting grooves and sonic atmospheres as they go. The process may not even be aimed at any specific project; it may simply be an ongoing exercise. "It's not like an artist who leaves the piano if nothing is happening," says Hank Shocklee, discussing the day-to-day work of the Bomb Squad. "We'll do something—a beat, some samples—and file it away. Then when we're thinking about a track, we'll call it up and try it out."[23] Similarly, for producer Al Eaton, working alone at his own One Little Indian Studios, the process of creating backing tracks is ongoing. "That is one way in which rap and hip hop production is a little different from other types of pop music," according to Eaton. "I write all the time, so I have a lot of the work done before the act ever comes in."[24] When a rapper comes in with lyrics, they are matched with a suitable backing track, if possible, which is then tailored to suit the particular project. And even if none of the archived material is appropriate, it still serves to get the process started and to help rapper and producer begin zeroing in on a direction for the track.

In band-oriented styles, on the other hand, a full band performance may be the only way to get an idiomatic sound. "I've always believed in recording a live backing track that holds some magical interaction between musicians," says John Leckie. He feels that such interaction "is almost impossible to obtain when doing singular overdubs." His approach, then, is to begin recording with "the bass, drums, a rhythm instrument and the vocal all happening together," and then to choose "the take that has this magical interaction or uplift or some spirited feeling that makes the song happen." For Leckie, methodically building a track one layer at a time renders the track somewhat lifeless. "When using a click track and starting with the drums, then bass and so on, you may never have more than one band member in the studio at the same time, and it's quite hard to keep a human essence or organic musical dialog."[25] In addition to the interaction among musicians this approach provides, many recordists prefer it for the separation it affords between "A" and "Z" "energies." Musicians can focus on playing together while engineers and producers handle the technical matters. Once a good basic track is on tape, the "organic musical dialog" is liable to undergo some degree of editing—replacing a part, fixing a mistake, altering a sound, and the like—and it will almost certainly have further layers added through overdubbing.

Time frames for recording projects vary enormously. The Beatles recorded the fourteen songs on *Please Please Me* (1963) in a day, but when they recorded *Sgt. Pepper's* four years later, it took them six months of studio time. Early Beach Boys singles were recorded in hours, but Brian Wilson spent six weeks recording "Good Vibrations" (1966). Trevor Horn spent three months on the Buggles single "Video Killed the Radio Star" (1979). And Rick Rubin characterized the sessions for Tom Petty's *Wildflowers* (1994) as "just a casual process of getting together every afternoon for two years."[26]

Because making a record can take a long time, some sort of efficiency must be maintained in the production process, not only for cost control but also to preserve the concentration of creative energies and prevent the project from becoming lost in a maze of endless, unfocused possibility. The longer and more involved the process is, the more problems are liable to arise, and many artists prefer to work quickly in order to avoid the potential pitfalls of the drawn out project. Describing Madonna as "quite a vibe merchant—a real viber in the studio,"[27] William Orbit recalls that on the sessions for her *Ray of Light* (1998) album her repeated reaction to his analytical painstaking was "Don't gild the lily," which he explains as a wariness of over-refinement. "By perfecting, you can lose the character . . . and she always had an eye out for that."[28] Indeed, an overabundance of time and choice can lead to diffusion of focus, a tendency to defer decisions, and general loss of expressive power, or "character." "De La Soul made an album in a week! . . . We need some of that," lamented U2's Bono as the sessions for *Zooropa* (1993) dragged on.[29] Of course, part of *Zooropa's* eclectic charm derives from the nature of its creative evolution. But the many experiments, which yielded so many possibilities for the album's ultimate makeup, might easily have resulted in chaos. "I learned from Steve Lillywhite and Dan Lanois to commit to sounds and performances early on," reports Kevin Killen. "The most important thing is to make decisions and not to leave choices until the last minute, because then you're left with too many options."[30]

Because consistency of expression and atmosphere—"vibe"—can be difficult to maintain in the studio, pre-production often serves as a vital preparatory stage during which an image of the record's shape and tone is developed, even if only in a rough form. Spending time preparing songs, arrangements, and performances before entering the studio means that the project is already underway before tape ever rolls and the team enters the studio with a sense of purpose. In the case of the Red Hot Chili Peppers' *Blood Sugar Sex Magik*, seven months were spent "working on the material," because in producer Rick Rubin's view, "the process of getting the music onto tape is very simple, but getting the music to the point where it's even ready to be recorded is very tough."[31] According to lead singer Anthony Kiedis, much of this time was spent "just soaking up life, creating music before we ever got into the studio." The process succeeded in heightening the band members' sensitivity to one another musically, allowing them to "develop a fluid musical conversation." Bassist Flea extends the communication metaphor to the psychic level. "By the time we made this record," he says, "we had an intense telepathic thing going musically." Because the Chili Peppers' interactive performances are so integral to the "material"—indeed, all band members are credited equally as songwriters on all tracks—honing their musical communication was a crucial aspect of pre-production. In a sequential and cumulative approach where jamming, songwriting, arranging, and rehearsal were stages that occurred prior to recording, the songs and arrangements developed in terms of their live representations, the sound of which became a point of reference throughout the process of making the record. "When I hear [this record]," says Flea, "I get a picture of a hand hitting a guitar, a string vibrating. This is four guys playing music."[32] The months of preparation made it possible for the picture that he describes to serve as the central image that guided the project. The aim was to "keep that band feel all the time," and while the record is in no sense a live album, rendering something of the sonic and expressive image and power of the band's live performance were the artistic goals.

For Rubin, as for so many recordists, the studio "is a place to make magic happen,"[33] which in the case of the Chili Peppers required a pure focus on high-intensity performance. Creating and capturing the feel of spontaneous expressive eruption that gives the record its vital character was the primary objective, and too many analytical decisions about songs and arrangements during the recording process would slow things down, diffusing the project's focus and potentially creating distractions for the band. This, in turn, might impede the fragile flow of energy required to infuse the recording with a life of its own. But the months of pre-production had provided the project with a clear direction. In the midst of the innumerable options and choices that crop up in the course of recording, having such an aesthetic anchor can be crucial for keeping a project on track.

Another common pre-production practice is the recording of songs in rough preliminary versions. Such "demo tapes" can range from a bare songwriter's sketch with a vocal and single-instrument accompaniment to more elaborate recordings that specify details of the groove and the arrangement. While demos may be meant simply to give a project a sense of direction prior to entering the studio, they are also recorded works in themselves. This presents an interesting problem often remarked on by recordists. Oftentimes, the sound of the demo acquires a certain degree of authority in the minds of the recordists, and the formal recording sessions may become frustrating attempts to remake sounds and recapture an elusive spirit. In the case of the demos for Los Lobos' *Kiko*, the sound offered enough specificity to indicate the direction that the record's sound should take—far beyond anything that a simple rendition of the song could have done—yet remained general enough to allow the recordists the freedom to pursue the effect in other ways. On the other hand, there is often a quality in the initial setting down of an idea that is somehow nontransferable, and complaints that the demo is in some way superior to the record are common. Many artists simply refuse to make demos. "I never make demos, and I've never understood how to do them," says Tom Petty. "What happens to me is that I do a demo and then I get frustrated because the record doesn't sound as good. I always put songs down on 24-track so if I want to make a record later, I can."[34] Similarly, Dave Edmunds is "much happier trying to capture the moment the first time," rather than making a preliminary recording that may have " a great feel that you can never recapture on the master."[35]

One of the most famous cases of problematic demos is Bruce Springsteen's *Nebraska* (1982). The eventual solution to the problem yielded one of the most unusual rock albums of the 1980s, and brought home to all those involved in the project just how inimitable the affective sense of a particular performance recorded at a particular time and place can be. Initially, Springsteen recorded a group of songs at his home on a four-track cassette recorder. The tracks were intended as demos to show the members of the E Street Band and manager/producer Jon Landau the direction he had in mind for the upcoming album project. According to Springsteen, the demos were meant simply to bring greater efficiency to the recording process (his three previous albums had each required many months of studio time). Those who heard them, however, found the stark atmosphere of the recordings captivating. Coproducer Chuck Plotkin recalls being "transfixed" when he first heard them; Landau worried that the tone and atmosphere of the tracks might be impossible to emulate with full band arrangements; band member Steve Van Zandt's reaction was simply, "This is an album."[36]

Nevertheless, the band learned the songs and began recording them. Although the E Street Band was in top form, everyone agreed that their recordings had far less character than the demos. "The stuff on the demo tape was astounding," recalled Plotkin. "It was an incredibly evocative piece of work. And we were losing more than we were picking up."[37] Landau summed up the futility of the effort: "If we were missing by a little, we could figure that out. But we're not in the ballpark. We're not even close."[38] It was clear to everyone involved that the expanded studio tracks only diminished the intimate immediacy of Springsteen's home recordings, and after two weeks the *Nebraska* material was set aside and the studio time, which had already been reserved, was used to record the material that would be released on *Born in the U.S.A.* two years later.

Springsteen, however, insisted that his next album release would consist of the *Nebraska* songs in some form. Gradually, a radical notion—release the demos themselves as a record—emerged and was agreed upon by the creative team. But this decision did not end the problems. When the four-track cassette master was transferred to a professional-quality multitrack for remixing, it was discovered that the primitive technical quality of the recordings seemed to have an affective integrity that the "better" technology could not match. "The better it sounded, the worse it sounded," recalled Plotkin. The "wonderful mixes" that were done in the studio "were also depriving the stuff of some important element of its particularness."[39]

Springsteen then tried to rerecord the songs with the same stripped-down arrangements and intimate mood, but under studio conditions. This, too, failed to capture the atmosphere of the original recordings. Finally, the original two-track mixes, which had been recorded on a "completely screwed up old battered blaster," were accepted as the master mixes. For all their limited frequency range, tape hiss, chair creaks, and other presumed shortcomings, these tracks captured the unique essence of *Nebraska.* The "particularness" of the confluence of songs, performances, and recording conditions represented an unrepeatable set of circumstances in which the work was born and to which it owed both its surface particularities and its essential character. *Nebraska* is a very unusual case, but it well illustrates how intimately the artwork and the process of its creation can be linked. Although the songs, the performer, and the arrangements were the same, changes in recording tools, place, and personnel altered the work's essence to a degree obvious to everyone involved.

The demo problem points us again to the inseparability, as far as rock is concerned, of musical ideas and their material form. Because the work exists as a manifestation, we are in the habit of grasping its phenomenal traces as identifying features. It is always possible to transfer musical parts to different instruments and to rerecord performances. But in the process of setting down a musical part in a particular way, the musical thought takes on the fullness of physical manifestation. This is what can be so difficult to duplicate. To do so requires returning to the music's pre-sounding state and then attempting to restore the sonic meaning in some more polished or developed way. But the effect of the initial recording cannot be erased. It remains a presence. Perhaps the demo serves as a guide, perhaps as a distraction or even an obstruction, but in any case it remains the first realized instance of the song as a track.

MIXING

Mixing is the stage in the record-making process when all the elements accumulated during the recording stage are brought together in a composite image of an apparently unitary musical performance. The mix defines the nature of the sound world in which the music is taking place and links the two in a unique and permanent relationship. The process involves placing the track's elements into an overall arrangement and refining the sounds and dramatic progression of the musical narrative. With the sounding work before them, like a canvas before a painter, recordists combine elements and shape their interactions to arrive at a desired result. And while in the modern studio every musical part and sonic process can be manipulated separately, all aspects of the mix are interdependent. Among the guiding principles of sound mixing, criteria concerning elements' interactions are fundamental.

Mixing is often compared to montage technique in filmmaking, but this accounts for only part of the mixing process. Montage is an additive technique whereby scenes are linked in a particular sequence to create a desired effect. The filmmaker Sergei Eisenstein explained the principle of montage in terms of Japanese ideograms. "For example: the picture for water and the picture of an eye signifies 'to weep.' . . . But this is—montage! Yes. It is exactly what we do in the cinema, combining shots that are depictive, single in meaning, neutral in content—into intellectual contexts and series."[40] Linking musical moments to create the timeline of an apparent performance also has such a narrative aspect. The effect of montage is especially apparent in the dub mix techniques pioneered by Jamaican reggae producers beginning in the 1960s. Dub mixes suddenly reorient the listener by abruptly changing the musical "scene,"—for example, by dropping instruments out of the mix unexpectedly. The technique, widely adopted throughout rock's genres in the 1980s with the advent of the 12-inch remix, can be applied in real time or in a spliced-together construct.

On the other hand, sound mixing also involves a vertical, or synchronic, type of assemblage; the musical moments of which the narrative mix is made have to be fashioned before any montage can take place. In film terms, this is like the composition of a shot, which "creates a sense of depth—both physical and psychological—to draw the viewer into what occurs within the frame."[41] Even if much of the track is cut live, each ingredient is still more or less compartmentalized on a separate tape track and console channel, and combining them requires an electronic balancing process, taking into account the complementary effects of musical parts, timbres, ambient images, spatial placement, and so forth. These are combined to create sonic images whose qualities may be characterized with such terms as "color," "density," "atmosphere," "lighting," "distance," and "focus." As these words imply, vertical assemblage creates a sense of dimensionality, that is, a perception of space—of left-to-right, near-to-far, high-to-low. Composing the "shot" means defining the configurations of these dimensions.

The mixing choices most apparent to the listener concern foreground elements. We can make out clearly the relative level of the voice, the brightness of the snare, or the panning of the guitar far off to one side of the stereo spectrum. But the mixing process has several layers of compositional activity, and much of what we hear is shaped behind the scenes. Sound processing, for instance, may be used obliquely to bring a sound into a desired shape and/or relationship with other sounds. An example would be using equalization or compression on a sound's ambient image, rather than on the sound itself. And multing, which we touched on in chapter 4, provides many options for working in the textural background in ways that affect foreground events. Engineer/producer Joe Chiccarelli illustrates:

> I'll typically bring up the snare drum on two faders. The main snare track will be EQ'd just the way I like it, but the additional snare track will have 1 kHz boosted like crazy to produce a real honking tone. When I creep the "honking" fader into the mix a little, the snare seems to pop out of the track a bit more and add a real aggressive snap.
> This trick also works great if I have some guitar tracks that sound nice but that could use a little more meat. In that case, I'll take all the guitars and assign them to a stereo subgroup that, in turn, is routed to a stereo compressor. Then, I'll really squish the subgrouped guitars and fade them underneath the main guitars to fill out the low-mid frequencies.
> On vocals, I usually use two compressors. My main lead-vocal

channel will have pretty conservative EQ and compression so that it just sits nicely into the track. But these settings may not help the vocal jump through the mix when all the other tracks are brought in around it. So I'll send the vocal to another fader and route the signal to something ugly, such as an old Urei 1176 compressor, and boost 4 kHz or 5 kHz to add bite. When this channel is tucked way underneath the main vocal track, it really adds personality to the voice and helps it cut through the mix.[42]

Thus, although the multiplied version of the foreground sound is materially present in the mix, its amplitude is so low that it has no apparent presence of its own. Rather, it is an agent by which the foreground can be manipulated "silently." In that the listener can be sure only of the effect, and not its source, such techniques contribute to what might be called the suspension of aural disbelief. If the source of an effect is not apparent, the impression grows that what we are hearing is not an effect at all but rather some kind of sonic reality all its own.

The many and varied approaches that recordists take to mixing reflect the same issues as other aspects of the record-making process—style of music, personal preferences, contingencies of the project, and so forth. Some build a mix beginning with the drums, some begin with the vocal. Some push up all the faders from the beginning, and work from there. Others proceed one part at a time. Some fashion the mix after an image of a live performance, while others are intent on creating a sonic world without real-world counterpart. Some kinds of music call for a hazy texture, others for sharp clarity. Some emphasize the groove, others the lyrics. Some recordists use minimal sound processing, others use it extensively. Whatever approach is taken, a central criterion for all projects is the impression mixers form in their minds of the sort of mix that will allow the track to realize its affective potential. Engineer Matt Wallace boils the problem down to a single question: "What kind of feeling do I want the listener to have at the end of the day? . . . It's really all about the emotion and feeling."[43] Most rock records are built around a song and a vocal performance, and these two elements are the mixer's touchstones, the primary sites of "emotion and feeling." "The essence is the song, after all," Arif Mardin reminds us. "This gadgetry should actually enhance, and not occupy us."[44] Indeed, the song provides a focal point and serves as a guide through the maze of mixing possibilities. "I really want the song to shine—that's the most important thing to me," says Tom Lord-Alge, whose mixes often involve extensive "gadgetry."[45] But, while he admits to taking creative license ("I like . . . to have my way, so to speak, with my clients' tapes"), which may include extreme sound processing such as chaining multiple compressors and equalizers on a single sound or altering musical arrangements, the aim is always "to do whatever it takes to make . . . the song come across better."[46]

George Massenburg describes his approach to mixing in a suggestive summary that lays out the basic principles involved in any mix:

> I mix like I'm decorating a four-dimensional "space." Starting with some essential structural elements, I craft artifact and gesture, all of which say something about themselves and often refer to other elements in the "space": shaking hands with (or, perhaps, conflicting with) other elements and usually supporting, flattering, or teasing the focal point—the center, the vocal.[47]

This economical statement encapsulates the project nicely, and unpacking it reveals many of the problems of mixing. Massenburg highlights the interactive nature of the relationships among individual elements and larger composites—artifacts and gestures—and points to the ongoing shifts in perspective that a record makes available through its manipulation of "four-dimensional space," which includes both vertical and narrative assemblage. Of these four dimensions, three are synchronic: the stereo soundstage (width), the configuration of the frequency spectrum (height), and the combination of elements that account for relations of prominence (depth). The fourth dimension is the progression of events, the narrative or montage. "Artifact and gesture" refers to relationships among components of differing size. In the vertical assemblage, an artifact may be an individual sound within a textural gesture, or it may be some textural subset—multiple guitars, say, in a texture that also contains bass, drums, and keyboard. In the narrative dimension, on the other hand, the artifact is a subset of a larger, temporal gesture. In a song where the verse and chorus have radically different textures— Garbage's "Supervixen" (1995), for example—the two together represent a narrative gesture in which each is an artifact, while on a more local level each is a gesture made of other artifacts. In other

words, in both the vertical and the narrative dimensions, such relationships are not static. As artifacts accumulate, they become gestures, which, in turn, are themselves artifacts within larger gestures.
Throughout the mixing process, perspective shifts continually as
individual elements and subsets are measured against larger gestures, and ultimately, the piece as a whole. Let's explore now each of
Massenburg's four dimensions in more detail.

STEREO

Stereo is a system of sound recording and reproduction that takes
advantage of the psychoacoustics of sound localization. Using two
loudspeakers separated in space, a sound can be assigned to one or
the other or any proportional combination of the two and thus
appear to emanate from any place along a horizontal plane. For the
recordist, the stereo space is a panoramic soundstage across which
elements can be positioned and moved about. The left-to-right orientation of each element is controlled by the panning knob on the
console, the position of which can be changed in real time during
mixdown. Stereo placement is one of the principal factors—along
with ambience and the development of textural depth—in shaping a
track's spatial dimensions. The more unique the space is, the less it
represents experiences of sound in the natural world and the more
the record takes on the quality of a dramatic stage.

The point of reference for a conventional stereo mix of a rock band
is the visual image presented to a listener facing a bandstand. The
vocalist is at center stage with the drummer just behind—the kick
and snare drums are dead center, the high hat to one side, toms and
cymbals spread from left to right. Because of its powerful sonic presence and its function as anchor of both groove and chord changes,
the bass is also usually placed in the center. Other instruments in the
arrangement are spread across the stereo spectrum as they would be
on stage, balanced in such a way that all can be clearly distinguished.
This "natural" image is often manipulated for expressive effect, however, and a distinctive stereo image is often a thematic feature of a
track. Recall in chapter 3, for example, Karl Wallinger's mix of "Way
Down Now," where the stereo space is set up in an oppositional
counterpoise of left and right drums, guitars, and voices—something like two different bands playing the same song simultaneously,

each in their own way. The configuration is unfamiliar, defying isomorphic analogy with live performance and demanding from the listener an interpretive engagement of some sort.

A track's stereo image may remain fixed, or it may change as the
track progresses. Animating the soundstage produces a range of
effects—from the purely auditory to ones linked in some way to a
song's lyrics or the track's narrative flow. The back-and-forth panning of the guitar in the introduction to Shawn Colvin's "Diamond in
the Rough" (1989) serves simply as an announcement, calling the
audience's attention to the stage on which the drama is about to be
set. The whimsical right-to-left bounce of the snare sound on Prince's
"Starfish and Coffee" (1990) reflects the general tone of the lyrics—
playful and childlike. It also produces a curious rhythmic/spatial
effect as the duration of the snare sound is matched by the speed of
its travel across the stereo spectrum. Sly Stone's left/right juxtaposi-
tions of rhythmic figures on the track "In Time" (1973) animate the
stereo field with an antiphonal energy. In this case too, stereo placement contributes to the track's rhythmic effect, emphasizing the
dancing interlace of parts and providing a crystalline clarity to the
rhythmic texture. In Bob Clearmountain's mix of Crowded House's
"Kill Eye" (1988) the arrangement of the stereo soundstage changes
according to a dramatic plan. During the song's verses, hard, violent
images are hurled at the song's subject, a criminal figure addressed
as "Kill Eye" by some narratorlike character playing the role of a
Greek chorus. At this point, the voice is the only presence in the center of the soundstage. The entire drum kit and the bass are placed on
the left side; all other instruments are on the right. The isolation of
the vocal conveys a sonically dispassionate quality—a starkness of
atmosphere—that enhances its pitiless accusatory tone. At the
refrain, the voice slips into the character of the song's subject, and the
stereo image abruptly shifts to a more conventional configuration;
the center is now shared by the voice and several instruments. Filling
out the timbral space in the track's center brings a fullness and
warmth to the refrain that is absent in the verse. As this shift occurs,
both vocal style and lyrics change from accusation to plaintive
plea—"I wanna be forgiven / I wanna life with children," sings the
increasingly desperate character. The narrative technique here is similar to the timbral/structural correspondence noted in U2's "Zoo

Station," but in the case of "Kill Eye" it is the stereo image that mirrors the song's sense and structure.

The stereo spectrum, then, can be employed quite literally as a dramatic stage on which a character's movements are choreographed and woven into the dramatic scheme. Consider the stereo spectacular of Led Zeppelin's "Whole Lotta Love" (1969). The setup for the guitar solo, which involves preparing and reserving a special place on the stage, is especially interesting. The track begins with a left-to-right movement that casts a shadow to the back far right of the stage. This is accomplished by placing the primary guitar riff on the left and its delayed ambient image on the right. Because of the much lower amplitude of the ambience and the distancing effect that ambience produces, the two images seem to be at different depths as well as different horizontal locations. When the rest of the band enters, the far right remains unfilled except for the guitar ambience, whose prominence now recedes further. The persistence of this configuration and the lack of a strong balancing presence opposite the guitar riff marks the right side of the stage as a shadowy place, an impression that is enhanced by the guitar glissando that enters at the chorus. In keeping with the track's stereo theme, the glissando moves from left to right, but as it reaches the right side it disappears abruptly only to reappear on the left. Each repetition is the same. As the glissando reaches the point where it might, by its prominence, claim the right side of the soundstage for itself, it vanishes, leaving the space to the ambient shadow.

At the beginning of the break after the second chorus, the right side begins to open up, first with a slowed-down guitar glissando, which now traverses the stereo plane more deliberately and fades slowly into the right-hand distance, and then with a conga/bongo part that serves as a transition into the next section. At this point the song structure is suspended, and with it, the track's spatial theme. The entire stereo spectrum now is put in play with random back-and-forth panning of various sounds, and all that is left of the initial stereo orientation is the drums. When the freely panning sound collage comes to an end, however, the original stereo picture drops back into place as the bass and the guitar resume their places. But now a new character is introduced. A solo guitar boldly steps forth at the right side of the soundstage, emerging, as it were, from the ambient shadow that has hovered there since the beginning of the track. It is the only time in the piece that there is an electric guitar in this position, and clearly the space has been reserved to heighten its dramatic entrance. In the track's stereo scheme the persistence of the nearly empty right side of the mix has been something of a mystery. But now as the spotlight shines on the solo guitar, the narrative sense of the scheme becomes apparent as the most individual instrumental character in the drama reveals that this has been its dwelling place all along.[48]

Stereo was not a factor in early rock recording. Although techniques for recording and reproducing binaural sound had been in existence since the late 1920s, it was only with the advent of magnetic tape that stereo began to make inroads into the home listening environment. In the late 1940s, tape recorders became popular consumer items, and stereo tapes offered a sound experience closer than ever to the acoustic conditions of live performances. But it was not until 1957 that record companies finally agreed among themselves on a standard system for producing stereo records. Even then, however, the format was intended not for the mass market but for audiophiles, who were, for the most part, collectors of classical recordings. The "prime artifact of rock 'n' roll"[49] was the mono 45-rpm single, the staple of both teenagers' record collections and AM radio, which did not broadcast in stereo. Aside from the issues of retail and radio exposure, mono recordings represented an aesthetic frame for musicians and producers, who had grown up with them. Phil Spector, for instance, never really took to stereo. When it became the standard format in the record industry, he began sporting a button demanding "Back to MONO," which later became the title of his retrospective compact disc boxed set.[50] Brian Wilson, too, believed that mono was the preferable format because it gave the recordist more precise control over the sound image:

> I look at sound like a painting, you have a balance and the balance is conceived in your mind. You finish the sound, dub it down, and you've stamped out a picture of your balance with the mono dubdown. But in stereo, you leave that dubdown to the listener—to his speaker placement and speaker balance. It just doesn't seem complete to me.[51]

In the mid-sixties, however, many recordists began to use stereo imaging in creative ways. This coincided both with the emergence of FM radio and with changes in the conception of rock's "prime artifact" from the single to the album. FM disc jockeys regularly played album tracks, and even entire album sides. And unlike AM radio, FM broadcast in stereo. For the Beatles, who at the time led the way in innovative record making, the emphasis shifted from single to album with *Rubber Soul* (1965), "the first album to present a new, growing Beatles to the world," according to George Martin. "For the first time," he recalls, "we began to think of albums as art on their own, as complete entities."[52] At the same time, though their records continued to be released in mono versions as well, the stereo space of Beatles tracks began to be treated with an imaginative flair similar to that exhibited by so many other aspects of their work. As noted earlier, many of the vocal images on *Revolver* (1966) took on a distinctive multiplicity as voices and their echoes became widely separated in the stereo field—one hard left, the other hard right. In such configurations, the voice is not only decentralized, it is not localized at all. Rather, the two halves of its presence delineate a field within which the other sounds of the track are contained. Thus, the voice takes on a purely formal function in addition to its more conventional role.

One *Revolver* track, "Eleanor Rigby," uses stereo in a thematic way that would be exploited on subsequent albums with increasing sophistication. Here, McCartney's solo voice is placed off to the right side during all of the verses, while in the chorus a double appears on the left, the two voices balanced on either side of the strings. As the stereo configuration mirrors the song's structure, it participates in the song's structural articulation. That is, it becomes a narrative device. With *Sgt. Pepper's* (1967), stereo placement is fully integrated into the musical arrangement and dramatic presentation of each track. From the opening of the album to the resounding E-major piano chord with which it ends, stereo configurations change like the sets in a play, each unique to a particular musical scene.

The record's final track, "A Day in the Life," presents two different characters embodied in the voices of Lennon and McCartney, each of whose disposition in the stereo space seems to have a programmatic significance. At the beginning of the track, Lennon's vocal is alone with its echo on the right side of the stage. The bass and drums are in the middle, and the piano, guitar, and maracas are on the left. As the second verse begins—with the line, "He blew his mind out in a car"—

the voice and its echo start to move in discrete steps towards the left, finally arriving at center stage on the word "lords." In the third verse the leftward motion continues, leaving the center and finishing with "I'd love to turn you on" at the extreme left of the stage along with the piano/guitar/maracas accompaniment. As the vocal finishes, from the now mostly vacant right side of the stage the ominous orchestral glissando/crescendo begins to emerge, eventually filling the entire stereo spectrum. The wandering quality of Lennon's vocal complements his dreamy delivery of the stream-of-consciousness imagery, and contributes to what Walter Everett has called a feeling of aimlessness in the first part of the song.[53]

After the orchestral glissando, the song breaks into its middle section. Written and sung by McCartney, this part of the song has an altogether different tone—dry and matter of fact in lyrics, vocal character, and sound. Like Lennon, McCartney enters alone at the right of the stage. Unlike Lennon's character, however, this one has no echo and it does not move. It lays claim to the side of the stage vacated by the first character and presents an image of stasis that, again, seems to reflect the tone and the sense of the vocal. When the section ends and McCartney's character goes "into a dream," ethereal vocal "aah"s emanate from the right side of the stage and sweep slowly across to the far left and back again to the right, traversing the entire spectrum in a single gesture that serves as a bridge back to the track's initial atmosphere. Lennon reenters where he had quit, at the left of the stage, but now the piano, guitar, and maraca accompaniment is on the right side, leaving the voice alone once again. Lennon's character finishes the song from this position, no longer wandering but rather, emphasizing the contrast with McCartney's character through separation and distance. In a curious final twist, when Lennon sings ". . . Albert Hall. / I'd love to turn you on," his voice appears on both left and right sides of the stage simultaneously, recalling the track's beginning as we arrive at its end. In its song structure and its arrangement, the track has a sense of journey about it that is reflected in the stereo moves. We shift between the two affective dimensions of Lennon's and McCartney's characters as between dream and waking, though it is left to the listener to determine which is which. Is McCartney's interruption the dream or the waking reality? Though more matter of fact in tone, it is introduced by a surreal orchestral intrusion and is left via a sweeping cloud of swooning voices. Lennon's character, on the other hand, emerges from the applause of the previous track. His sections have dreamlike lyrics and vocal style, but the images are taken literally from daily news events. On its own, the song only hints at the underlying significance of its binary structure and the questions it raises. The arrangement and performances sharpen the song's dramatic focus, and the animated stereo space adds further to the interpretive problem as it heightens the contrast between the characters and what they have to say.

FREQUENCY RANGE

The configuration of a track's frequency range is determined first of all by the individual sounds and the musical arrangement. Each timbre has particular frequency characteristics, which suggest ways that it might fit into the overall scheme. And the arrangement presents a set of timbral combinations that denotes the basic form of the track's textures. In a model for a conventional mix, certain instruments, inhabiting specific frequency ranges, combine to form a balanced aural image spanning the audible frequency spectrum. In the basic voice/guitar/bass/drums ensemble, for example, the low frequency range is anchored by the bass guitar and the kick drum; the low-to-middle midrange is shared by snare drum, tom-toms, and the fundamental pitches of the guitar and voice; the upper midrange and high end are represented by the high hat and cymbals, guitar and voice overtones, and ambient air. In addition, the high and low ranges among the percussion have general rhythmic roles. The bass and snare drums anchor the meter while higher frequency instruments such as the high hat, shaker, and tambourine play the rhythmic subdivisions. Furthermore, some sounds "sparkle," others "crunch," while still others "rumble." Inasmuch as each of these can be assigned a frequency range—high, middle, and low, respectively—areas of the frequency spectrum can be said to carry a potential affective meaning.

The inherent properties of a musical arrangement can be either enhanced or altered as timbres are manipulated electronically. Recall in chapter 4 Butch Vig's approach to fitting together multiple guitar parts on the first Garbage album. Left unprocessed, such a texture soon becomes muddy as the guitars battle over the same frequency space, in effect canceling one another out. But with appropriate equalization, the guitars, now emptied of some of their frequency content, can be brought into a complementary relationship, and the texture can take on the complex and detailed character that is the aim of such layering. The principle is simply that too much information in too small a space reduces sonic intelligibility. The massed weight of multiple instruments can actually result in a small sound. Some of the information must be filtered out—a practice often called "subtractive equalization"—so that each part can come through. Tom Tucker speaks of using subtractive equalization to "build holes in the musical spectrum," whereby he removes content from the mix's lower midrange. He locates this "mud area" between about 150Hz and 1,500Hz and endeavors to open it up so that the various parts that occupy it—especially the vocal—can "speak through."[54] Used this way, electronic arranging overlaps with arranging in the traditional sense, and the ultimate effect of a texture is a product of this combination.

As they craft the configuration of the frequency range, recordists have various things in mind. The aim may simply be clarity, smoothness, and tonal balance. But very often some sort of unique sound or expressive effect is intended, leading mixers to emphasize some portion of the frequency range in a particular way—hence characterizations of a mix such as "bright," "warm," or "bottom-heavy." Engineer Dave Way thinks of frequencies in terms of "emotional levels," treating the ranges differently according to the "kind of feelings and emotions [one is] trying to bring out of this song or this artist."[55] An emphasis on certain areas of the frequency spectrum may also serve as a stylistic hallmark for a particular record, an era, or a genre. A great many tracks from the 1980s, for example, are characterized by an exaggerated brightness, which often includes an element of thinness in some area of the overall frequency picture. The Bangles' "If She Knew What She Wants" (1985), for instance, has some very thin guitar sounds to go along with the emphatic high-frequency splash of the snare and the lightly ticking high hat. The guitars' midrange weight has been sucked out of them. The Thompson Twins' "Doctor Doctor" (1984) has a lean, brittle quality—typical not only of their style but also in many ways of mid-eighties British pop mixes in general—where even the kick drum has the upper-register click of its attack emphasized. On ABC's "Many Happy Returns" (1982) the kick drum is scarcely more than a click, providing little in the way of low-end presence, and the bass cuts a similarly slim figure. Steve Winwood's "Higher Love"(1985) has a solid foundation in the low end provided by a thudding kick and a synthesizer bass sound. But above this is an arrangement filled with high-frequency percussion instruments—high hat, shaker, agogo, timbale—and scratching rhythm guitar, all bubbling away with sixteenth-note syncopations. These are joined by shiny metallic synthesizer timbres, bright stabs of synthesized brass, Chaka Khan's backing vocals, and a snare that sounds something like a burst of high-frequency white noise. On top of it all is Winwood's high tenor voice. The overall color is sharp and electric, well-matched to the track's teeming rhythmic energy. The tom-tom fills are welcome contrasts to the persistently vivid texture as they roll through the mix at points of structural articulation.

On the other hand, many styles of rock emphasize the physical power of the bass register, and none does so more than rap. "For me," says engineer Steve Ett, "rap is a matter of pumping the shit out of the low end."[56] The bass drum sound of the Roland 808 drum machine at high level, "the loudest thing on the record," sets the tone for innumerable rap mixes, pushing the bass register to extremes. Kurtis Blow likewise sings the praises of the Roland 808 kick drum: "It's a car speaker destroyer. That's what we try to do as rap producers—break car speakers and house speakers and boom boxes. And the 808 does it."[57] "I like to distort the bass levels," says Kris Parker (KRS-One), whose own preferred drum machine is the Emu SP-12, another hip-hop favorite. "There's actually an art to distortion; there's an art to a kick drum that's too loud." In this music, pumping up the low end is a matter not only of personal aesthetic but of speaking the sonic language. "If the kick isn't 'boom, boom, boom,' you're not in the competition."[58] Parker's *By All Means Necessary* (1988) has a variety of booming kicks, none fatter than on the track "Illegal Business."

The low end of a track is its most physical area. The low frequencies are the ones that make the chest cavity resonate with the beat of the music, and a track may create an altogether different effect if its low-end content is attenuated or obscured in some way. The curious impression left by the original mix of Iggy Pop and the Stooges' *Raw Power,* for example, is largely a result of a lack of low end. In this version, the record seems to be misnamed at the least, as Pop implies when he characterizes it as an "eccentric, odd little record" that "always sounded fragile and rickety." Although he claims to be "very proud" of the initial effort, which was produced by David Bowie, Pop acknowledges that "there's no bottom, no power." Some twenty years later, he remixed the album, restoring some of the Stooges' characteristic sonic intensity and allowing the record's sound to resonate finally with its title.[59]

Configuration of the frequency range need not be consistent for an entire album; it may be shaped for an expressive effect appropriate to a specific track. TLC's "Red Light Special" (1995), for example, which was produced by Babyface (Kenneth Edmonds) and mixed by Way, has a thick, blooming quality about it. Its lower midrange and low end are filled with keyboard textures, alto vocals, bass, and bass drum, which meld together in a warm bath of sound, forming a suggestive atmosphere fitting the expression of sexual desire in the song's lyrics. The higher parts—high hat, shaker, the high snap of the hand claps, and the pinging attack of one of the synthesizer sounds—add a frequency layer that provides just enough sizzle, but the overall character is best described by the song's title. Because of the concentration of lower frequencies, higher-register events, like the guitar solo, that occur in the course of the track provide a contrasting relief. The high voice in the bridge, which continues over the top of the final chorus, has a similar effect. In the context of the album, however, an even greater contrast becomes apparent as we move to the track immediately following. Unlike the warm cloak of "Red Light Special," "Waterfalls" begins with a low end represented only by a bass drum, which though quite full is also dry—the spaces left between the drum's attacks have no low-frequency content at all. Thus from one track to the next the light seems to change. The listener moves from an enveloping low-light atmosphere out into the day. And even when the full arrangement starts in, the track retains a transparency—not a crystalline brightness like "Higher Love," but a clarity. "Waterfalls" is a song about a young person attempting to negotiate the unforgiving reality of the streets—the appealing allure and the mortal danger of drugs, sex, and money—and ultimately, the song is a declaration of faith in oneself. The message is obviously different from that in "Red Light Special," and before any lyrics are heard, the shift in overall tone color signals that the story has changed.

As with all aspects of the mix—and much like traditional orchestration—the frequency space is filled with interactive relationships. Frequency characteristics of different timbres can work together in complementary ways, creating an assortment of dovetail effects. On Matthew Sweet's "Sick of Myself" (1995), for example, some of the most prominent instrumental sounds are the heavily distorted guitar timbres, which emphasize midrange presence but have little high-end content. The effect, though aggressive, is somewhat muffled and contained. In the song's choruses the cymbals, whose amplitude is quite a bit lower than that of the guitars, begin to play continuously. Their attacks are largely subsumed in their sustained noise, which provides a canopy of high-frequency sheen above the guitars. In this particular balance the cymbals function more as a timbral effect than a discrete musical part. As they dovetail with the frequency content of the guitars' distortion noise, they effectively extend the timbral range of the guitars during the choruses, opening up the top of the frequency range and expanding the guitars' basic character. On this track the proportions of the mix thus help to define the roles played by the parts of the musical arrangement with respect to one another. The frequency characteristics of the different instruments combine to form a composite character in the frequency space. Furthermore, the frequency space itself interacts with other mix parameters; for the effect is not simply a matter of complementary frequency ranges, but includes their amplitudinal balance as well. Because the cymbals are softer, they are "behind" the guitars in textural space. The relationship between the two, then, is not simply one of frequency, but also of relative prominence.

PROMINENCE

Relations of prominence are analogous to "depth," among Massenburg's four dimensions of a mix. They impart impressions of proximity and emphasis along with whatever associations these may have. The more prominent a sound is, the more forward it appears to be in relation to other sounds on the track and the more it claims a listener's attention. A particular matrix of prominence relationships—or more simply, a particular balance—defines the terms of discourse among a track's elements and informs our sense of what the record is about. Such relations, however, are shaped not only *among* sounds but also *within* individual sounds. Because sound recording and processing are capable of revealing minute sonic details, the proportion between the most apparent aspect of a sound (say, a stick hitting a snare drum head) and its lower-level details (the high-frequency rattle of the snare) may be configured in various ways. Thus depth perception works at many levels of the mix, ranging from the individual event to the overall texture, and when we listen to a record our perspective shifts continually among these levels. These shifts are choreographed to some degree by the mixer, and with repeated listenings we no doubt fall into repetitive listening habits. But one of the great delights of listening to a well-mixed record lies in exploring aurally its textural recesses, its middle ground and background, and discovering that it offers levels of sonic experience far beyond its obvious surface moves. "I try to provide things so that upon repeated listening there will be some new things to find that are cool," says Andy Wallace, "something that will continue to augment whatever I'm trying to get out of that mix on further and further subterranean levels."[60] Evidence of his success can be heard on albums ranging in style from *Rage against the Machine* by the group with the same name and *Kettle Whistle* by Jane's Addiction to Ben Folds Five's *Whatever and Ever Amen* and Jeff Buckley's *Grace*.

I use the term "prominence" instead of "loudness" to emphasize the multifaceted nature of prominence perception. It's true that when we think of prominence, the first thing that usually comes to mind is loudness, but on a record loudness is only one of many factors that influence such impressions. In the area of timbre, for instance, the frequency spectrum can be configured so that certain sounds take on prominence simply by inhabiting a space where there is little competition from other sounds. Also, equalization can sharpen a sound's presence without raising its overall amplitude. That is, prominence may be increased by amplifying or attenuating specific areas of a sound's frequency content. The focusing effect of compression is also very important. Simply increasing a sound's amplitude may have little effect on its prominence if it remains too diffuse in the mix. Paradoxically, a sound made louder may become more indistinct if it dulls the overall clarity of the mix. Ambience can also affect the sharpness of a sound's image and its sense of distance from the listener. And because sounds at or near the center of the stereo field have greater psychoacoustic impact, a sound's stereo placement can affect its prominence. In short, like texture, the principle of prominence encompasses all of the other parameters of the mix.

This interrelatedness of parameters affects a track's textural "gestures" as well as its "artifacts." Changes in equalization or loudness among middle-ground sounds, for example, can account for significant differences in the perception of sounds in the foreground. A sound that at one amplitude adds a certain "subterranean" quality to the texture may, when increased, begin to mask a foreground element that inhabits a similar area of the frequency spectrum or the stereo space. The conflict may be quite subtle. While the foreground element may appear to be diminished in some way, the culprit may be difficult to identify. The mixer must, therefore, have a keen sense of how the perception of prominence functions and must keep track of each sound's effect on the overall texture. The problem in this example might be corrected by a change of equalization or placement rather than a change of amplitude.

Unlike frequency range and stereo, prominence is perceptible only in relationship. That is, to assess prominence we need a frame of reference. In the introduction to Marvin Gaye's "What's Going On" (1970) we first hear a group of men at a party. The scene in itself has a degree of aural depth of field represented by the varying prominence of the voices. When the instruments come in, however, the perspective changes. The instrumental track is more prominent than the voices, and our attention shifts as the voices recede into what is now a deeper field. Finally, the lead vocal enters, more prominent still, and once again our sense of perspective changes. The singer is clearly at the mix's front and center. Our ears have in effect zoomed out from their initial focus. Thus the basic frame of reference comes into being gradually as relationships among elements form and settle into place. The changes in perspective orient us to the track's depth of field, and because we have been alerted to the deeper levels of the mix by the zooming maneuver, we remain in touch with them. After all, for a moment, they were the foreground, and that memory remains. As the backing vocals take over from the party voices, occupying the same level, they appear to be happening in the same place as the party was a moment ago. So in fact the party has not stopped. Rather, the men have joined in a communal sing, a gesture that surely resonates with the theme of the song.

The voice is usually the standard by which relations of prominence are judged. It is usually the single most important element in the track because, both as an expressive element and as the conveyor of verbal meaning, it is the focal point for listeners. As such, its relative prominence affects both the sense of the song and the place of other sounds in the track. But while listeners may key in to the voice, recordists do not automatically place it in a position of prominence. Its rhetorical power is such that it engages the listener no matter where it is placed in the mix, and deemphasizing it in some way—say, making it softer or placing it off to one side—can serve a range of expressive purposes. Consider the Rolling Stones' "Tumbling Dice" (1972): The voice is well back in the mix, which, together with Mick Jagger's diction style, deemphasizes the words' linguistic function and highlights instead their purely sensory effect as vocal sounds. With a rough equivalence among the mix's characters, we are presented with a great deal of textural activity in the foreground of the track. The composite sound is a representation not so much of voice and supporting instruments but of an aggregate whose various constituents continually play off of one another, imparting a sense of unrefined energy that spills forth in a glorious, anarchic noise. This is a characteristic quality of Stones records, as Velvet Underground guitarist Sterling Morrison pointed out. He contrasted this type of mix with what he called the "closet mixes" of *The Velvet Underground* (1969), the group's third album. The original mixes for this album, which were done by engineer Val Valentin, were fairly conventional in terms of balances and stereo placements, but Lou Reed remixed the tracks to, as Morrison put it, "bring the voices up and put the instruments down."[61] Indeed, whereas in the original mixes the voice is laid in among the other instruments, in the remixed versions it takes up virtually all of the foreground. Its prominent, dry image standing alone at the center of the mix demands our full attention.[62]

Where the Reed mixes are most unconventional, however, is in the treatment of Maureen Tucker's drums and Doug Yule's bass. The drums are a quiet presence off to the side on all but one track on the album, and the bass is submerged and indistinct. Thus, rather than the driving physical force that typifies their role in rock, these instruments, to use Berio's words again, "assume the estranged character of quotations of themselves."[63] Even on an animated rhythmic track like "I'm Beginning to See the Light," the drums are a distant accompaniment, shunted off to the left and placed behind the strumming acoustic guitar. Whereas in "Tumbling Dice" Tucker's favorite drummer, Charlie Watts, takes up more foreground space at the center of the mix than Jagger's vocal, the *Velvet Underground* remixes force us to delve into a track's dimly lit recesses to pick up its primal sonic elements. Rather than feeling them pulsing from the loudspeakers, we grope for them. It's a disorienting experience, as relationships of sonic power are configured in ways that contradict natural experience. "Candy says / 'I've come to hate my body'" begins the album's opening song about transvestite Candy Darling, and the mix presents an image of a musical ensemble, a musical body, whose parts are arranged in an unfamiliar way. I can't say that I have a preference for either the Valentin or the Reed mixes. They are interesting and successful in different ways. As they present the same songs and performance in different proportional relationships, they put the record in different lights, produce different aesthetic effects, invite different interpretive possibilities. This is not surprising since the two are, in effect, different works.

While some of the conventions of prominence relations are dictated by musical style—for example, the central role of distorted electric guitars in heavy metal or the bass drum in hip-hop—the details are specific to the track and are configured around the song to create a particular impression. Thus, although on many albums a general mix configuration may remain fairly constant from track to track, it is not uncommon for tracks on the same album to be mixed quite differently, depending upon the sense of the song and the intended effect. In the course of Sinéad O'Connor's *The Lion and the Cobra* (1987) we hear a number of different prominence configurations on different tracks over the course of the album. The last three tracks treat both the voice and the instrumental ensemble in markedly different ways, each highlighting different characters. The progression represents an intensification of the technique used throughout the album and as such serves as the culmination of an overarching kind of sonic narrative. In "I Want Your (Hands on Me)," an aggressive drum track is the primary foil to the voice, and the overall loudness projects the track forcefully from the speakers. On the next track, "Drink before the War," the drums recede to a thin, middle-ground presence and the voice likewise begins at a level just above a whisper, while the most prominent character in terms of loudness is the organ, situated at the sides of the mix. The center of the track seems to have collapsed. Our sense of foreground is radically altered as we are forced to probe more deeply into the track to locate the characters—voice and drums—that were so powerful only moments ago on the preceding track. After about a minute, a guitar begins to strum a chord on the second beat of each bar. This sound seems even more distant, an impression created both by its low amplitude and its ambient image, which imparts the sense of a large space. As the guitar increases the sense of distance in the track, the vocal begins to come forward gradually, eventually becoming the most dominant presence. The overall depth of field thus expands in two directions at once. Through the subsequent course of the track these various degrees of textural distance are invoked in ways that complement O'Connor's dramatic vocal delivery, which alternates between hushed undertone and anguished cry.

Finally, on "Just Call Me Joe" a distorted electric guitar sound takes center stage, its arpeggiated figures supported by distorted rhythm guitars pulsing on either side. All other elements, including the voice and its double, are placed around the guitar, forming a large sonic cluster that spans both the frequency and the stereo spectra. A persistent theme throughout the album is the elusiveness of the voice. Its image is smeared across a portion of the central area in the stereo field, but unlike the shadow effect of Peter Gabriel's "Love to Be Loved," discussed in chapter 3, it lacks a strong originating presence. Through various processing techniques and a prominent echo that is noticeably separated from the main vocal in stereo space, the overall vocal image is given a diffuse quality, like a phantasmic presence whose face is never clearly in focus and whose precise location we cannot pinpoint. Now on the album's last track, the voice and its double are clearly separated by the guitar, one on either side. With the guitar holding the place of central prominence, the voices emanate from its margins and ultimately drown in the distortion and ambience of the track's coda.

NARRATIVE

The deliberate construction techniques used in fashioning the three dimensions represented by stereo, frequency range, and prominence are subsumed ultimately in temporal experience. That is, whatever constructive feats a mix entails, they are presented in the context of its fourth dimension, time. It is here, in their roles as participants in an unfolding sound drama, that the mix's various "shots" assume their contextual meaning. As noted earlier, a track's textural narrative has its own design whose unfolding may or may not coincide with that of the song. Even when its most obvious points of articulation do synchronize with those of the song, however, there are myriad textural variations that keep the mix fluid within structural subdivisions. As the track unfolds, the configurations of its three "spatial" dimensions modulate through various textural states; and as phenomenal particulars fuse with musical arrangement in a sequence of textural events, the track takes on a narrative shape both in its large outline and in its details. The mixer may have played some small section of the track dozens of times in succession, refining the image; the listener, unaware of this, will hear that section only in relation to what surrounds it. Although the mixing process allows for all sorts of artifice, the mixer must not lose sight of the ultimate aim, which is to present an effective image of a musical performance.

Mixing is itself a kind of performance. Its primary instrument is the console, which the mixer "plays" with a combination of technical skill and musical sensitivity. Prior to computer automation, mixes were performed in real time, sometimes with many hands on the console making changes in loudness, equalization, processing, stereo placement, and so forth as the multitrack master played. Oftentimes, complex mixes with tricky choreography were created in small sections, which were then spliced together. Nowadays, most mixes are automated, at least to some extent. That is, the mix itself is recorded; its moves are programmed into a computer. It can therefore be built just as deliberately as a composite vocal track or any other performance. The principle of "A and Z energies," however, applies here as well. Zooming back and forth between the small detail and the expressive gestalt, the mixer seeks the combination of emotional sweep and critical refinement that will animate the track's aura.

The narrative aspect of the mix is what reconnects the project with its origins. It cements both the conceptual and the practical connections between recording and mixing. Performances have been gathered—often in ways that seem to contradict the very notion of musical performance—and become artifacts subject to deliberate compositional decision making. Now, the piecemeal construction process must yield to the temporal gesture that began it all. If many of the compositional concerns that mixing entails require working in dimensions that are analogous to space, finally, the track must assume a shape in musical time. While there are structuring processes by which relationships among a track's formative elements are shaped, ultimately, the structure is perceived as motion, activity, performance. Though the recorded utterances have been transmuted into material components, they retain their connection to the performative moment, to which they transport the listener each time the record is played. Still, the performance is mediated. It bears the traces of transmutation. While the techniques of the transmutation process may be artfully hidden from the listener, the perceived performances are usually something quite different in their sonic form from what the musicians actually produced.

6

Engineers and Producers

Nobody does an album by themselves. I work with great
people, I have a lot of help.

Tom Waits

Making records is intrinsically a collaborative creative process,
involving the efforts of a "composition team" whose members interact in various ways.[1] As a matter of form, the "artist" on a recording
is usually the person or group who receives top billing on the album
cover, but in fact most of the tasks involved in making a record
require some measure of artistry. Social relationships among the
team members also contribute to the outcome of a recording project.
Indeed, pre-production can include getting acquainted and in tune
on a number of levels. When Robert Plant and Jimmy Page asked
Steve Albini to work with them on *Walking into Clarksdale* (1998), he
suggested that they "do a short session together to see if our working
methods were compatible."[2] Producer and engineer Dave Jerden,
too, speaks of the importance of forging a partnership before embarking on a project:

> The point being, if you are going to do something important in the
> creative world, you have to look beyond just pushing around faders;
> there has to be a bond made between the producer, the band and the
> engineer. It's almost like a family, and you have to understand each
> other and establish trust.[3]

The interplay between different participants' sets of skills and
points of view can be as much a source of creative energy as the skills
themselves. In the liner notes to *Acadie* (1989), Daniel Lanois points to
significant moments in each track's development. Describing the creation of "White Mustang II," he captures the flavor of the collaborative process in a suggestive nutshell:

On a small portable recorder I did 20 takes of this guitar instrumental—my friend Pierre Marchand listened to them all and picked out the best. In England, Brian [Eno] played many beautiful keyboard parts—a sort of sound sculpture behind a lonely guitar. James May, a New Orleans trumpet player, was playing outside my window. I invited him to do an overdub. Much later Malcolm [Burn] did the mix.[4]

In general, the tasks involved in record making are songwriting, arranging, performing, engineering, and producing.[5] These are the nominal categories of contributors that usually appear in an album's credits, and they reflect the coordinated creative effort involved. The process, however, is fluid, and tasks often merge or overlap. A vocalist may reshape the work of a songwriter through improvised embellishments. A mixing engineer can affect a track's arrangement simply by manipulating the equalization and loudness controls on the mixing console. Producers may act as arrangers, performers, songwriters, or engineers. In short, tracks develop in an organic way, and distinctions among roles need not be definitive. Rather, collaboration fuels a catalytic responsive flow that can take many forms as ideas circulate among a project's participants and the project moves through its various stages. As Jerry Wexler puts it, "[I]t's like who does what to whom in bed. Nobody knows. . . . Nobody knows what goes on at a record session unless you're sitting there. . . . In the long run, what emerges is that the credit accrues to the whole team."[6] This chapter focuses on the creative roles of engineers and producers, two members of the team whose efforts remain, for the most part, behind the scenes.

ENGINEERS

am standing there writing WHAAAT? on my favorite wall
when who should pass by in a jet plane but my recording
engineer "i'm here t pick up you and your latest works
of art. do you need any help with anything?" . . . an so i
answer my recording engineer "yes, well i could use some
help in getting this wall in the plane"

Bob Dylan

As we have seen, Leopold Stokowski grasped the importance of the sound engineer's role as soon as he began to make radio broadcasts in the 1920s. Edward Kealy has noted that with the advent in the 1940s of magnetic tape, which brought increased flexibility in editing, engineers became even more influential; "the recording medium gained a whole new range of aesthetic decision points" in which "the sound mixer was directly involved."[7] Although the contributions of sound engineers are now commonly celebrated in the popular press, Kealy is one of the few scholarly writers on popular music who when speaking to the "multiplicity of authorial voices in the musical text," acknowledges in some detail the voice of the engineer.[8] We have already come across quite a lot of evidence of that voice in examples throughout this book. I would now like to explore some of the specific duties that fall within the engineer's job description.

Engineers are in fact responsible for much of what we hear on a recording—from the quality of the sound colors to the refinement of the smallest details in the mix. Beginning with their decisions about microphone selection and placement, engineers participate fully in the process of shaping the musical work, and their involvement deepens as the project progresses. They are both craftsmen and shamans, harnessing the power of the machine and deftly manipulating its magical secrets to effect the transformation of the musical moment into a musical text. They are the participants in the process who best understand the technological tools in terms of their potential for realizing musical aims—for getting the "wall in the plane." Throughout the recording project, songwriters, performers, and producers are reliant upon them to shepherd intuitive musical visions that are often only partly formed, perhaps technically naive yet artistically sensible, through a daunting technical and analytical process.

The engineer is, in a sense, a translator for the other members of the recording team. Musical ideas, human presence, artistic personalities, the sounds of instruments, voices, and rooms must all be translated from their original state into the medium of the recording. Communication and empathy are critical. Working on *Kiko* (1992), *Latin Playboys* (1994), and *Colossal Head* (1996), the members of Los Lobos developed a quick, intuitive communication with engineer Tchad Blake. By the time they reached the *Colossal Head* sessions, Blake was coproducing (along with Mitchell Froom). The instinctive musical understanding that had developed between engineer and writer/musicians allowed the project—which was begun without any finished songs yet completed in a month—to proceed in ways that while sometimes unorthodox, kept the focus on intuitive creativity. Technical methodology was simply absorbed into the overall creative gestalt of the process. In a Los Lobos interview David Hidalgo recalled, "We'd say something that sounded off the wall, they would say, 'Oh, OK, cool, let's do it.' " "In three seconds," added Cesar Rosas, "Tchad would go [he mimes Blake punching something up on a board] 'tchk, tchk, tchk, tchk.' 'Like that?' 'Yeah, like that.' " Saxophonist Steve Berlin continued, "Tchad's artistry is that he starts in a place that's very, very colorful, and he frees you to think abstractly. It's not like you have to get from A to B to C to D. If you want to start at Y with him, you can see a whole range of possibilities."[9] Blake's grasp of the project's creative flow meant that the series of steps that often becomes the procedural habit of a recording project could be rearranged at will to present new perspectives without fear of becoming lost in a maze of trial and error.

As the preceding example shows, one aspect of an engineer's task is to afford performers a sense of well-being in the studio, keeping technical worries from impeding the creative flow and preserving the inspiration of the intuitive moment in the midst of what is often a tedious process. Tom Flye remembers that for his album *Fresh* (1973) Sly Stone recorded overdubs at several different locations—at the Record Plant in Sausalito, California, at Stone's home studios in Los Angeles and New York, and at his mother's home in San Francisco, depending on where Stone felt like working. The changes in recording spaces and equipment made the engineer's life difficult. Flye recalls at one point punching in every eight bars with "a different guitar, a different sound, different board, different everything" from what had been recorded already.[10] Mindful of his technical responsibilities, Flye was worried initially: there was no way that the sounds would match. Reassured to some extent by Stone's admonishment to "just do it," Flye "started punching in every other eight bars and it *was* totally different—but it was great; it worked great that way."[11] While Flye, or probably any other engineer, would not recommend such a technique as a standard practice, in this case it served a creative need. The early Sly and the Family Stone records featured live ensemble playing, but beginning with *There's a Riot Goin' On* (1971) Stone began to record instruments one at a time, playing most of them himself. He worked incessantly but not systematically—a guitar part here, a bass part there, "almost like needlepoint," recalled

Epic Records A&R-man Stephen Paley.[12] Moving from track to track, Stone responded to what he heard on tape and added new parts. If nothing occurred to him, another track was put up. "Sometimes, he could go through ten or fifteen tracks before he found something that he wanted to work on," recalls Flye.[13] In what became a very disorganized, piecemeal process, it fell to the engineer to give some consistency to the sound and to maintain a positive view of what many saw as a waste of time and money. For though the method was inefficient, it was Stone's way of maximizing his ability at the time, and the success of the results is undeniable. Summing up his role, Flye speaks for many engineers when he says: "You have to give the artist the freedom to be creative, or everything is going to sound the same. I don't want to sit around and make Tom Flye records. I was happy to help Sly do the records he wanted to do."[14]

Engineers are charged first of all with capturing the sounds of the musical performances at the recording session and doing so in a way that allows musicians to sound their best. This means working quickly and efficiently to get the session into tracking mode as soon as possible, and managing any technical vagaries as unobtrusively as possible. A drummer who has spent two hours hitting a snare drum while the engineer adjusts microphone placement, sets recording levels, decides on equalization, and so forth, will be hard-pressed to then produce an inspired performance. Besides the "time equals money" maxim that rules the professional recording environment, there is a concern for "capturing the moment," that is, capturing the musicians' energy before the adrenaline slows to a trickle and boredom sets in. "John [Lennon] was a one or two take man," recalls EMI engineer Peter Vince. "If you didn't get him then, or if you didn't put the right amount of echo in his cans [headphones], you just wouldn't get the performance from him."[15] On the other hand, some artists work gradually toward the definitive performance, as we've seen in the case of Elvis Presley. Either way, the engineer must accommodate. As Vince suggests, engineers must also provide a suitable sonic environment for the performers via their headphone mix. The musician might, for example, have a particular equalization and reverb added to the headphone mix, creating a sound environment that stimulates the performance but is not printed to tape. Meanwhile, the producer in the control room may require a different mix—a harsher light in which to make critical judgments. The engineer must meet these needs simultaneously, alternating between two different sonic environments and sets of criteria.

Because so many things affect sound between its point of production and its appearance in the monitors and headphones, when engineers "get sounds," they are not simply setting up microphones and monitoring record levels; they are balancing a complex network of interactive mediating elements that color the sound and may affect the musicians' performance as well as the decision making of the recording team. The best engineers draw on their reservoir of knowledge and experience to manage the interface between music and machine, art and technology, with a sensitivity to musical expression guiding their own technical "performance." "I'm not really a musician in my own right," says Kevin Killen. "What I play is the console, and I interpret the ideas and get them to tape."[16] Likewise, Tom Lord-Alge refers to the Solid State Logic console as his "instrument."[17] As engineers select microphones, preamps, compressors, equalizers, effects, and recording media and determine how to use them according to the general aesthetic aims of the project, they also bring their personal style to the recording. They "interpret the ideas and get them to tape." Each has favorite pieces of equipment for a given application. Indeed, many engineers carry their own collections of gear from one project to another. They have, moreover, their own techniques, which are informed by experience, by the way they perceive sound, and by their attitude toward sonic treatment. Engineer Richard Dodd points out that "what a sound is and how we perceive it are two different things."[18] In other words, dealing with sound inevitably involves the engineer's sonic imagination. Dodd speaks of using compression, for instance, "to achieve my perceived envelope—to add excitement and sensitivity or presence, or change or add perspective," all of which lie in the realm of subjective aesthetic sense.[19] Interviews with engineers are filled with questions about equipment choices, miking techniques, approaches to using compression and equalization, mixing techniques, and so forth; and the answers to these question often have much in common. A Shure SM57 microphone seems to be most people's favorite for a snare drum, for example. But deeper questions—regarding such things as capturing a vocal (both in terms of sound and performance), dealing with the issue of ambience, the aesthetics of sound processing, and so forth—prompt answers that vary widely. The refined sense of sonic nuance and sonic meaning as it relates to musical expression that engineers bring to a project is the result of personal experience with recorded sound. The degree to which an engineer's individual style can leave its mark on a record is summed up well by Glyn Johns: "If one of the engineers in there and myself, if we both did a session with identically the same set-ups, even, and the same musicians, the same piece of music, it'd sound totally different."[20]

In addition to a thorough grounding in the nature and handling of sound, engineers need a variety of other related abilities. Paramount is an understanding the workings of musical elements—the form of a song, the shape and nuances of a phrase, the progression of events in an arrangement or a performance. This is invaluable in any kind of editing process—whether splicing tape, bouncing tracks, or assembling composite performances—as well as in keeping an ear on the "overall noise": the way that the musical arrangement plays out in sound. An awareness of musical structure also allows the engineer to find the exact place where an overdub is required, and to get there as quickly as possible to minimize any disruption in the session's flow. From a strictly organizational standpoint, the engineer must keep track of which takes have been determined acceptable, which may be questionable, and which need to be redone. In the compartmentalized environment of the multitrack medium, all the various musical parts inhabit their own separate places, and the engineer needs to know at all times the location and status of all the elements of the track. If drop-ins are required, for instance, it is the engineer's responsibility to punch the machine in and out of "record" at precisely the right spots. These may be in the middle of phrases, where a mistake will erase something intended to be kept.

George Massenburg, who as an engineer, producer, and electronics designer spends his life grappling with the musical/mechanical interface, offers the following view of what makes a great engineer: "What I listen for is transparency, where the idea moves from its inception to the listener with the least amount of forces impeding it."[21] In other words, engineers' work requires a deft, sometimes invisible, hand. For their manipulation of sonic reality must become for the listener a reality in itself—not an apparent replacement or a representation. Such "transparency" is a demanding criterion requiring musical, organizational, and interpersonal skills as well as technological expertise. Moreover, inasmuch as the work of the various participants in the recording process is interdependent, it demands a sensitivity to the overall artistic aims of the project. "Certain producers . . . choose their engineers very carefully, because the producers know that those engineers are going to bring certain aspects to the record," says Killen, who has worked as both engineer (for U2, Patti Smith, Roy Orbison, and Kate Bush) and producer (for Peter Gabriel and Elvis Costello). In Killen's opinion, "whether you call that person an engineer, a co-producer or a producer, it's all nomenclature at that point. The industry likes to put things into nice little boxes, but most engineers do feel that they play a large part in the artistic end of a record."[22] Mitchell Froom has no doubt on this point. He characterizes his relationship with Blake as a "creative partnership."[23] Similarly, in the liner notes for her second album Sheryl Crow acknowledges the helpful collaboration and aesthetic empathy of engineer Trina Shoemaker by offering "deep felt thanks . . . for being willing to try anything while I figured out how to make this record."[24] And producer Jack Douglas is very clear about the nature and significance of an engineer's role:

> I'll take the tracks to where I think they should be, and then when I'm out in the studio running it down with the band that super class of engineer has taken it to twice what I heard while I was in [the control room]. I'll come back in and get a great big surprise. Engineering is really an art, and there are some real good artists out there.[25]

The engineer/producer partnership can be something of an alterego situation with both parties working on different aspects of the same picture. Such partnerships often last for many years—examples include Jerry Wexler and Tom Dowd, George Martin and Geoff Emerick, Phil Spector and Larry Levine, Quincy Jones and Bruce Swedien, Stevie Wonder and Gary Olazabal. Nominally, the engineer and producer are responsible for different kinds of decisions, which each trusts the other to make—the producer focuses on songs, arrangements, and performances, while the engineer brings all of these together sonically. Of course, in keeping with the fluidity of the process, such neat assignments of duties inevitably give way to more complex overlaps. As Killen says, in many cases, "it's all nomenclature." Many experienced engineers assume production duties, taking on a role that one of rock and roll's original engineers, Cosimo

Matassa, calls the "subtle sub-producer."[26] Most producers, on the other hand, if not engineers themselves, are at least well aware of the basics. As Arif Mardin summarizes the relationship, "One of the processes of production is that you bounce off of other people."[27]

A clear mark of the engineer's importance to the record-making process is the responsibility he or she assumes for the track's final mix. The mix brings into a coherent whole the ideas and expressive intentions that have been articulated by the project's participants; until there is a mix, there is no piece. Yet setting up the basic dimensions of the mix is usually left to the engineer alone. In order to preserve a fresh perspective, the producer and any others who are still involved at this stage usually avoid the studio while the engineer goes about bringing the recorded material into a coherent sonic and musical frame. Says Bob Clearmountain of Bruce Springsteen:

> As most producers do, he gives me a few hours to get my mix together and listens to my concept. If he doesn't like it, he'll just tell me it isn't what he had in mind. He'll point me in a new direction. But usually he likes what I come up with and he'll just go through a bunch of different options.[28]

In order to "come up with" a mix that is close to the artist's mental image of the finished piece, the engineer must come to it with a sense of the stylistic history of the genre and the artist's previous work. This provides a context for approaching the myriad decisions that a mix entails. Whether the project at hand aims for a general continuity with past work or a new direction, some sort of benchmark is required that provides a sense of the stylistic significance implied by specific choices.

Clearmountain's musical, technical, and empathic abilities make him a popular choice as mix engineer on many artists' albums with which he has not been involved during the recording phase. Daryl Hall claims that "Bob Clearmountain is one person . . . that you can give something to and let him fly blind with it, and he'll come out with the right thing. He's supernatural when it comes to that. He's the only person I know who can do that, and I guess that's why I use him all the time."[29] Clearly, the "right thing" is a realization of what Hall envisioned the work to be, which is as good a summary as any of the engineer's compositional input. Engineers are charged with objectifying the musical ideas and performances of other members of the recording team and fashioning technically sound solutions to aesthetic problems.

Much of an engineer's work is done after hours. Once the formal recording session is over and the musicians have left the studio, the engineer often stays to work on edits, sounds, mix ideas, and so forth. According to Bill Flanagan, during the sometimes lengthy and intense negotiations that took place in the studio during the making of U2's *Zooropa*, the engineer, Flood, listened in silence. But night after night, "when everyone else [was] talked out, exhausted, and home in bed," he remained behind to continue work on the tracks, "making it sound the way he want[ed]." The point where he left off was the point at which the others began when they arrived the next day. Thus, the engineer quietly, yet tellingly, nudges the project along. "A lot of the time I'm like this junior partner," says Flood. "It's almost like you go around with the broom afterwards."[30]

PRODUCERS

For "Watching the Wheels," which he [John Lennon] played like a Bob Dylan song with just him on acoustic guitar, his instructions were: "This is angular, make it circular."

Jack Douglas

The question often arises: "What exactly does a record producer do?" While their work includes things as mundane as budget management, it can also tend to the enigmatic, as the quote from Jack Douglas suggests. Conceptions of the producer's role vary greatly among producers themselves and from one era to another, and the scope of the role is limited only by the number of tasks on a given project. From the standpoint of the record company, the producer is the person who is responsible for delivering a given project on time and on budget, and there have been producers who do little more than pay bills and keep the project on schedule, leaving creative tasks to writers, arrangers, musicians, and engineers. But most rock producers play some sort of aesthetic role as well, which may overlap with songwriting, arranging, performing, and engineering, either in actual participation or in lending critical judgment or advice. Most importantly, producers must nurture the overall process and preserve a larger creative vision as the process moves through myriad mundane details. Paul Fox puts it this way:

> [A]s a producer, you have so many different bags that you have to dip into. . . . You have to be somebody who is aware of all the different levels that go into being an artist. There's a little bit of being a psychologist, a teacher, the musician and arranger. Then there's being the engineer and the sound sculptor. . . . I'm the guy who flies the helicopter above the trees to look down and get the overview.[31]

In the following discussion I cover a range of approaches to production, drawing in producers from various historical eras. It is worth remembering that in addition to philosophical differences among producers, certain historical factors have wrought changes in the producer's role and function. These include technological developments, increased economic power and artistic autonomy on the part of recording artists (especially those who write their own songs), changes in the structure of the music business, and most recently, the dramatically lowered costs of producing professional-quality recordings outside of professional studios. Nevertheless, there is an element that successful producers of all eras and stylistic persuasions have in common: good instincts—about people, art, and commerce.

The nature of the producer's influence varies as much as the nature of the role. It might be immediately apparent in the sound of the record; some producers have a distinctive personal style that is reflected in the sounds and musical arrangements of whatever project they work on. Or, the producer's influence might be behind the scenes—putting together the right chemistry among the musicians, for instance, or finding an appropriate song for a given artist. Some producers are associated with a particular style of music and might be sought for their sense of stylistic nuance. Others are especially sympathetic to the needs and vision of a particular recording artist, providing him or her with creative direction and guidance and coaxing forth performances that will stand the test of time. While no two producers have quite the same combination of skills, each must have the ability to draw together diverse elements and to manage the dynamics of collaborative creativity among the members of the recording team.

Memphis producer Jim Dickinson offers this characterization of a producer's role:

Music has a spirit beyond notes and rhythm. To foster that spirit and to cause it to flourish—to capture it at its peak—is the producer's task. . . . As a producer, I try to remain aware and attuned to the peculiar harmonic properties of the events as they unfold. This is not just musical. I'm talking about how the balance is gonna change in the room constantly during the process, just because of the process itself. It's in the life of the event where you find the soul, and that's what you're trying to capture.[32]

Dickinson's comment is beautifully expressed; it both captures the essence of a process whose nature is organic, chaotic, empirical, and infinitely variable, and points to the producer's primary concern—attending to "the process itself" and "the life of the event." Fellow Memphian Sam Phillips has spoken of becoming "lost in the process" of recording in the same way that he saw Howlin' Wolf—his favorite singer among all those he recorded—become completely absorbed in a song and in the moment of performance.[33] Remember, as we saw in chapter 5, that for Phillips the process itself could bring out "a person's innate, possibly unknown talents." He has characterized his own role as producer thus: "My greatest contribution, I think, was to open up an area of freedom within the artist himself, to help him to express what *he* believed his message to be."[34] This opening up occurred in the process of recording. Recording is the moment of what I have called aura transferal in chapter 1. It is the time of searching for "that indefinable thing," the time to "bottle lightning," and it is the producer's job to foster the spirit that enables this and to recognize when the transferal has occurred.

It is easy to point to the specific contributions of producers such as George Martin or Mitchell Froom, who have often participated as arrangers and performers on projects that they have produced. But Dickinson's characterization allows us to also understand the importance of a producer such as Jerry Wexler, the sort of producer who "begins as an amateur, an impassioned fan, and somehow finds himself in charge of sessions with no special cachet."[35] Perhaps Wexler's most important contribution was his sensitivity to musicians and his sensibility about records, developed over decades of being "an impassioned fan." For many years, beginning in the 1960s, the New York native produced records in the South, first in Memphis and then in Florence, Alabama. While he was drawn to the feel with which the southern musicians played, as well the lower fees they charged, a main reason why he returned again and again was that his production style was suited to the loose, collaborative environment in which these musicians worked. There was an element of spontaneity in the recording process itself that reflected the feel of the music and that allowed the inspiration of the intuitive moment to flourish. The energy of ideas in dynamic interaction was powerful and unpredictable, and defining moments in recording sessions might emerge unexpectedly. The famous story of Wilson Pickett's "In the Midnight Hour" (1965) is a good example. Unsatisfied with the feel of the groove that the Stax rhythm section was playing, Wexler, in his first session at Stax as anything other than an observer, "suddenly realized [he] was on the wrong side of the glass." He burst out of the control room doing a popular dance, "shaking [his] booty to a groove made popular by the Larks' 'The Jerk,' a mid-sixties hit."[36] In 1968, Steve Cropper, who cowrote the song with Pickett and played guitar on the session, told an interviewer, "When I wrote the tune I had it going a completely different way. Basically the changes were the same, basic feel was the same, but there was a different color about it." Bassist Duck Dunn concurred and elaborated: "The bass thing was really Jerry Wexler's idea. . . . [W]e had it going another way. Jerry came out and did the jerk dance."[37] The point of Wexler's demonstration was that the accent should be shifted from the downbeat to emphasize the weaker beats of the measure, especially the second. "Why don't you pick up on this thing here?" he urged the band, making the rhythm with his body. "The idea was to push the second beat while holding back the fourth—something easier demonstrated than explained."[38] Evidently, the difference was profound. "To tell you really," says drummer Al Jackson, "you wouldn't believe the way it was played on the floor and the way it is now."[39] Not only was the record a hit, the groove became something of a formula for the band. "Al and I have been using that as a natural thing now," Cropper enthused. "It turned us on to a heck of a thing."[40]

Wexler defines the roles of the producer according to three categories:

> The first is the documentarian, like Leonard Chess, who took Muddy Waters's Delta blues and recorded them just as Muddy played them—raw, unadorned, and real. Leonard replicated in the studio what he heard in the bar.
>
> I fit into the second category—the producer as servant of the

project. . . . His job is to enhance: meaning find the right song, the right arranger, the right band, the right studio—in short, do whatever it takes to get the best out of the artist.

Phil [Spector] is the prime example of the third category: producer as star, as artist, as unifying force.[41]

As "servant of the project" Wexler produced some of the most memorable records of the 1960s. His success lay in his feel for musical style and sound, in the interactive working environment he fostered, and in his understanding of and respect for the artists he produced. As "an onlooker, organizer, encourager, and, ultimately, promoter," he brought elements together and set collaborations in motion.[42] His contributions to the success of "Midnight Hour" began some time before he began dancing for the band. He took Pickett, who had been languishing for a year after signing with Atlantic, to Memphis in search of a breakthrough. He put Pickett and Cropper together "in a hotel room with a bottle of Jack Daniel's and the simple exhortation—'Write!' "[43] Thus, without contributing any actual music himself, Wexler was in part responsible for the song as well as the record.

Another such breakthrough was Aretha Franklin's "I Never Loved a Man (The Way I Love You)." Franklin had been recognized as a fine singer and pianist while still in her teens, and John Hammond was instrumental in bringing her to Columbia Records, where she remained for six years and recorded eight albums. Her Columbia recordings, however, met with little success, and in 1967 Wexler signed Franklin to Atlantic and became her producer. Once again, he headed south, this time to Rick Hall's Fame Studios in Florence, Alabama, where he had begun recording with Pickett the previous year, using the regular studio rhythm section of Chips Moman (guitar), Tommy Cogbill (bass), Spooner Oldham (keyboards), Roger Hawkins (drums), and Jimmy Johnson (rhythm guitar). In February, 1967, they all went into the studio to record "I Never Loved a Man," Franklin's first Atlantic single. "I had no lofty notions of correcting Columbia's mistakes," recalls Wexler. "My idea was to make good tracks, use the best players, put Aretha back on piano, and let the lady wail."[44] According to Wexler's account, the session began with Franklin playing the song for the rhythm section. Then, as the band learned the song and worked out the rhythm arrangement, saxophonist Charlie Chalmers "went into Rick (Hall's) office to write out the horn parts, and when he came out with the arrangement, we played the whole band together."[45] Franklin's over-dubbed vocal harmony in the chorus—a moment whose sensual impact irresistibly sets the track's "hook"—was Chips Moman's idea, Wexler recalls, almost an afterthought. It all sounds quite simple and straightforward, but success in such a process is elusive. The particular combination of musical sensibilities that Wexler brought together and the free flow of ideas among them created the atmosphere in which Franklin's talent as a performer could finally be transformed into a successful recording—her first top-ten record and the first of many hits she would have on Atlantic.

It was Wexler's intuitive understanding of Franklin's talent and the dynamics of the collaborative relationship that set the session on the right track. For one thing, he knew enough to "let the lady wail." At Atlantic, Franklin "remained the central orchestrator of her own sound, the essential contributor and final arbiter of what fit or did not fit her musical persona."[46] He also knew that the group of musicians he introduced her to at Fame would understand that persona. "The minute Aretha touched the piano and sang one note, the musicians were captivated. They caught the fever and raced for their instruments." Songwriter Dan Penn, who was present at the session, recalls: "When she hit that first chord we knew everything was gonna be all right."[47]

The first and third of Wexler's categories—the producer as documentarian and the producer as star—are useful in a conceptual sense, but it's rare to find producers who fit neatly into either of them. More commonly, a producer manifests characteristics from all three categories. With regard to the first, documentary-style realism is simply not what rock records are about. With the exception of Chuck Berry, Leonard Chess's Chess Records was primarily a blues and R&B label. These were idioms with established performance traditions, and representing them on records was a matter of some transparency. However, even a "documentarian" brings an aesthetic sense to the presentation of "what he heard in the bar." Though the aim of such an approach is to recreate the effect of an experience as one perceives it, that perception is, of course, subjective. But whether one chooses to represent an actual experience or one that exists in the aural imagination, the record is what counts. Even in rock styles for which a more or less documentary presentation is an ethical issue, studio artifice is enlisted to create the desired image. Recall in chapter 3 Butch Vig's editing of Nirvana's tracks on *Nevermind*. Another famous punk album, the Sex Pistols' *Never Mind the Bollocks Here's the Sex Pistols* (1977), benefited from the experience and skills of producer Chris Thomas, whose résumé at that time included projects with Roxy Music, Pink Floyd, and the Beatles. Thomas recalls that the album that many assumed was played live in the studio was in fact "quite labored," with numerous overdubs and edits. The goal was to make a record that would have a strength of impact similar to the Sex Pistols' aggressive style in live performance, and Thomas's job was to create that feeling by whatever means necessary. As a documentary, "Anarchy in the U. K." consisted of Johnny Rotten "basically just scream[ing] into the microphone," a single guitar part, and a basic track that "was very loose between bass and drums." But once Thomas won Lydon's confidence and convinced him that he "didn't think [the vocal] was going to work like that," the two worked together "bit by bit" toward achieving the results that we hear on the record.[48] Similarly, the guitar part was augmented by "something like a dozen" others, which Thomas orchestrated and mixed. And a day was spent piecing together a tighter groove between the bass and drums by combining bits of many takes.

In his third category of producer, Wexler names Spector, who with his image as something of a rock *auteur* (as Evan Eisenberg has characterized him), is a rare and controversial bird. Jack Nitzsche, the arranger on many Spector sessions, believed that Spector "is the best record producer—no, I mean he is the only artist/record producer. He was firstly an artist."[49] "Artist" here means not simply someone who contributes artistry to the project, but rather "recording artist," that is, the person who claims top billing. In the 1960s, before beginning his association with the Beatles and then George Harrison and John Lennon, this was Spector's public image. In 1965, Rolling Stones manager Andrew Loog Oldham took out a congratulatory ad in *Melody Maker* touting the Righteous Brothers' recording of the Barry Mann/Cynthia Weil song "You've Lost That Lovin' Feelin' " as "the great new PHIL SPECTOR Record."[50] Beginning in 1963, Spector released on his own Philles label album-length collections of his productions for various artists, including, among others, the Crystals, Darlene Love, the Ronettes, and Bob B. Soxx and the Blue Jeans, but the featured attraction was clearly Phil Spector. In fact, oftentimes the groups' personnel were not consistent; vocalists were cast and recast like actors playing roles. In 1976, Spector began to reissue his works in collections with titles such as *Rare Masters* and *Phil Spector's Greatest Hits*. Furthermore, when his business position was strong enough to demand it, he insisted on sharing songwriting credit equally with songwriters. In his view, the songs were not really finished until he had produced them.

This is quite a contrast to George Martin, who, though responsible for much of the Beatles' success as recording artists, was always a "servant of the project" first of all. Comparing himself to Martin, Spector has said, "I don't consider myself in the same situation or league. . . . I don't consider him with me. He's somewhere else. He's an arranger, that's all."[51] Far more than an arranger, Martin was a collaborator and a facilitator in the studio. But for Spector record making was, above all, a matter of the producer's self-expression, the producer's voice. Whatever particular sound an individual track might have, it was a manifestation of a larger, encompassing vision—his. "I don't have a sound, a Phil Spector sound," he told Jan Wenner in 1969. "I have a style, and my style is just a particular way of making records."[52]

But the idea that a producer should be such an *auteur*—imposing his or her own sound and vision on diverse projects—is controversial, as is the "artist/record producer" conflation (unless, of course, the producer is also the featured performer). "The main part of the job is to stay absolutely out of the way when you're not needed," says Mitchell Froom. "If you can't make the decision to leave a good thing alone, you've no business being a producer."[53] By contrast, Spector used recording artists as vehicles. "I loved them," Spector said of the Righteous Brothers. "I thought they were a tremendous expression for myself. I think they resented being an expression."[54] Rick Hall—founder of Fame Studios and central figure in the development of the "Muscle Shoals sound"—has an equally imperious view of musicians. Comparing his approach to that of Wexler, Hall says, "Jerry thinks that musicians are the answer to hit records. I say musicians are like basketball players, they need a manager to tell them when to drop a play. My engineering ability and advice on licks and beats contributes more than the individual musicians."[55]

Comparing the roles of record producer and film director—from which the *auteur* concept is borrowed—Don Was characterizes the former as "a little more of a nebulous thing." For Was, the "film director is the artist and it's really his vision, and the actors and the entire crew are there to serve him. Whereas if you are producing a record, you make the same types of decisions, but, theoretically, they are towards furthering the artist's vision."[56] Was is credited as a creative collaborator by the artists he works with, but there is clearly some line that delimits the scope of his creative contributions and distinguishes his role as a producer from the role he inhabits as an artist when making his own records. As he himself puts it, referring to his own Was (Not Was) albums, "If I'm going to lapse into being the artist, I might as well really do it."[57]

The conflicting views of producers' roles just surveyed are drawn from different historical periods and circumstances. The historical trend has generally favored producers who can empathize with the artist. Indeed, Spector retained his mastery of the studio process through his final recording project—the Ramones' *End of the Century* (1980). But artists were less and less inclined to work with a man who, when frustrated, went for his pistol, as he is said to have done with Lennon and Dee Dee Ramone, among others. As recording artists gained ever-greater autonomy beginning from the mid-sixties, they sought producers who could work from within the artist's creative sphere, helping to draw out and focus the most characteristic aspects of their artistic personae, rather than imposing a perhaps-conflicting musical vision from the outside. "The main criterion is that the producer provides a camaraderie, more than a technical expertise," says Rickie Lee Jones. "I want them to relate to the work, to dig it and help to bring an atmosphere of confidence."[58] This trend toward greater autonomy for recording artists has led to partnerships in which the production credit is shared between the producer and the artist, or, simply the artist and the engineer. This is the sort of arrangement where women producers are most often found. For although historically few women have been producers in the traditional sense, many recording artists have done much or all of their own production work. These include Joni Mitchell, Sheryl Crow, Kate Bush, Lauryn Hill, Sinéad O'Connor, Liz Phair, and Björk.

Far from receding in importance, however, producers now enjoy unprecedented visibility. There has been "a marked transition in the role of record producer"[59] from the record companies' A&R men who matched songs with artists, hired musicians and arrangers, and supervised recording sessions—men like John Hammond and Mitch Miller—to the independent contractors of today. The trend has accelerated in the last twenty years. "Producers seem to be getting known by the public nowadays and I don't think that's a good thing. It's the band that's all important, all the time," protested Steve Lillywhite in 1981.[60] At the time, however, Lillywhite was at the forefront of the young British producers who were responsible for the ever-more-experimental sonic treatments that took records further and further from acoustic reality. The records they made demanded to be heard on their own sonic terms. As it became common practice to problematize conventional sounds as never before—as variations on the massive drum sounds of Peter Gabriel's third album, for instance, turned up on Lillywhite's 1983 productions for U2 (*War*) and Big Country (*The Crossing*)—audiences became more curious than ever about who other than the musicians had a hand in shaping the sounds. "Listeners' ears have gotten very sophisticated, and demand a good-sounding record, and a well put together record," Joe Chiccarelli told an interviewer in 1986. As the audience became accustomed to a sonic culture where technologies such as digital delay and reverb, automated mixing, and sampling allowed recordists "to go a lot further soundwise . . . experimenting more and more," listeners, informed increasingly by the popular press about the people behind the console, developed a greater awareness of sound per se and a greater appreciation of producers' "voices."[61]

British recordings of the early 1980s marked a turning point in terms of both sound and public awareness. With an abundance of sound processing, new electronic instruments,[62] and resurgent experimental attitudes, the distance between the natural sound world and the sound of records increased markedly; and the audience response, as measured in record sales, was enthusiastic. Working with producer Robert "Mutt" Lange, a transplanted South African, engineer Mike Shipley remembers it as a time when "[w]e'd have to invent types of drum sounds, because his thing was always, 'Let's do something different. It can't ever be the same, it can't ever be just a boring drum sound, it has to be *Star Wars*! . . . Let's make it big, different, larger than life.'"[63] Though he won the Grammy for Producer of the Year in 1985, American producer David Foster was quite emphatic in telling an interviewer where the inspiration for many of his most recent production techniques had originated:

Now, in one sense, all that sounds like we're doing pretty well. But on the other hand, when I listen to the stuff that's coming out of Britain, it just blows me away. I mean guys like Trevor Horn are absolutely brilliant, and I think in terms of state-of-the-art production they're simply miles ahead of us. We're just loping along, trying to keep up with them. Just listen to what Horn did with Frankie Goes to Hollywood. Whether you like the group or not, there's no denying that his production is just amazing.[64]

Of course, by further expanding rock's sonic palette young producers like Horn, Lillywhite, Lange, and Hugh Padgham were simply doing what so many before them had done. When George Martin recalls that "before and even after the Beatles arrived—the record producer was basically an organiser," he is thinking of his experience as an employee at a large corporation where procedural rules were part of company policy.[65] In America, on the other hand, where small independent record companies were responsible for so much early rock and roll, there were producers breaking the A&R mold from the beginning, making records whose sound bore the producer's mark. Clearly, Sam Phillips was far more than an "organiser." And there were many other independent engineer/producers around the country—Norman Petty in Clovis, New Mexico; Lee Hazelwood in Phoenix, Arizona; Cosimo Matassa in New Orleans; Bill Putnam as well as the Chess brothers in Chicago; the Erteguns with Tom Dowd in New York—all working at making distinctive, unique-sounding records. One legendary engineer/producer of the 1950s and 1960s, Joe Meek, was a fellow countryman of Martin. Unlike Martin, however, he began in the mid-fifties to work as an independent in his own small studio. In pursuit of sounds that he first imagined and then set about creating—even if doing so required that he build equipment from scratch or modify an existing piece—he used recording techniques that would have been forbidden in the studios of any of the major record labels. He is credited with some of the earliest radical sound treatments in rock, employing reverb, echo, compression, equalization, distortion, unusual microphone placement, and tape speed variation to create sound worlds—and hit records—unlike any of the time.[66]

Today there are many producers who are at least as well known as the artists they produce, and in many cases they make records of their own. Examples include "Baby Face," Butch Vig, Mitchell

Froom, Sean "Puffy" Combs, Daniel Lanois, and Dr. Dre. Artists turn to production as well: Pink Floyd's David Gilmour (Dream Academy, *The Dream Academy*), Nine Inch Nails's Trent Reznor (Marilyn Manson, *Antichrist Superstar*), John Mellencamp (James McMurtry, *Too Long in the Wasteland*), Electric Light Orchestra's Jeff Lynne (Tom Petty, *Full Moon Fever*), Phil Collins (Frida, *Something's Going On*). Those involved in the art of record making gain experience in different aspects of the process, and many are able to move beyond their initial roles to explore new ones. For whether they begin as performers, songwriters, arrangers, engineers, or producers, all are working on the same thing, the record. With that as the central focus, what Dickinson calls "the process itself . . . the life of the event" becomes paramount, and anyone with the ability to foster it in some way may rightly claim the title of "producer."

7

Resonance

To me, specific records and specific songs are even more
important than the artist. There's something about pop
music that makes you not really care that much about
Buddy Knox . . . but you really want to hear "Party Doll."

Don Dixon

By way of conclusion, I would like to probe a little further into the
resonant atmosphere in which recordists work and which influences
their creative imaginations and aesthetic decisions. In the course of
the preceding chapters, I have often used words like "convention,"
"association," "resonance," "allusion," "reference," and "rhetoric."
Until now, I've skirted the implications of such terms, but now I'd
like to bring them into the discussion directly, for they suggest the
workings of an aesthetic system whose very nature shapes the production and reception of its constituent works.

Throughout the poetic/aesthetic economy of rock—among
artists, fans, critics, and historians—records are commonly interpreted in terms of other records. Meanings accumulate through a
continual process of interaction that connects individual works to a
field of works past, present, and future. The resulting web is a backdrop to every new undertaking, and its presence influences artists
and audiences alike. Consider this record review: "The arrangements
feature prominent acoustic guitars, piano, occasional pedal steel,
and, most notably, trumpet; think Van Morrison circa *Inarticulate
Speech of the Heart* and you've got it."[1] The reviewer is telling us
something about how the record sounds not only by naming instruments in the arrangements but also by making an associative connection to an earlier record. The connection is personal, but he and
his editor obviously believe that it will resonate sufficiently with
their readers.

Similarly, describing Richard Manuel's vocal style, Greil Marcus has written:

> There are times when Richard Manuel sounds like the ghost of Johnny Ace (that sweet-voiced fifties R&B singer who died in a game of Russian roulette)—Johnny Ace condemned to haunt a gloomy radio, from which "Pledging My Love" . . . issues every time you spin the dial. There are times when the tone is desperate, close to the panicky feeling Marvin Gaye got on "I Heard It through the Grapevine." But more often than not, the music is simply ominous.[2]

Here again, we have a characterization couched in terms of the writer's personal associations. The connection between Manuel, Ace, and Gaye is an interpretive act on Marcus's part, based on his perception of the evocative qualities of a collection of voices emanating from a loudspeaker. The suggestive resonance of his characterization is at once impressionistic and precise. Anyone who knows the three singers' styles and the emotional aura surrounding their work can sense what Marcus is getting at. The effectiveness of such an interpretation derives from the fact that the practice of intertextual reference—in the broadest sense—is so prevalent in rock. It serves as a contextualizing force that situates the individual recording within a galaxy of other recordings and provides the listener with all sorts of clues as to style, rhetorical sense, and aesthetic stance.[3]

Connections among records can be subtle, obvious, or any shade in between—from wispy allusions to direct quotations. And the association may occur in a number of ways—through lyrics or musical syntactic elements like grooves or chord progressions, of course, but also through sounds, performance practices, and recording techniques. That is, resonances may occur at the level of song, arrangement, or track. Furthermore, associations may refer to a general style—amounting to little more than a sharing of conventions—or more directly to a particular artist or work. Slapback echo is recognized as a characteristic feature of rockabilly style, and every post-rockabilly band from the Flaming Groovies to the Stray Cats has used it to situate themselves stylistically. Tom Petty, who has often alluded to other artists' work in various ways, clearly emulates Bob Dylan's singing style circa *Blonde on Blonde* in his vocal for the track "Echo" (1999). On Karl Wallinger's "Sunshine" (1993), the most immediately apparent associations include a guitar riff reminiscent of Hendrix's "Hey Joe" (1967) in both syntax and sound; a chord progression, twelve-string acoustic, and slide guitar sounds that allude to the Rolling Stones' "Wild Horses" (1971); and some rhythmic heavy breathing à la Paul McCartney's "Kreen Akrore" (1970). In a collage of Beatlesisms—or, more precisely, *Revolver*isms—Beck's "The New Pollution" (1996) combines allusions to the bass line from "Taxman," the drum groove and ambience from "Tomorrow Never Knows," and George Harrison's swooping Indian-influenced vocal style on "Love You To." In the deep ambience that permeates Cocteau Twins records we hear a nod to Phil Spector, as Robin Guthrie has made clear.[4] Lenny Kravitz borrows with gusto, as track after track alludes now to Hendrix, now to Lennon, now to Thom Bell. The kaleidoscope of references, coupled with his ability to make them convincingly, is a central feature of a style that in the end is all his own.

Whatever the degree and nature of the connection, interpreting its meaning is a personal matter for the listener. Records circulate and connect with one another through the agency of listeners, whose accumulated listening experience, sensitivity, and reasons for listening differ from one to another. Of course, artists are listeners as well. Indeed, they are listeners first. Their vocabulary is formed initially by the sounds that they absorb. In their youth, impressions were formed in their budding artistic consciousness by the records that they loved, and in maturity their work is informed by what is going on around them. Collectively, rock recordists partake, both consciously and unconsciously, of a common pool of musical and sonic resources. As they follow their artistic impulses, creating their own individual works, they draw from the well of their sonic experience, which, filled as it is with the works of other artists, is the basis of their understanding of what amounts to the language of record making.

Writings about music bear witness to a long history of analogy with language aimed both at explaining musical practice and the apprehension of musical meaning. Comparisons between rhetoric and music have been especially popular. Rhetoric provides its practitioners with effective ways of imparting meaning to an audience using a set of conventional resources: words and grammar, of course, but also figures of speech, modes of delivery, and arrangement of an argument. The individual rhetorical utterance is particular to the speaker, but the material and tools with which it is made are commonly held and understood. Musicians, too, practice their art and craft before audiences, and it is easy to see why the analogy between rhetoric and musical composition became as widespread as it did, especially in German composition treatises from the seventeenth and eighteenth centuries, when shared conventions were still prized among artists and audiences. In the nineteenth century, composers of concert music, reflecting the ideological currents of the time, began to move away from a foundation based in conventional practices in pursuit of an expression that was above all personal. As Leonard Meyer has observed, the shift was accompanied by a "change from a conceptual model derived from language to one based on organic growth."[5] Indeed, the epithet "mere rhetoric" became an expression applied to anything thought to be hollow in meaning and showing little imagination. But popular musics, by definition, rely on familiar materials and practices for their success. The tradition of invoking rhetoric, therefore, would seem to extend naturally to rock, whose styles all have committed core audiences whose knowledge of both stylistic norms and individual nuance can be quite comprehensive. As David Brackett points out, rhetoric "emphasizes conventions governing the relationships between pieces," and as a basis for musical analysis, it stresses "the importance of the musical *surface* rather than seeking to explicate the hidden depths of structure."[6] For a musical idiom where surface is essence and intertextual relationships are rife, the "metaphor of the oration" seems like a perfect fit.[7]

But we must be careful here. The practice of making analogies between music and rhetoric dates back to Aristotle. Remote as this history may seem in relation to rock, the concept of rhetorical analogy carries historical associations, and if we are to invoke rhetoric in thinking about rock music, we need to be clear about what we mean in doing so. For writers such as Joachim Burmeister (1564–1629), Christoph Bernhard (1627–1692), and Johann Mattheson (1681–1764), the principles of rhetoric provided a handy means of explaining many of music's formative, structural, and expressive concepts. As a central component of a liberal education, rhetoric was a widely familiar linguistic discipline, and theorists took advantage of this to explain the more abstract discipline of musical construction, just as contemporary composers apparently employed rhetorical principles in their musical expression. Such analogies could be quite systematic, equating specific rhetorical and musical devices, especially in the realm of elaboration. But the fact that there are "numerous conflicts in terminology and definition among the various writers, and there is clearly no one systematic doctrine of musical figures" evinces the intrinsically interpretive nature of the enterprise.[8] Music is far more impressionistic than language, and analogies between the two cannot support literal parallelisms. The correspondences are in a sense metaphorical, though I don't want to make too much of that either. Let's just say that they are loose. Heinrich Koch (1749–1816) admits as much in his treatise instructing students in the principles of composing in the late-eighteenth-century Classical style. "Generally speaking, only feeling can determine both the places in the melody where resting points of the mind [*Geist*] occur and also the character of these resting points," he writes somewhat reluctantly on the subject of phrase endings.[9] He goes on to say that if music were more like language in its mechanisms of syntactic sense, he could be more precise in his directions; but as it is, all he can do is to leave the matter in the realm of "feeling." It may seem, once again, that we are far afield, but there is something to be learned from such distant historical affinities. For there is a common ground for the Classical style and rock that is more elemental than their stylistic features or context of presentation. The similarity lies in aesthetic principle. In both aesthetic systems individual musical style is built on a foundation of conventional procedures and resources, which, in turn, enables the resonant atmosphere in which artists, their works, and their audiences negotiate meaning. As Edward Cone has written, "during the period of the Viennese Classics, original musical thought and generally accepted procedures find not only mutual accommodation but mutual reinforcement." The statement is equally true of rock, as is the upshot: "the results are happy for composer and audience alike."[10]

In calling attention to rock's intertextual processes, then, I am not proposing any systematic correspondence with linguistic practices, nor appealing for a taxonomic accounting of rock's rhetorical devices, but simply drawing upon the broad principle of conventional understanding. In language, grammar provides normative procedures—rules—for ensuring correctness and coherence within a given conventional system at a particular time in that system's history, while rhetoric is the artful manipulation of the rules, the play of the individual imagination within a conventional framework. In music, normative expectations develop as practices repeat themselves and develop into conventions. But this does not mean that such things become *rules* in the grammatical sense. While rhetorical practice in music involves playing with conventions, the play is far more empirical, and fanciful, than is possible with language. This is why rock recordists, though they share musical and technological resources and are influenced by stylistic and commercial guidelines that can be quite specific, stress repeatedly that there are no rules. What they mean—and this is reminiscent of Koch—is that even working within a conventional system with all sorts of stylistic guidelines and normative procedures, the success of their rhetorical flourishes depends upon creative musical imagination, not logical justification. For though it works within boundaries, the creative musical spirit values the "lucky find" far above the deliberate argument.[11]

As Mark Evan Bonds has pointed out, rhetoric "is at least in part an aesthetic category."[12] I would say that for rock—and one might make the case for other musics as well—it is *mostly* "an aesthetic category." While the metaphor of rhetorical display is often appropriate for specific instances, as a general characterization of intertextual practice or events I would prefer to leave things at the level of association, a term that is at once more neutral and more encompassing. For while rhetoric involves an intentional act directed from one party to another, as in the "art of persuasion," association is simply a property available within a conventional system. It may take the concrete form of a more or less isomorphic correspondence, with a dance, say, or a specific event—Neil Young's "Ohio" (1970), for instance.[13] Or it may call forth a nostalgic reminiscence, or provide stylistic orientation. For a given listener, association can work in any number of ways, or not at all. That is, it exists always as a potential but is manifested only through agency, on the part of either artist or listener or both. It may lie dormant, unperceived yet present. Association gives rise to an ever-fluid process where meaning flows in all directions independently of artist intention or audience awareness. It can arise in an individual consciousness at any time, often quite unexpectedly. Furthermore, association encompasses nuances of connection whose significance as symbols, allusions, quotations, or references—to say nothing of irony, parody, synecdoche, and all the rest—may be impossible to articulate. Sounds are filled with nuances that echo experiences that have become deeply embedded in consciousness. Most listeners probably could not say why a particular sort of snare rattle or the sound of a plectrum scraping across guitar strings in a particular way brings a sense of delight and satisfaction. They may not even notice the details consciously. But they know well when the sound strikes them as right and good, and that is a result of their ability to locate the sound within the context of their own listening experience.

Let me give a personal example: a connection between R. E. M.'s "Tongue" (1994) and The Band's recording of Bob Dylan's "I Shall Be Released" (1968) made through purely sonic clues and without any conscious effort on my part. In the introductions to both tracks, a simple solo piano part is placed on the left side of the stereo sound-stage with its ambience projected to the right. Although the piano parts are alike only in their rhythmic feel—slow, measured pulsations articulated in a deliberate sort of way—their timbral type and stereo juxtaposition of source and reverb are substantially similar. In each case, the brief piano intro is followed by the entrance of a pleading falsetto vocal and organ sounds that, while quite different in themselves, share a similarly wet ambient image. This is not Michael Stipe's normal singing voice, and it might call to mind any number of singers. The lyrics certainly seem unrelated to those of "I Shall Be Released." Yet following this particular introduction, it reminds *me* of Richard Manuel, who sang the lead on "I Shall Be Released." Manuel—"the ghost of Johnny Ace"—is one of rock's tragic figures. Long before he took his own life, his singing style expressed a yearning sadness. "Sometimes I thought you felt too much," sings Robbie Robertson in "Fallen Angel" (1986), his tribute to Manuel. Indeed, the vulnerability and rawness of a soul too open and knowing for its own good is a characteristic mark of Manuel's artistic persona, and he portrays the hope against hope of the character in "I Shall Be Released" with a resigned clarity.

As I make this association, "Tongue" takes on a deeper aura. If the track on its own engages me with its sound, the associations forming in my mind hold an intellectual and emotional fascination. The association is slight and momentary yet strong in its effect, for it amounts to an assertion of my power as a listener, of my ability to discern connections between artworks through the lens of personal experience. At the same time, it affirms the resonant nature of the idiom that makes such associations possible. Simply by changing his tone of voice, Stipe has demanded an interpretive engagement, which in turn makes one listen more closely to the track's other elements and wonder what is meant. As one wonders, the mind darts about involuntarily, seeking an explanation. Of course, it is not the artist's job to explain anything; it is from the listener's own experience that the connection is made. And the result of such interpretive forays is a meaning grasped not through the workings of connotation, but as a direct connection between records—the sort of thing that Richard Middleton calls "primary signification."[14] While connotation may follow as the listener reflects on what he or she has discovered, the initial sense is one of records in dialogue. The association process is an ever-present and evolving part of the listening experience. Associations occur, recede, shift, mutate. And as they do, they enrich one's sense not only of the track at hand but also of the overall aesthetic system. Both artists and listeners benefit from the workings of such a system. Artists' works speak louder in a resonant atmosphere, and part of what they say amounts to an invitation for listeners to claim an active, participatory role.

Furthermore, the mere possibility of associations lends the system a sense of integrity. Because they make one aware that there is a relational field, perceived connections among artworks automatically amount to some sort of meaning. They create a sense of shared understandings from which develop conventional associations, expectations, and ultimately, traditions. Whether or not such connections have specific meanings doesn't really matter. Noticing them is enough. The fact that it is possible to make such connections gives listeners the impression that *something* meaningful is happening as they traverse the aesthetic space between themselves and the musical works that they encounter. We are always free to take interpretation as far as we like, but it's not necessary in order to appreciate or delight in what is taking place. I can make a case, for example, that the distorted acoustic guitar sound on the Beatles' "I'm Only Sleeping" makes for an edgy emotional counterpoint to the dreamy vocal, a subtext that resonates with the veiled desperation of the song's isolated protagonist. Or I can simply note that this is not your average acoustic guitar sound—an observation whose significance increases as one's listening experience grows—and take my delight from its unusual sonic texture. I know that the sound is distinctive because I have heard lots of acoustic guitars on rock records. This one is not like the Everlys' or Bob Dylan's or even the Beatles' own guitars on earlier albums. By its raw, harsh tone it has gotten my attention, and even if I cannot put it into words, I know that it is saying *something*.

If this leaves things fuzzy, so be it. The very lack of specificity resonates with recordists' repeated references to "cool sounds." On its face, "cool sounds" is subjectively impressionistic and nonspecific to the point of being meaningless. Furthermore, "cool" seems almost impossible to unpack for any solid clues to physical characteristics or aesthetic value. But because the rock recordist's aesthetic world is deeply infused with a knowledge of sound acquired by listening to records, impressions of "cool" are formed against a field. When recordists say that a particular move on a record—a sound, part of an arrangement, a performance—is cool, they are saying simply that it strikes them as distinctive. The fact that they are making the assessment in relation to a field of more or less commonly known works allows us to get a sense, through a sort of triangulation process, of the significance of "cool." This is the same process that gives shape and definition to George Martin's "infinite palette of musical colours," whose terms otherwise seem to contradict the very notion of convention. The vagueness of the designation "cool" reflects to a certain extent the ineffable nature of music, the fact that musicians have little need for precise linguistic distinctions, and the disingenuous strain of apparent anti-intellectualism that rockers pay lip service to. But more importantly, it speaks to the integrity of the musical system in which they work. Relying on the implied sense that resonant connections impart, recordists develop expressive styles imbued with all the nuanced shades of their record-listening experience, confident that much of that experience is common among their audience and that simply foregrounding possibilities of association will place their work into a larger resonant frame.

Although record making is extremely technical, comments on the nature of its process and criteria—even by those responsible for its most technical aspects—routinely deemphasize theoretical principles or justifications. "If I like something I keep it," says Karl Wallinger. "If something bothers me I get rid of it, and it's on to the next thing."[15] Thomas Dolby has characterized his work as "mainly intuitive and motivated by a puerile sense of mischief."[16] Tony Visconti, acknowledging that "the range of options is incredible," narrows the choices by "gut feeling." "If it sounds good, I record it and don't ask questions."[17] Nicky Ryan, who produces Enya's richly layered tracks, states, "I don't have a preconceived picture. We work on it until it's right, and only your ears can tell you that."[18] The reason "your ears can tell you that" is that they are working with a firm basis for intuiting the sense of a sound in relation to other sounds. The accumulated works and conventional practices of rock recording provide a context in which recordists can make referential use of sound and enhance the sense of their work by connecting it with others. The ways in which particular sounds—or aspects of sounds, nuances—have been used on prior recordings influences how they are used on subsequent ones. The distinctiveness may be in the form of contrast, variation, transformation, or uniqueness; but in any case, it is assessed and understood against a referential field.

"[W]e thought, 'This sounds cool,' " recalls Butch Vig of a digital feedback sound that he and his cohorts in Garbage stumbled upon while working on their first album. They used the sound on the track "Stupid Girl" (1995) during the song's pre-chorus sections. "It made sense for us to drop the bass out and put that in its place. I have no idea why."[19] This isn't quite true. For one thing, Vig knows that any time the bass drops out of a rock track, it creates a sense of expectancy. Moreover, the sound "gave the song a real tense quality in that section, like something is being stretched. In a way it almost becomes a hook. Even though it has no real musical character, it does create tension, especially with Shirley [Manson] singing high in her range at that point in the song."[20] Despite his protestation, Vig clearly has a very good idea of the effect the sound creates. In his reluctant analysis we can admire both his respect for the mystery of artistic intuition and his grasp of record-making language, which is the basis for his sense of the sound's distinctive quality. More curious than the digital feedback, however, is the obvious reference made at the track's opening to the Beatles' "Back in the U. S. S. R." (1968). The Beatles' track begins with the sound of a jet plane flying across the stereo spectrum, creating a Doppleresque effect. "Stupid Girl" starts out with a similar sound, though here it is a composite made up of what sound like guitar glissandi. Because the sound is not sampled from the original or even produced by the same general timbral source, it comes across as a sort of mutated allusion. But why is it there at all? The two songs seem completely unconnected. Is there some symbolic point to the allusion? If so, I don't get it. What's more,

I don't care. For what I do get is a sense of delight as I recognize it. It alerts me to the artist's sense of field, as well as to my own. I am reminded once again that the work I am focused on at the moment reaches far beyond itself and thereby gains a resonant aura of association quite in addition to its own actual features. Furthermore, I sense artists in dialogue. And as the reference joins the individual instance to something larger, I sense tradition.

What I am calling association is similar in some ways to the cultural processes that some writers characterize as discursive or dialogic. Robert Walser, for example, looks to the "concept of discourse" to provide a perspective on both the "formal characteristics of [musical] genres" and the "range of understandings shared among musicians and fans concerning the interpretation of those characteristics."[21] Samuel Floyd describes the interchanges between "the complementary oppositions of African- and European-derived musical processes and events" as "dialogical music making."[22] However one characterizes it, the workings of any such process depend on the context provided by a cultural field, a notion that Thomas McFarland has developed with some sensitivity. In a counter to Harold Bloom's well-known theories of influence, McFarland senses connections not only in confrontations between "strong poets" but in cultural "parataxes," which may amount to only "minimal and almost imperceptible relationships."[23] He substitutes the term "parataxis," meaning "simple juxtaposition," for "influence" in an effort to grasp the nature of cultural fields filled with events of every sort of magnitude. "To look at cultural events," he writes, "is like looking at stars in the night sky. We look up with unaided vision and see stars, more than we can count, and of varying brightness and no immediately discernible pattern." As our awareness grows, "we see more stars and we see them in more detail; but there are still more than we can count, and we infer that there are many more we do not see." With still more experience, "we begin to ascribe patterns to the seemingly random configuration of the stars," and finally, "to connect constellations of cultural patterns, by which with deeper observation we can locate whole galaxies."

The connections that we make among the juxtaposed events are possible only because there exists "a field anterior to any particular works in it." It is "the unity supplied by the anteriority of field" that allows us to sense the significance of a work, a body of works, or the features of a style:

> The rule derived thus seems invariable: first there is field, then constellation, and only as a third awareness is there object considered as focus of observation. . . .
> Furthermore, though our primary intuition of the stars is of number and brightness and scattering, and only our secondary view, enhanced by meditation and magnification, begins to find pattern and interrelationship, that enhanced secondary view reveals to us that starry events differ in more ways than mere brightness or proximity. . . . [T]here are stars of differing intensity and size, and there are planets and moons; and what look like stars sometimes turn out to be whole galaxies, which again take different shapes: pinwheels, blobs, rings—there is even one identified as the "sombrero" galaxy. There are in addition quasars and pulsars and black holes. In the same way, the actual content of cultural field in its constellational groupings is not limited to poetry and strong poets but reveals other cultural configurations as well.

Thus, it is field, in all its complexity, that enables rhetoric, dialogue, influence, association, and the rest. For as McFarland reminds us, looking into the night sky, "we do not see the drift of stars: we see stars in simple juxtaposition. Conceptions of current are derived from the anteriority of field, not from the parataxes themselves. The river, as Wordsworth says, is our own mind." That is, we each participate in cultural dialogue—both as individuals and collectively—to the extent that we choose to look or to listen more closely. Artists listen more closely than most, and they absorb sounds through the filter of their own artistic identity. "Influences are infinitely numerous; writers are infinitely sensitive; each writer has a different sensibility," Virginia Woolf tells us.[24] And the currents that form in the minds of recordists flow not only between works but among all the "infinitely numerous" sonic details of records' formal elements. The sounds on records represent a broad range of significance—artistic, historical, great, and small. Both the artist's expressive gesture and the listener's interpretation are infused with an awareness of field that allows minimal, momentary, and inexplicable allusions, references, and rhetorical gambits to resonate in a frame far larger than themselves. The overall resonant frame amplifies, as it were, the smallest nuances with which records are filled, even as it contains the

broadest gestures—songs, personalities, utterances. As Steven Feld
says, the

> boundary or frame represents the notion that potentially very gen-
> eral and very specific messages emerge simultaneously in the con-
> sciousness of the interpreting listener. The boundary or frame is both
> a closed and open door to this process; it can lock in or compact a
> summary of all interacting interpretive constructs, or it can let them
> scatter and draw more attention to its own position among those
> elements.[25]

Feld's formulation of "interpretive moves" framed by "expressive
ideology," "identity," and "coherence systems" that connect the sens-
ing of musical meaning with other kinds of cultural experience presents a picture of associations that potentially move in all directions at
once and connect all aspects of the listening experience.[26] Again, the
currents are formed through the perceptions of individuals, and any
aspect of a track can trigger an association. The process is dynamic,
the flow ongoing.

Hank Shocklee says that his brother Keith "knows records like an
encyclopedia."[27] The simile suggests that record collections are
repositories of knowledge and that they represent accumulated tradition. In addition to artistic expression, they represent historical
documents and instruments of instruction that provide both ground
and atmosphere. Beck Hansen began recording his *Odelay* album
(1996) with no songs written. He and producers Mike Simpson and
John King (a.k.a. the Dust Brothers) began the project by "listening to
records for inspiration both sonically and melodically."[28] They began
a journey of personal expression with a trip through worlds created
by other travelers. This is not to say that records are made only in
terms of other records. Artists create in terms of their own experience
of the world. But inasmuch as the expression of an artistic impulse
requires some kind of medium, it is sound recording that gives
recordists their voice, and it is to records that they appeal, consciously or not, for guidance in shaping the articulation of their own
sensibility. Record making is a compositional practice, a poetic language. It continually renews itself as creative consciousness moves
freely about the ever-expanding galaxy of records, forming and re-
forming new associations all the time. The galaxy is indeed filled
with stars and events of every sort and magnitude. Casting about

with our ears, we may come upon Richie Valens or Moby; the Crystals or Sonic Youth; Blue Cheer or the Temptations; Abba or AC/DC; King Crimson or the Ramones or Grandmaster Flash; Metallica, the Supremes, or the Smiths; the Hollies, Nine Inch Nails, or the Go Gos; Nico or Whitney Houston or Joan Jett or Cibo Matto. The names are symbols for groups of collaborators and the works that bear the traces of their creative acts. It is the richness and diversity of expression, and the range of talents and skills involved, that makes rock such a robust idiom. At the same time, it is the willingness of artists to participate in a conventional system, to share common formative resources while molding them to their own ends, aiming their own creative projects at developing a unique resonant space within a definite cultural field, that allows for connections to be made among such disparate artworks. The connections that listeners of all sorts make among records covering an expanse of historical time and stylistic appearance lend strength to the fabric of the overall system. I have stressed that records are first of all about themselves, the physical impressions that they impart. But as they become part of our consciousness and we begin to recognize associations among them, a larger picture emerges. Collectively, records present an image of a cultural practice whose conceptual coherence is assured—once again, for artists and audiences alike—by the shared perception that its works possess the power of resonance. For the culture of rock recording both demands and insures that, in the end, records are about far more than themselves.

Notes

INTRODUCTION

1. See engineer and producer credits at the back of the book for an overview of the records represented.

2. Stephen Blum, "Theory and Method: Analysis of Musical Style," in *Ethnomusicology: An Introduction*, ed. Helen Myers (New York: W. W. Norton, 1992), p. 213.

3. Edward Lippman, *A History of Western Musical Aesthetics* (Lincoln: University of Nebraska Press, 1992).

4. Igor Stravinsky, *Poetics of Music in the Form of Six Lessons* (Cambridge: Harvard University Press, 1974), p. 4. (Emphasis in original.)

1. WRITING RECORDS

Source for chapter epigraph: Susanne Langer, "A Note on the Film," in *Feeling and Form* (New York: Scribner, 1953), p. 411.

1. This characterization is borrowed from the title of Lydia Goehr's *The Imaginary Museum of Musical Works: An Essay in the Philosophy of Music* (Oxford: Clarendon Press, 1992). This title, in turn, is borrowed from Franz Liszt's "On the Position of Artists and Their Place in Society," in which he calls for the "foundation of a musical Museum" dedicated to the performance and preservation of "all the works that are considered best"; in Alan Walker, *Franz Liszt: The Virtuoso Years, 1811–1847* (Ithaca: Cornell University Press, 1987), pp. 159–60.

2. Soon after this recording was made, Germany invaded Austria and the Jewish members of the orchestra were expelled. Walter, who was out of the country at the time, would not see Austria again until after the war.

3. See Robert M. W. Dixon and John Godrich, *Recording the Blues* (New York: Stein and Day, 1970).

4. Douglas Kahn, "Introduction: Histories of Sound Once Removed," in *Wireless Imagination: Sound, Radio, and the Avant-Garde*, ed. Douglas Kahn and Gregory Whitehead (Cambridge: MIT Press, 1992), p. 5.

5. Dziga Vertov, "Speech of 5 April 1935," cited in Seth Feldman, *Evolution of Style in the Early Works of Dziga Vertov* (New York: Arno Press, 1977), p. 13; and in Kahn, "Introduction," p. 10.

6. Laszlo Moholy-Nagy, "Problems of the Modern Film," in *Moholy-Nagy*, ed. Richard Kostelanetz (New York: Praeger, 1970), p. 135.

7. Laszlo Moholy-Nagy, *Vision in Motion* (Chicago: Paul Theobald, 1969), p. 277.

8. Ibid.

9. Igor Stravinsky, *An Autobiography* (New York: Simon and Schuster, 1936), pp. 150–54.

10. Béla Bartók, "Mechanical Music" in *Béla Bartók Essays*, ed. Benjamin Suchoff (Lincoln: University of Nebraska Press, 1976), p. 292.

11. Ibid., p. 298.

12. Kurt Weill, "Radio and the Restructuring of Musical Life," in *Writings of German Composers*, trans. and ed. Michael Gilbert, Jost Hermand, and James Steakly (New York: Continuum, 1984), p. 263.

13. Ibid.

14. Carlos Chavez, *Toward a New Music: Music and Electricity*, trans. Herbert Weinstock (New York: W. W. Norton, 1937), p. 175.

15. Ibid., p. 87.

16. Mezz Mezzrow, with Bernard Wolfe, *Really the Blues* (London: Flamingo, 1993), pp. 325–26.

17. For a study of sound recording's effect on violin performance practice, see Mark Katz, "The Phonograph Effect: The Influence of Recording on Listener, Performer, Composer, 1900–1940" (Ph.D. dissertation: University of Michigan, 1999).

18. Oliver Daniel, *Stokowski: A Counterpoint of Views* (New York: Dodd, Mead and Co., 1982), p. 306.

19. Ibid., p. 309.

20. Ibid., p. 311.

21. See Glenn Gould, "Stokowski in Six Scenes" in *The Glenn Gould Reader*, ed. Tim Page (New York, Alfred A. Knopf, 1984).

22. Glenn Gould, "The Prospects of Recording," in *The Glenn Gould Reader*, pp. 338–39.

23. This account is from a conversation with Gene Paul (September 18, 1996).

24. Mary Alice Schaughnessy, *Les Paul: An American Original* (New York: William Morrow, 1993), p. 181.

25. Bruce Swedien, "Tear Down the Walls," *EQ* (June 1991), p. 40.

26. Mr. Bonzai, "Bruce Swedien: The Master Touch," *Mix* (January 1992), p. 95.

27. Carl Belz, *The Story of Rock* (New York: Oxford University Press, 1969), p. viii.

28. Ibid., p. 46.

29. Charlie Gillett, *The Sound of the City: The Rise of Rock and Roll* (New York: Pantheon Books, 1984).

30. Peter Wicke, *Rock Music: Culture, Aesthetics, and Sociology*, trans. Rachel Fogg (Cambridge: Cambridge University Press, 1990), p. 4.

31. Thodore Gracyk, *Rhythm and Noise: An Aesthetics of Rock* (Durham: Duke University Press, 1996), p. 13.

32. Ibid., p. 52. (Emphasis in original.)

33. Scottie Moore and James Dickerson, *That's Alright, Elvis* (New York: Schirmer Books, 1997), p. 57.

34. Peter Guralnick, *Last Train to Memphis: The Rise of Elvis Presley* (Boston: Little, Brown and Co., 1994), p. 93.

35. Quincy Jones, "Producing Records," in *Making Music: The Guide to Writing, Performing and Recording,* ed. George Martin (London: Pan Books, 1983), p. 286.

36. The tape machine was four-track, but because of the liberal use of track bouncing the project was actually more complex. For a detailed account see George Martin, with William Pearson, *Summer of Love: The Making of Sgt. Pepper* (London: Macmillan, 1994).

37. Ted Fox, *In the Groove: The People behind the Music* (New York: St. Martin's Press, 1986), p. 175.

38. The sonic treatment was not always intentional, but rather, was a matter of contingency. Most early rock and roll records were made under relatively primitive conditions where hi-fi transparency was not possible, even had it been desired.

39. Mark Ribowsky, *He's a Rebel* (New York: E. P. Dutton, 1989), p. 29.

40. George Martin, *All You Need Is Ears* (London: Macmillan, 1979), p. 35.

41. Walter Benjamin, "The Work of Art in the Age of Mechanical Reproduction," in *Illuminations,* trans. Harry Zohn, ed. Hannah Arendt (New York: Schocken Books, 1969), pp. 217–51.

42. Richard Middleton, *Studying Popular Music* (Milton Keynes, U. K.: Open University Press, 1990), p. 65.

43. Benjamin, *Illuminations,* p. 229 footnote: "Luigi Pirandello, *Si Gira,* quoted by Léon Pierre-Quint, 'Signification du cinéma,' *L'Art cinématographique, op. cit.,* pp. 14–15."

44. Langer, "A Note on the Film," p. 413.

45. Fox, *In the Groove,* p. 166.

46. Jones, "Producing Records," p. 286.

47. Ibid.

48. John Pareles and Patricia Romanowski, eds., *The Rolling Stone Encyclopedia of Rock & Roll* (New York: Rolling Stone Press/Summit Books, 1983), p. 322.

49. Belz, *Story of Rock,* p. 46.

50. Gracyk, *Rhythm and Noise,* p. 36.

51. Nelson Goodman, *Languages of Art: An Approach to a Theory of Symbols,* 2nd ed. (New York: Hackett, 1976), pp. 112–13.

52. Ibid., p. 121.

53. Gracyk, *Rhythm and Noise,* p. 32.

54. Ibid.

55. Larry the O, "To Sir with Love: Conversations with and about Sir George Martin," *Electronic Musician* (February 1999), p. 60.

56. Fox, *In the Groove,* p. 334.

57. Robert L. Doerschuk, "Twelve Who Count: Brian Eno," *Keyboard* (March 1995), p. 51.
  58. Langer, "A Note on the Film," pp. 412–13.

2. TRACKS

Source for chapter epigraph: David Leaf, *Pet Sounds* CD booklet (Capitol, 1990), p. 21.
  1. Edward Jablonski and Lawrence D. Stewart, *The Gershwin Years: George and Ira* (New York: Da Capo Press, 1996), pp. 293–94.
  2. Sting, "Songwriting," in *Making Music: The Guide to Writing, Performing and Recording*, ed. George Martin (London: Pan Books, 1983), p. 72.
  3. Many songwriters and music publishers had offices in the Brill Building at 1619 Broadway and across the street at 1650 Broadway in New York City. During the late 1950s and early 1960s, numerous pop hits were written here by songwriting teams such as Gerry Goffin and Carole King ("Will You Still Love Me Tomorrow?"), Doc Pomus and Mort Schuman ("Save the Last Dance for Me"), Jeff Barry and Ellie Greenwich ("Be My Baby"), and Barry Mann and Cynthia Weil ("You've Lost that Lovin' Feelin'")."Tin Pan Alley" is also a reference to a concentration of New York songwriters and music publishers. However, the "Alley" was more a concept than a place. In the 1890s it moved from East 14th Street to West 28th Street, and then between the World Wars, to a group of buildings on Broadway around West 50th Street including the Brill Building. Some of the most famous songwriters associated with the Tin Pan Alley tag were George Gershwin, Irving Berlin, Jerome Kern, and Richard Rodgers.
  4. Iain Blair, "Rick Rubin: Forever Def," *Mix* (January, 1992), p. 148. Rubin is speaking here of the Red Hot Chili Peppers' *Blood Sugar Sex Magik* album (1991), for which seven months were spent in pre-production. His input as a producer for Tom Petty, whose *Wildflowers* (1994) was recorded in bits and pieces over a two-year period, was quite different. I have more to say about the pre-production process of *Blood Sugar Sex Magik* in later chapters.
  5. Paula Parisi, "Steve Lillywhite: From Ultravox to the Stones," *Mix* (May 1986), p. 115.
  6. Camran Afsari, "John Leckie: From Abbey Road to the Stone Roses," *Mix* (January 1993), p. 62.
  7. Mr. Bonzai, "Lindsey Buckingham: Endlessly Rocking," *Mix* (September 1992), p. 48.
  8. Ibid., p. 47.
  9. David Leaf, *The Beach Boys* (Philadelphia: Courage Books, 1985), p. 78.
  10. Leaf, *Pet Sounds* CD booklet, p. 8.
  11. Michael Molenda, "Production Values: Audio Visionary," *Electronic Musician* (October 1995), p. 42.
  12. Blair Jackson, "Producer Chris Thomas: Three Decades on the Cutting Edge and the Charts," *Mix* (January 1999), p. 36.

13. Bill Flanagan, *U2 at the End of the World* (New York: Delacorte Press, 1995), p. 183.

14. Dominic Milano, "Peter Gabriel: Identity," *Keyboard* (October 1989), p. 44.

15. Richard Buskin, "Digging Deep with Peter Gabriel," *Mix* (March 1993), p. 44.

16. Milano, "Peter Gabriel," p. 44.

17. Ibid.

18. Buskin, "Digging Deep with Peter Gabriel," p. 45.

19. Ibid., p. 47.

20. Mr. Bonzai, "Hugh Padgham: Studio Synchronicity," *Mix* (October 1990), p. 84.

21. Michael Molenda, "Production Values: Listen to the Music," *Electronic Musician* (April 1996), p. 69.

22. Ruth Finnegan, *The Hidden Musicians: Music-Making in an English Town* (Cambridge: Cambridge University Press, 1989), pp. 160–79.

23. Blair Jackson, "Los Lobos Paint Their Masterpiece," *Mix* (October 1992), p. 202.

24. Mark Lewisohn, *The Beatles Recording Sessions* (New York: Harmony Books, 1988), p. 59.

25. Martin, *All You Need Is Ears*, pp. 199–200. A mono mix of this version can be heard on *The Beatles Anthology*, vol. 2 (Capitol, 1996).

26. This effect is created by recording with the tape running backwards. When the resulting recording is played back normally, the recorded sound's envelope is reversed.

27. Martin, *All You Need Is Ears*, p. 200.

28. Walter Everett, *The Beatles as Musicians: Revolver through the Anthology* (New York: Oxford University Press, 1999), pp. 79–80.

29. Blair Jackson, "Karl Wallinger: Still Hosting His World Party," *Mix* (November 1997), p. 183.

30. Erwin Panofsky, *Meaning in the Visual Arts* (Garden City, N.Y.: Doubleday Anchor Books, 1955), p. 22.

31. Lippman, *A History of Western Musical Aesthetics*, p. 24.

32. Goehr, *Imaginary Museum of Musical Works*, p. 218.

33. E. T. A. Hoffman, "Beethoven's Instrumental Music," in *Source Readings in Music History*, sel. and annot. Oliver Strunk (New York: W. W. Norton, 1950), p. 775.

34. Ibid., p. 777.

35. G. W. F. Hegel, "Aesthetik," in *Werke (Jubiläumsausgabe)*. Excerpted in "Georg Wilhelm Friedrich Hegel," in *Music and Aesthetics in the Eighteenth and Early-Nineteenth Centuries*, trans. and ed. Peter le Huray and James Day (Cambridge: Cambridge University Press, 1981), p. 343. (Emphasis in original.)

36. Eduard Hanslick, *On the Musically Beautiful: A Contribution towards the Revision of the Aesthetics of Music*, trans. and ed. Geoffrey Payzant (Indianapolis: Hackett, 1986), p. 78.

37. Carl Dahlhaus, *Nineteenth-Century Music*, trans. J. Bradford Robinson (Berkeley: University of California Press, 1989), p. 10.

38. Ibid.

39. Arnold Schoenberg, "New Music, Outmoded Music, Style and Idea," in *Style and Idea: Selected Writings of Arnold Schoenberg*, trans. Leo Black, ed. Leonard Stein (New York: St. Martin's Press, 1975), pp. 113–24; Charles E. Ives, "Essays before a Sonata," in *Essays before a Sonata, The Majority, and other writings of Charles Ives*, ed. Howard Boatwright (New York: W. W. Norton, 1970).

40. Ives, "Essays before a Sonata," p. 84. (Emphasis in original.)

41. Benjamin Boretz, "Nelson Goodman's *Languages of Art* from a Musical Point of View," in *Perspectives on Contemporary Music Theory*, ed. Benjamin Boretz and Edward T. Cone (New York: W. W. Norton, 1972), p. 41.

42. Regarding the matter, Kendall Walton has written: "One of the most fundamental questions of musical aesthetics is this: Which is of primary importance, musical works (symphonies, songs, sonatas, etc.) or performances of musical works? Are works or performances the basic objects of musical attention, musical appreciation, and musical judgment?" He stresses in a footnote that the question as he sees it has to do with how the two are regarded in "our cultural institution of music," among "composers, performers, and appreciators. Neither works nor performances are *intrinsically* primary, apart from their place in some cultural institution." Kendall L. Walton, "The Presentation and Portrayal of Sound Patterns," in *Human Agency: Language, Duty, and Value*, ed. Jonathan Dancy, J. M. E. Moravcsik, and C. C. W. Taylor (Stanford: Stanford University Press, 1988), p. 237. See also: Goodman, *Languages of Art*; Roman Ingarden, *The Work of Music and the Problem of Its Identity*, trans. A. Czerniawski (Berkeley: University of California Press, 1986).

43. Boretz, "Nelson Goodman's *Languages of Art*," p. 34.

44. Roger Reynolds, "Thoughts on What a Record Records," in *The Phonograph and Our Musical Life*, ed. H. Wiley Hitchcock (Brooklyn: Institute for Studies in American Music, 1980), pp. 28–36.

45. Milton Babbitt, *Milton Babbitt: Words about Music*, ed. Stephen Dembski and Joseph N. Straus (Madison: University of Wisconsin Press, 1987), p. 181.

46. Goehr, *Imaginary Museum of Musical Works*, p. 206.

47. Middleton, *Studying Popular Music*, p. 83.

48. Simon Frith, "Try to Dig What We All Say," *The Listener* (June 26, 1980), p. 882; cited in Paul Clarke, " 'A Magic Science': Rock Music as a Recording Art," *Popular Music* 3 (1983), p. 205.

49. Susan Sontag, "Against Interpretation," in *Against Interpretation and Other Essays* (New York: Doubleday Anchor Books, 1990). All subsequent citations of Sontag are taken from this essay.

50. Leo Treitler, "Medieval Improvisation," *The World of Music* 3 (1991), p. 67.

51. Hanslick, *On the Musically Beautiful*, p. 80.

52. Ibid., p. 81. It should be pointed out that Hanslick's conception of sound is complex. Failure to acknowledge the "beauty residing in the purely musical" is a result of "the undervaluation of the sensuous." But by sensuous he does not mean the physical only. "The auditory imagination . . . which is something entirely different from the sense of hearing regarded as a mere funnel open to the surface of appearances, enjoys in conscious sensuousness the sounding shapes, the self-constructing tones, and dwells in free and immediate contemplation of them" (29–30).

53. Ibid., p. 29.

54. Ibid., p. 83.

55. Hanslick criticizes, for example, the notion that the "content of the theme is the series of intervals as such," for "this is not a musical determination but an abstraction" (81). And with regard to autonomy: "Even though aesthetical investigation must stick to the artwork itself, this autonomous artwork turns out to be in fact an efficacious mediator between two kinetic powers, its whence and its whither, i.e., the composer and the hearer. In the psyches of these two, the artistic activity of the imagination cannot be extracted as pure metal in such a way as to be deposited in the complete, objective work. Rather, it operates in their psyches always in close interrelation with feeling and sensation. Thus the feelings will retain a significance, before and after completion of the work, first in the composer and then in the hearer, from which we cannot withhold consideration" (45).

Also, Hanslick did not deny the ability of music to evoke emotions or images—as it did, in fact in his own critical writing. For example, writing about Bach's *St. Matthew Passion:* "In the first chorus . . . we have a polyphonic wonder whose enormous craftsmanship one admires without being oppressed or overwhelmed by it. . . . One can imagine no more majestic portal to the Gothic cathedral, with which the *St. Matthew Passion* is so often— and correctly—compared. . . . Can anyone have failed to notice the inspired device of surrounding every utterance of Christ with long-sustained tones of the violin, as if to suggest a transfiguring light, or halo . . . ." Eduard Hanslick, *Hanslick's Music Criticisms*, trans. and ed. Henry Pleasants (New York: Dover, 1950), pp. 96–97.

56. H. Stith Bennett, *On Becoming a Rock Musician* (Amherst: University of Massachusetts Press, 1980), p. 119. This refers to the various perspectives provided by multiple microphones, each presenting a separate acoustic point of view.

3. SOUND AS FORM

Sources for chapter epigraphs: Page 48: Richard Buskin, "Jerry Wexler: Atlantic Adventure," *Studio Sound* (April 1999), p. 58. Page 85: Alan di Perna, "Ed Cherney: Capturing Musical Dialogs," *Mix* (September 1991), p. 86.

1. Dylan's often-cited characterization is from a January 1978 *Playboy* interview conducted by Ron Rosenbaum: "The closest I ever got to the

sound I hear in my mind was on individual bands in the *Blonde on Blonde* album. It's that thin, that wild mercury sound. It's metallic and bright gold, with whatever that conjures up. That's my particular sound. I haven't been able to succeed in getting it all the time."

2. Roger Sessions, *The Musical Experience of Composer, Performer, Listener* (Princeton: Princeton University Press, 1974), pp. 70–71.

3. Leo Sacks, *The Best of Wilson Pickett* CD booklet (Rhino, 1992), p. 4.

4. Blair Jackson, "Imagine There's a Box Set: Rob Stevens on Assembling *The John Lennon Box Set*," *Mix* (Feb. 1999), p. 222.

5. Billy Gibbons: "I gotta hand it to that Mark Knopfler for the 'Money for Nothing' number on that last Dire Straits album. That guy must have called me three or four times to find out what I did with my guitar so that he could copy it for that song. . . . He didn't do a half-bad job, either, considering that I never told him a goddamned thing." Timothy White, "ZZ Top: The Ongoing Legend of Texan Rock's Rough Boys," *Musician* (January 1986), p. 65.

6. Jon Fitzgerald, "Motown Crossover Hits 1963–1966 and the Creative Process," *Popular Music* (January 1995), pp. 2–3.

7. Rick Clark, "Emmylou Harris: The Making of *Wrecking Ball*," *Mix* (February 1996), p. 184 (emphasis added). "Bleeding into the microphone" refers to leakage of the sound from one instrument into the microphone of another.

8. Ibid.

9. Paul Tingen, "Mitchell Froom," *Keyboard* (April 1993), p. 44.

10. Buskin, "Digging Deep with Peter Gabriel," p. 48.

11. This analytic breakdown of performances is a basic principle underlying computer-based sequencers. They record no sound at all, only performance data. All performance parameters—pitch, attack, duration, dynamics, pedaling, pitch bend, and so forth—are automatically recorded separately and can therefore be edited individually.

12. E.g., "Free As a Bird" (*The Beatles Anthology*, vol. 1, Capitol, 1995), where Paul McCartney, George Harrison, and Ringo Starr created a new Beatles track using John Lennon demos as a foundation.

13. Bill Milkowski, "Roy Halee: Capturing *The Rhythm of the Saints*," *Mix* (October 1990), p. 58.

14. Dan Daley, "Lou Reed Acquits Himself Well with *Mistrial*," *Mix* (October 1986), pp. 112–13.

15. Blair Jackson, "Digital Signal Processing at the Top of the Charts," *Mix* (March 1992), p. 37.

16. Mark Ribowsky, *He's a Rebel*, p. 93. (Emphasis in original.)

17. Ibid.

18. Ibid., p. 123.

19. Ibid., p. 255.

20. Steve La Cerra, "Bonnie Raitt's 'Sneakin' Up on You,'" *EQ* (May 1995), p. 36.

21. Milano, "Peter Gabriel," p. 36.

22. Dan Daley, "Russ Titelman: Production as Destiny," *Mix* (June 1986), p. 38.

23. Robert Walser, *Running with the Devil: Power, Gender, and Madness in Heavy Metal Music* (Hanover, N.H.: University Press of New England, 1993), p. 41.

24. Afsari, "John Leckie," p. 62.

25. The organ's thematic importance has been noted by Greil Marcus: "Garth Hudson's satanic organ playing . . . is the key to 'Chest Fever'—the words couldn't be, no one has ever deciphered them anyway." Greil Marcus, *Mystery Train: Images of America in Rock 'n' Roll Music* (New York: E. P. Dutton, 1976), p. 55.

26. Of "Mr. Tambourine Man," David Fricke has written: "There are few sounds in rock & roll as immediately recognizable, physically exhilarating and historically pivotal as the opening guitar riff on the Byrds' 1965 debut single, 'Mr. Tambourine Man.' The riff itself . . . was quite unusual. . . . But the actual *sound* of it—the clarion churchbell ring of Roger McGuinn's electric 12-string Rickenbacker, glistening with harmonic overtones—was something else again, a bracing guitar *reveille* for a brand new rock & roll day." David Fricke, "An Historical Essay," in the CD booklet accompanying *The Byrds* boxed set (Columbia, 1990), p. 14.

27. Luciano Berio, "Commenti al Rock," *Nuova rivista musicale italiana* 1 (May/June 1967), p. 130: "Quando con le chitarre elettriche (o al loro posto) vengono usati strumenti come la tromba, il clavicembalo, il quartetto d'archi, il flauto dritto ecc. (quasi mai il pianoforte), essi sembrano assumere il carattere straniato di una citazione di se stessi."

28. Ibid., p. 132: "Alcuni pezzi, infine (soprattutto quelli registrati), propongono un superamento dell'idea stessa di *song*, sviluppando una sorta di dramaturgia sonora fatta di frammenti di dialogo, di montaggi, sovrapposizioni di registrazioni diverse e di qualche manipolazione elettro-acustica: in questi casi la forma è il *collage*. Quei pezzi dei Rolling Stones, dei Tops, dei Mothers of Invention, dei Grateful Dead e, soprattutto, dei Beatles, che sono particolarmente legati alle tecniche di studio, sono praticamente ineseguibili dal vivo. Queste manipolazioni, proposte per la prima volta dai Beatles, evitano gli effetti e le trovatine sonore: il richiamo surrealista è ovvio.

"Quando un gruppo *rock* usa altri strumenti oltre alle chitarre, la batteria e l'organo elettrico, lo fa senza troppi compromessi: gli strumenti 'extra' vengono adoperati come oggetti puliti, come se venissero da lontano, in un modo, tutto sommato, che suggerisce l'utopia del 'ritorno alle origini'." (Emphasis in original.)

29. Lewisohn, *The Beatles Recording Sessions*, p. 59.

30. Martin, *All You Need Is Ears*, p. 167.

31. Ibid., p. 76.

32. Bruce Swedien, "Foreword" to *Music Producers: Conversations with Today's Top Record Makers*, ed. Terri Stone (Winona, Minn.: Hal Leonard, 1992), p. v.

33. David P. Szatmary, *Rockin' in Time: A Social History of Rock-and-Roll*, 3d ed. (Upper Saddle River, N.J.: Prentice Hall, 1996), p. 256.

34. Lewisohn, *The Beatles Recording Sessions*, p. 11. (Emphasis in original.)

35. Richard Buskin, "Use It or Abuse It," *Studio Sound* (March 1997), p. 61.

36. Mark Cunningham, *Good Vibrations: A History of Record Production* (London: Sanctuary Publishing, 1998), p. 273.

37. Rick Clark, "Radical Recording: Creative Chaos in the Control Room," *Mix* (May 1998), p. 38.

38. Eric Olsen, with Paul Verna and Carlo Wolff, *The Encyclopedia of Record Producers* (New York: Billboard Books, 1999), p. 128.

39. E.g., "Puddin' and Tain'" (1962), "(Today I Met) The Boy I'm Gonna Marry" (1963), "Fine Fine Boy" (1963).

40. This track is also the subject of a recent essay by Susan Fast. See: "Music, Contexts, and Meaning in U2," in *Expression in Pop-Rock Music: A Collection of Critical and Analytical Essays*, ed. Walter Everett (New York: Garland Publishing, 2000).

41. Eric Tamm, *Brian Eno: His Music and the Vertical Color of Sound* (Boston: Faber and Faber, 1989), p. 64.

42. Ibid., p. 173. Eno chose the term "ambient" to refer to a group of his instrumental pieces favoring minimal musical syntactical content and presented in a slowly unfolding soundscape (e.g., *Discreet Music, Music for Airports*).

43. Guralnick, *Last Train to Memphis*, pp. 235–39.

44. Lewisohn, *The Beatles Recording Sessions*, p. 74.

45. See Paul Théberge, *Any Sound You Can Imagine: Making Music/Consuming Technology* (Hanover, N.H.: University Press of New England, 1997); and Steve Jones, *Rock Formation: Music, Technology, and Mass Communication* (Newbury Park, Calif.: Sage Publications, 1992).

46. Clark, "Radical Recording," p. 36.

47. Blair Jackson, "Classic Tracks: David Bowie's 'Heroes,' " *Mix* (February 1997), p. 162.

48. The further away the microphone is placed from the sound source, the more room sound it will capture. Also, microphones have different directional patterns that affect their response to room ambience. For more on this, see chapter 4.

49. Mr. Bonzai, "Lunching with Bonzai: Jack Nitzsche," *Mix* (January 1987), p. 38.

50. Ribowsky, *He's a Rebel*, p. 44.

51. Ibid., pp. 185–86.

52. Lewisohn, *The Beatles Recording Sessions*, p. 15.

53. Ibid.

54. Cunningham, *Good Vibrations*, p. 323.

55. Paula Parisi, "Steve Lillywhite," *Mix* (May 1986), p. 114.

56. Pareles and Romanowski, *Rolling Stone Encyclopedia*, p. 510.

57. Dan Daley, "KRS-One—He's Fresh. Word!" *Mix* (October 1989), p. 76.

58. Mr. Bonzai, "Red Hot Chili Peppers: Some Like It Hotter," *Mix* (October 1991), p. 114.

59. Blair, "Rick Rubin," p. 150.

60. Robert Erickson, *Sound Structure in Music* (Berkeley: University of California Press, 1975), p. 139.

61. Richard Williams, *Out of His Head: The Sound of Phil Spector* (New York: Outerbridge and Lazard, 1972), p. 164.

62. Brian Wilson, with Todd Gold, *Wouldn't It Be Nice: My Own Story* (New York: Harper Collins, 1991), p. 82.

63. Leaf, *Pet Sounds* CD booklet, p. 21.

64. Wilson has said of Spector's influence: "I think that he was there just to let me know how to create a record." From David Leaf's interview with Brian Wilson in the CD booklet, *The Making of Pet Sounds* (p. 10), which accompanies *The Beach Boys: The Pet Sounds Sessions* (Capitol, 1996).

65. *Pet Sounds* repaid the Beatles' influence on Wilson. Impressed by the consistent quality and variety of the tracks on the Beatles' *Rubber Soul*, he wanted to move beyond singles and surf music toward "a new type of sophisticated-feeling music" (Leaf, *Pet Sounds* CD booklet, p. 5) and an expressive statement that spanned an entire album. In a 1990 interview, McCartney testified to Wilson's success: "It was *Pet Sounds* that blew me out of the water. I love the album so much. I've just bought my kids a copy of it for their education in life ... I figure no one is educated musically 'til they've heard that album ... I love the orchestra, the arrangements ... it may be going overboard to say it's the classic of this century ... but to me, it is a total, classic record that is unbeatable in many ways ... I've often played *Pet Sounds* and cried." (David Leaf, *Good Vibrations: Thirty Years of the Beach Boys* CD booklet [Capitol, 1993], p. 36) Moreover, the timing of the release of *Pet Sounds* (May 1966) ties it to *Sgt. Pepper's*. McCartney listened to *Pet Sounds* a great deal during the months leading up to the *Sgt. Pepper's* sessions and has credited it as his "inspiration for making *Sgt. Pepper's* ... the big influence" (Leaf, *Pet Sounds*, pp. 20–21). As far as the Beatles' other principal songwriter, John Lennon, is concerned, McCartney says, "I played it to John so much that it would be difficult for him to escape the influence ... It was the record of the time" (Leaf, *Good Vibrations*, p. 36).

66. Wilson, *Wouldn't It Be Nice*, p. 139.

67. Working versions and alternate mixes can be heard on *The Pet Sounds Sessions*.

68. By setting the balance control hard left or hard right, each of the two guitars can be heard on its own.

69. Nirvana's first hit, "Smells Like Teen Spirit," is a paradigmatic example, but think also of Led Zeppelin's "Ramble On" (1969) or the Beach Boys' "Good Vibrations."

70. Frank Zappa, with Peter Occhiogrosso, *The Real Frank Zappa Book* (New York: Poseidon Press, 1989), p. 188. (Emphasis in original.)

4. PLACES AND TOOLS

Source for chapter epigraph: Page 119: Doerschuk, "Twelve Who Count: Brian Eno," p. 51.

1. For an account of technical pre-production for *Set the Twilight Reeling,* see Bob Ludwig, "True Lou," *EQ* (April 1996), pp. 66–78, 123. This is an interview with Reed and engineer Steve Rosenthal conducted by one of the world's foremost mastering engineers, Bob Ludwig.

2. Robyn Flans, "The Tractors: A Fresh Breeze from Tulsa," *Mix* (March 1999), p. 179.

3. Jackson, "Los Lobos Paint Their Masterpiece," p. 202.

4. Ibid., p. 203.

5. The unusual character of the album's sonic textures was noted by many critics at the time. David Okamoto, for one, wrote in his June 25, 1992 *Rolling Stone* review: "[*Kiko*] sets tales of hope and despair against rhythmic backdrops spiked with feedback, distortion, sound bites, and other studio shenanigans that defy roots rock tradition" (41).

6. Ribowsky, *He's a Rebel,* p. 88.

7. Lewisohn, *The Beatles Recording Sessions,* p. 11.

8. John La Grou, "Recording the Acoustic Guitar: Tips from Top Engineers," *Mix* (June 1993), p. 56.

9. Ribowsky, *He's a Rebel,* p. 246.

10. Ibid.

11. The Led Zeppelin album is untitled but is often referred to as "the Runes album" or "Zoso."

12. Bill Milkowsky, "Understanding Bill Laswell," *Mix* (August 1986), p. 117.

13. Robert Pruter, *Doowop: The Chicago Scene* (Urbana: University of Illinois Press, 1996), pp. 16–17.

14. Jerry Hopkins, *Elvis: a Biography* (New York: Simon and Schuster, 1971), p. 120.

15. Barbara Schultz, "The Ramones' 'Teenage Lobotomy,' " *Mix* (June 1998), p. 201.

16. Iain Blair, "Daniel Lanois: Sonic Atmospheres," *Mix* (February 1990), p. 77.

17. Ibid., p. 82.

18. Rick Clark, "Brian Ahern," *Mix* (July 1996), p. 114.

19. Rick Clark, "Getting That Great Drum Sound: Advice from Both Sides of the Glass," *Mix* (June 1996), p. 55.

20. Blair Jackson, "Buddy Holly's 'Not Fade Away,'" *Mix* (April 1996), pp. 202, 212–16.

21. Peter Guralnick, *Lost Highway: Journeys and Arrivals of American Musicians* (New York, Harper and Row, 1989), p. 134.

22. Rob Bowman, "The Stax Sound: A Musicological Analysis," *Popular Music* (Fall 1995), p. 309.

23. In addition to Muscle Shoals, the immediate area includes the towns

of Sheffield, Tuscumbia, and Florence. The region is commonly referred to simply as Muscle Shoals.

24. Fox, *In the Groove*, p. 137.

25. Ibid.

26. Chip Stern, "The Serious Metafoolishness of Father Funkadelic, George Clinton," in *The Rock Musician*, ed. Tony Scherman (New York: St. Martin's Press, 1994), p. 9.

27. Malcolm Chisholm, "How to Design and Construct a Modern Control Room," *Mix* (August 1992), p. 52.

28. Larry Todd, "Reflecting on Studio Acoustics: Peter D'Antonio," *Mix* (October 1991), p. 75.

29. Chisholm, "How to Design," p. 52.

30. Bonzai, "Red Hot Chili Peppers," p. 105.

31. Ibid., p. 114.

32. Early on in this two-year period, The Band spent several months playing with Dylan, whom they had earlier backed up on his last world tour before his motorcycle accident and subsequent seclusion in Woodstock. The recordings of a small portion of these informal jam sessions were eventually released in 1975 on *The Basement Tapes*. Of these sessions Dylan told *Rolling Stone* interviewer Jan Wenner, "You know, that's really the way to do a recording—in a peaceful, relaxed setting, in somebody's basement, with the windows open and a dog lying on the floor." Jan Wenner, "Bob Dylan," in *The Rolling Stone Interviews* (New York: Warner Paperback Library, 1971), 1:302.

33. Barney Hoskyns, *Across the Great Divide: The Band and America* (New York: Hyperion, 1993), p. 180.

34. Ibid., p. 176.

35. Ibid., p. 180.

36. Ibid., p. 178.

37. Blair Jackson, "Tom Lord-Alge: The Grammy-Winning Engineer/Producer Is on a Roll," *Mix* (May 1989), p. 56.

38. Stephen Dark, "That Which Cannot Be Spoken: Divining the Heavenly Sound of Cocteau Twins," *Option* (May/June 1987), p. 32, cited in Jones, *Rock Formation*.

39. Michael Molenda, "Audio Visionary," *Electronic Musician* (October 1995), p. 45.

40. Roland Barthes, "The Grain of the Voice," in *Image, Music, Text* (New York: Hill and Wang, 1977), pp. 179–89.

41. John Woram, *Sound Recording Handbook* (Indianapolis: Howard W. Sams, 1989), p. 61.

42. Mr. Bonzai, "Stephen Paul: Microphone Doctor," *Mix* (April 1987), p. 47.

43. Ibid., p. 53.

44. Steve Albini, "The Secret to Miking Guitar Amps," *EQ* (August 1994), p. 36.

45. Ibid.

46. Swedien, "Tear Down the Walls," p. 38.

47. Bonzai, "Hugh Padgham," p. 84.

48. Blair, "Daniel Lanois," p. 80.

49. Clark, "Emmylou Harris," p. 184.

50. Rick Clark, "Mixing It Up with Analog and Digital," *Mix* (June 1995), p. 32.

51. Bob Clearmountain and Robbie Robertson, "A Conversation about Destroying the Myths of Digital Recording," *Mix* (July 1992), p. 83.

52. "National Academy of Recording Arts and Sciences (NARAS) Roundtable: Modern Recording and Production Techniques," from the September, 1990 Audio Engineering Society Convention, excerpted in *Mix* (February 1991), p. 64.

53. Godfrey Cheshire, "Don Dixon: Southern Indie Roots," *Mix* (June 1991), p. 55.

54. Clearmountain and Robertson, "Myths of Digital Recording," p. 81.

55. "NARAS Roundtable," p. 65.

56. Ibid., p. 66.

57. Clearmountain and Robertson, "Myths of Digital Recording," p. 86.

58. Ibid., p. 84.

59. Ibid., p. 86.

60. Clark, "Mixing It Up," p. 34.

61. Ibid., pp. 34, 37.

62. Ibid., p. 37.

63. Cited in Oliver Read and Walter L. Welch, *From Tin Foil to Stereo: Evolution of the Phonograph* (Indianapolis: Howard W. Sams, 1959), pp. 385–86.

64. Sarah Jones, "The Dream Machine: Grammy Nominees Speak Out on Reference Monitors," *Mix* (April 1996), p. 36.

65. Ibid., p. 30.

66. Brian Eno, "The Studio as Compositional Tool—Part II," *Down Beat* (August 1983), p. 52.

67. George Petersen, "Point of Reference: Engineers and Producers Speak Out on Small Monitors," *Mix* (February 1987), p. 24.

68. Sarah Jones, "The Dream Machine," p. 36.

69. Mel Lambert, "George Massenburg: Pro Audio Innovator," *Mix* (October 1997), p. 36.

70. Rick Clark, "Mixing Forum: Four Top Professionals Talk Gear and Techniques," *Mix* (May 1997), p. 50.

71. Steve La Cerra, "Butch Vig: Garbage Man," *EQ* (September 1997), p. 74.

72. Bobby Owsinski, "You Don't Know Jack," *EQ* (May 1996), p. 55.

73. Clark, "Mixing It Up," p. 37. (Emphasis in original.)

74. Bob Doerschuk, "In Control with Jam & Lewis Engineer Steve Hodge," *Keyboard* (May 1987), p. 76.

75. Clark, "Emmylou Harris," p. 184.

76. Rick Clark, "Creative Compression: Pushing the Envelope," *Mix* (January 1998), p. 58.

77. See, for example, Rick Clark, "Production Sickness Secrets Revealed," *Mix* (September 1995), pp. 30–44; Maureen Droney, "Radical Recording '99: From Retro to Destructo," *Mix* (July 1999), pp. 31–42.

5. TRACKING AND MIXING

1. Jackson, "Tom Lord-Alge," p. 59.

2. Aaron Copland, "The Sonorous Image," in *Music and Imagination* (Cambridge: Harvard University Press, 1952), p. 21.

3. Jackson, "Karl Wallinger," p. 105.

4. Adam Beyda and Anne Eickelberg, "Pell Mell: The Tchad Blake Way to *Star City*," *Mix* (May 1998), p. 202.

5. Ibid., p. 204.

6. Maureen Droney, "Mike Shipley: Having Too Much Fun to Stop," *Mix* (June 1999), p. 78.

7. Alternate or preliminary mixes have become a fertile source for sketch studies. See, for example, Everett, *The Beatles as Musicians*.

8. Evan Eisenberg, *The Recording Angel: Explorations in Phonography* (New York: McGraw-Hill, 1987), p. 109.

9. Paul F. Berliner, *Thinking in Jazz: The Infinite Art of Improvisation* (Chicago: University of Chicago Press, 1994).

10. Dave Marsh, *Glory Days: Bruce Springsteen in the 1980s* (New York: Pantheon Books, 1987), p. 121. (Emphasis in original.)

11. Blair Jackson, "An Invitation to Karl Wallinger's World Party," *Mix* (June 1993), p. 113.

12. Paul Clarke, " 'A Magic Science': Rock Music as a Recording Art," *Popular Music* 3 (1983), p. 201.

13. Marcus, *Mystery Train*, p. 173. Marcus's impressions are based upon the account in Hopkins, *Elvis*.

14. Hopkins, *Elvis*, p. 117.

15. Guralnick, *Last Train to Memphis*, p. 132.

16. John Pugh, interview with Phillips, *Country Music* (November 1973); cited in Marcus, *Mystery Train*, p. 168.

17. Ellis Amburn, *Dark Star: The Roy Orbison Story* (New York: Carol Publishing Group, 1990), p. 47. (Emphasis added.)

18. Milano, "Peter Gabriel."

19. Jackson, "Tom Lord-Alge," p. 60.

20. Thomas Dolby, for one, has spoken of his preference for developing tracks starting with nothing more than a song title: "My songs usually start with a title, often a title that is memorable and suggestive enough that the music and the rest of the words follow on . . . 'Airwaves,' 'One of Our Submarines,' 'Mulu the Rain Forest,' 'Screen Kiss.' Then there follows this strange exploration of the mystery that the title conjures up. For example on 'Mulu' I started with a rhythm made up of tsikada insects and trees falling

down in a jungle, then blew over the top of a milk bottle to make a Fairlight [digital sampler] pan pipe sound and found a melody. As I hummed along, words started to form which often tied in with the subject—'dreamtime/ faultline,' 'warming/morning dew/Mulu,' etc. It's all about atmosphere, really. I just try to climb inside my subject and squeeze out every drop of detail that adds to it, until one night I can sit back and listen and know it's all there, and then I mix it . . . which I suppose is not much more than the art of making all those impressions onto a piece of half-inch tape." Craig Anderton, "Thomas Dolby," *Electronic Musician* (June 1986), pp. 56–57.

21. Brian Eno, "The Studio as Compositional Tool—Part I," *Down Beat* (July 1983), p. 57.

22. Nicholas Schaffner, *Saucerful of Secrets: The Pink Floyd Odyssey* (New York: Harmony Books, 1991), p. 164.

23. Tom Moon, "Public Enemy's Bomb Squad," *Musician* (October 1991), pp. 69–70.

24. Mary Cosola, "A Day in the Life: House Party," *Electronic Musician* (April 1995), p. 71.

25. Afsari, "John Leckie," p. 58.

26. Fred Schruers, "Tom Petty: On the Road," *Rolling Stone* (May 4, 1995), p. 52.

27. Greg Rule, "William Orbit: The Methods and Machinery behind Madonna's *Ray of Light,*" *Keyboard* (July 1998), p. 38.

28. Ibid., p. 34.

29. Flanagan, *U2 at the End of the World,* pp. 195–96.

30. Maureen Droney, "Kevin Killen: On Recording Peter Gabriel, Elvis Costello and More," *Mix* (May 1999), p. 130.

31. Blair, "Rick Rubin," p. 148.

32. The quotes from Anthony Kiedis and Flea were taken from a Warner Brothers website (www.wbr.com/chilipeppers/chilibio.htm) on May 26, 1998.

33. Blair, "Rick Rubin," p. 148.

34. Iain Blair, "Tom Petty's Solo Fever," *Mix* (October 1989), pp. 185–6

35. Iain Blair, "Dave Edmunds: Back to Basics," *Mix* (June 1990), pp. 85–6.

36. Marsh, *Glory Days,* p. 113.

37. Ibid., p. 115.

38. Ibid., p. 120.

39. Ibid., p. 123.

40. Sergei Eisenstein, "The Cinematographic Principle and the Ideogram," in *Film Form: Essays in Film Theory,* trans. and ed. Jay Leyda (San Diego: Harcourt Brace Jovanovich, 1949).

41. John Harrington, *The Rhetoric of Film* (New York: Holt, Rinehart and Winston, 1973), p. 25.

42. Brian Knave and Michael Molenda, "The Sophisticated Mix," *Electronic Musician* (April 1996), p. 64.

43. Clark, "Mixing Forum," p. 46.

44. Robin Tolleson, "Arif Mardin," *Mix* (February 1987), p. 36.

45. Maureen Droney, "Mix Masters: Tom Lord-Alge," *Mix* (January 1998), p. 92.

46. Ibid., p. 235.

47. Glen Ballou, ed., *Handbook for Sound Engineers: The New Audio Cyclopedia*, 2nd ed. (Carmel, Minn.: SAMS, 1991), p. 1158. Massenburg's description has something in common with the analytic frame posited by Allan Moore in his formulation of the "sound-box." See: Allan F. Moore, *Rock, The Primary Text: Developing a Musicology of Rock* (Milton Keynes, U. K.: Open University Press, 1993), pp. 104–10.

48. This characterization is based on the 1994 compact disc version, which producer Jimmy Page remastered from the original tapes. The general effect is the same on the original LP version, but there are differences in some of the details.

49. Andre Millard, *America on Record: A History of Recorded Sound* (Cambridge: Cambridge University Press, 1995), p. 224.

50. Spector's first stereo recording was "Black Pearl" (1969) by Sonny Charles and the Checkmates.

51. Leaf, *Good Vibrations* CD booklet, p. 30.

52. Lewisohn, *The Beatles Recording Sessions*, p. 69.

53. Everett, *The Beatles as Musicians*, p. 117.

54. Clark, "Mixing Forum," p. 48.

55. Maureen Droney, "Dave Way: Mixer on a Hot Streak," *Mix* (April 2000), p. 44.

56. Mark Dery and Bob Doerschuk, "Drum Some Kill: The Beat behind the Rap," *Keyboard* (November 1988), pp. 34–35.

57. Ibid.

58. Daley, "KRS-One," p. 77.

59. Iggy Pop interview conducted by Arthur Levy for the CD booklet accompanying the *Raw Power* reissue (Columbia, 1997).

60. Maureen Droney, "Mix Masters: Andy Wallace," *Mix* (May 1998), p. 88.

61. David Fricke, essay accompanying the CD boxed set, *The Velvet Underground: Peel Slowly and See* (Polydor, 1995), p. 63.

62. The original mixes were reissued in 1986 (Polydor 31453 1252 2).

63. Berio, "Commenti al Rock," p. 130. For the full quotation in the original Italian, see note 28 for chapter 3.

6. ENGINEERS AND PRODUCERS

Source for chapter epigraphs: Page 163: Bill Flanagan, *Written in My Soul: Conversations with Rock's Great Songwriters* (Chicago: Contemporary Books, 1987), p. 389. Page 164: Bob Dylan, *Bringing It All Back Home* (Columbia, 1965), cited in Kealy, "The Real Rock Revolution," p. ii. Page 172: Owsinski, "You Don't Know Jack," p. 55.

1. "Composition team" is George Martin's term for his working relationship with the Beatles. Martin, *All You Need Is Ears*, p. 35.

2. Steve Albini, "Recording Page and Plant's *Walking into Clarksdale*," *Mix* (July 1998), p. 184.

3. Maureen Droney, "Dave Jerden: Fundamentals from Jane's to Chains," *Mix* (December 1998), pp. 104–6.

4. Daniel Lanois, *Acadie* CD booklet (Opal/Warner Bros., 1989), p. 6.

5. Interestingly, these designations are retained even when they all apply to a single person. For instance, Prince's *1999* (Warner Bros., 1982) was "produced, arranged, composed and performed by Prince"; Stevie Wonder's *Innervisions* (Motown, 1973) was "written, produced and arranged by Stevie Wonder."

6. Fox, *In the Groove*, p. 136.

7. Kealy, "Real Rock Revolution," p. 44.

8. David Brackett, *Interpreting Popular Music* (Cambridge: Cambridge University Press, 1995), p. 15.

9. Chris Morris, "We're an American Band," *Pulse* (April 1996), p. 45. In the quotation from Rosas, the brackets are in the original.

10. Blair Jackson, "Sly and the Family Stone's 'If You Want Me to Stay,' " *Mix* (December 1998), p. 173.

11. Ibid. (Emphasis in original.)

12. Joel Selvin, *Sly and the Family Stone: An Oral History* (New York: Avon Books, 1998), p. 166.

13. Ibid., p. 165.

14. Jackson, "Sly and the Family Stone's 'If You Want Me to Stay,' " p. 178.

15. Lewisohn, *The Beatles Recording Sessions*, p. 70.

16. Dan Daley, "Kevin Killen: The Engineer Becomes Producer," *Mix* (October 1989), p. 64.

17. Jackson, "Tom Lord-Alge," p. 59.

18. Clark, "Creative Compression," p. 52.

19. Ibid.

20. Michael Wale, *Voxpop* (London, 1972), p. 224, cited in Simon Frith, *Sound Effects: Youth, Leisure, and the Politics of Rock* (London: Constable, 1983), p. 112.

21. Mr. Bonzai, "George Massenburg: In Search of the Lost Nanoweber," *Mix* (November 1985), p. 204.

22. Daley, "Kevin Killen," p. 64.

23. Molenda, "Production Values: Listen to the Music," p. 69.

24. *Sheryl Crow* CD booklet (A & M, 1996).

25. Owsinski, "You Don't Know Jack," p. 52.

26. Jay Gallagher, "Cosimo: A Conversation with the Dean of New Orleans Recording," *Mix* (March 1996), p. 99.

27. Tolleson, "Arif Mardin," p. 32.

28. Mr. Bonzai, "Bob Clearmountain: Sound Ideas," *Mix* (October 1989), p. 92.

29. Bruce C. Pilato, "Daryl Hall: Standing Solo," *Mix* (November 1986), p. 283.

30. Flanagan, *U2 at the End of the World*, p. 190.

31. Maureen Droney, "Paul Fox: The Band's the Thing," *Mix* (February 1996), pp. 115–16.

32. Rick Clark, "Jim Dickinson: Memphis Maverick," *Mix* (October 1992), pp. 186–87.

33. From a 1998 interview by Terry Gross on National Public Radio's *Fresh Air.*

34. Guralnick, *Lost Highway*, p. 330. (Emphasis in original.)

35. Jerry Wexler and David Ritz, *Rhythm and the Blues: A Life in American Music* (New York: Alfred A. Knopf, 1993), p. 143.

36. Ibid., p. 176.

37. Jan Wenner, "Booker T and the MGs," in *The Rolling Stone Interviews*, 1:134.

38. Wexler and Ritz, *Rhythm and the Blues*, p. 176.

39. Wenner, "Booker T and the MGs," p. 135.

40. Ibid., p. 134.

41. Wexler and Ritz, *Rhythm and the Blues*, p. 143.

42. Ibid., p. 189.

43. Ibid., p. 175.

44. Ibid., p. 207.

45. Charlie Gillett, *Making Tracks: Atlantic Records and the Growth of a Multi-Billion-Dollar Industry* (New York: E. P. Dutton, 1974), p. 209.

46. Wexler and Ritz, *Rhythm and Blues*, p. 206.

47. Ibid., p. 210.

48. Jackson, "Producer Chris Thomas," p. 210.

49. Bonzai, "Jack Nitzsche," p. 38.

50. Ribowsky, *He's a Rebel*, p. 187.

51. Williams, *Out of His Head*, pp. 156–58.

52. Jan Wenner, "Phil Spector," in *The Rolling Stone Interviews*, 1:258.

53. Molenda, "Production Values: Listen to the Music," p. 72.

54. Wenner, "Phil Spector," p. 258.

55. Gillett, *Making Tracks*, p. 207.

56. Erik Philbrook, "The Wizard of Was," *ASCAP Playback* (November-December 1994), p. 5.

57. Ibid.

58. Mr. Bonzai, "Rickie Lee Jones: Sweet and Spicy," *Mix* (April 1992), p. 74

59. Bruce Swedien, Foreword to *Music Producers*, ed. Terri Stone, p. v.

60. Paul Colbert, "Steve Lillywhite—the 3D Producer," *Melody Maker* (January 24, 1981), pp. 31–32.

61. Linda Jackson and Blair Jackson, "Producers and Engineers Talk Budgets," *Mix* (February 1986), p. 74.

62. For instance, Fairlight and Synclavier samplers, Linn, Oberheim, and Roland drum machines, and Yamaha's DX-7 digital synthesizer.

63. Droney, "Mike Shipley," p. 76.

64. Iain Blair, "David Foster Can't Slow Down," *Mix* (September 1985), p. 22.

65. Martin, *All You Need Is Ears*, p. 104.

66. Meek's memory is preserved by the Joe Meek Appreciation Society, which publishes the magazine *Thunderbolt*. See also: John Repsch, *The Legendary Joe Meek: The Telstar Man* (London: Woodford House, 1989). A collection of Meek's recordings can be heard on *It's Hard to Believe It: The Amazing World of Joe Meek* (Razor and Tie, 1995).

7. RESONANCE

Source for chapter epigraph: Anthony DeCurtis, "Don Dixon and the Sounds of the New Southeast," *Mix* (October 1984), p. 212.

1. Dave DiMartino, Review of the Apartments' *A Life Full of Farewells*, *Musician* (August 1995), p. 92.

2. Marcus, *Mystery Train*, p. 54.

3. My discussion here focuses on sounds. For a musical syntactic approach to intertextual play, see John Covach, "The Rutles and the Use of Specific Models in Musical Satire," *Indiana Theory Review*, vol. 11 (1990), pp. 119–44.

4. "I've been an obsessive collector of Phil Spector's stuff, I've got loads and loads on vinyl, a lot of rarities. Nice tunes, big sounds—yeah, it was an obvious influence." Robin Guthrie, "Robin Guthrie of Cocteau Twins Talks about the Records That Changed His Life," *Melody Maker* (November 6, 1993), p. 27.

5. Leonard B. Meyer, *Style and Music: Theory, History, and Ideology* (Philadelphia: University of Pennsylvania Press, 1989), p. 166.

6. Brackett, *Interpreting Popular Music*, p. 25. (Emphasis in original.)

7. Mark Evan Bonds, *Wordless Rhetoric: Musical Form and the Metaphor of the Oration* (Cambridge: Harvard University Press, 1991).

8. George J. Buelow, "Rhetoric and Music," in *The New Grove Dictionary of Music and Musicians*, ed. Stanley Sadie (London: Macmillan, 1980), 15:794.

9. Heinrich Christoph Koch, *Versuch einer Anleitung zur Composition* (Rudolstadt and Leipzig, 1782–93; facsimile, Hildesheim: Georg Olms, 1969), 2: 349. Partial translation by Nancy Kovaleff Baker, *Introductory Essay on Composition* (New Haven, Yale University Press, 1983). I have used Baker's translation but have reinstated *Geist*, which she omits.

10. Edward T. Cone, "The Uses of Convention: Stravinsky and His Models," *The Musical Quarterly* (July 1962), p. 287.

11. Stravinsky, *Poetics of Music*, p. 53.

12. Bonds, *Wordless Rhetoric*, p. 69.

13. The refrain line in this song is "four dead in Ohio," referring to the shooting of protesters by National Guardsmen at Kent State University in 1970.

14. Middleton, *Studying Popular Music*, pp. 220–32.

15. Jackson, " Invitation to Wallinger's World Party," p. 114.

16. Anderton, "Thomas Dolby," p. 60.

17. Molenda, "Production Values: Audio Visionary," pp. 44–45.

18. Blair Jackson, "In the Studio with Enya," *Mix* (May 1992), p. 135.

19. La Cerra, "Butch Vig," p. 109.

20. Ibid.

21. Walser, *Running with the Devil*, p. 28.

22. Samuel A. Floyd, Jr., *The Power of Black Music: Interpreting Its History from Africa to the United States* (New York: Oxford University Press, 1995), p. 235.

23. Thomas McFarland, *Originality and Imagination* (Baltimore: Johns Hopkins University Press, 1985). All of the quotations that follow are taken from chapter 2, "Field, Constellation, and Aesthetic Object." Bloom's theories are set forth in *The Anxiety of Influence: A Theory of Poetry* (Oxford: Oxford University Press, 1973); *A Map of Misreading* (Oxford: Oxford University Press, 1975); *Poetry and Repression: Revisionism from Blake to Stevens* (New Haven: Yale University Press, 1976); and *Kaballah and Criticism* (New York: Continuum Publishing Company, 1983).

24. Virginia Woolf, "The Leaning Tower," in *Collected Essays*, vol. 2 (London: Hogarth Press, 1966), p. 163; cited in McFarland, *Originality and Imagination*, pp. 42–43.

25. Steven Feld, "Communication, Music, and Speech about Music," in *Music Grooves: Essays and Dialogues*, by Charles Keil and Steven Feld (Chicago: University of Chicago Press, 1994), p. 90.

26. Ibid., pp. 90–91.

27. Moon, "Public Enemy's Bomb Squad," p. 70.

28. Alan di Perna, "Digging the Dust Brothers," *EQ* (November 1997), p. 60.

Glossary

ADT. Artificial double tracking. An electronic process that simulates the doubling of a vocal or instrumental part.

ambience. The acoustical character of an enclosed space. In record production, it usually refers to the effect produced by reverberation.

amplifier. A device that increases the power, and hence the amplitude, of an audio signal.

analog audio. An electrical representation of sound pressure; changes in pressure are translated into changes in voltage.

attack. The initial onset of a sound.

bandwidth. A particular frequency span. In equalization, for example, bandwidth refers to the range of frequencies surrounding a selected central frequency.

basic tracks. Recordings of the foundational musical parts of an arrangement, usually drums, bass, and any parts that are primarily harmonic, such as rhythm guitars.

bus. A point in a circuit where several signals merge. The stereo mix bus on a console, for example, groups all of the signals present in the console down to two channels.

channel strip. On a console, a channel strip is a module to which a signal can be routed and then controlled and mixed with other signals. Controls include level, panning, equalization, and on professional consoles, gating and compression.

chorusing. A timbral effect created by continuously varying the delay time of a repeated sound by 15 to 35 milliseconds while combining it with the original sound.

click track. A referential pulse to which overdubs are synchronized.

compression. A process whereby a signal's dynamic range is reduced by a defined ratio.

condenser microphone. A microphone that translates sound into electrical signals by registering variations—caused by sound pressure—in the distance between two plates, one fixed, the other movable. Condensers respond very quickly to transients (rapid changes in sound pressure) and have a wide frequency response, making them well-suited for recording vocals and certain percussion instruments.

console. A device that allows for individual control of many separate signals and provides the means for combining them into a composite audio image.

cover version. A recording of a song that has been recorded previously by another artist.

DAT. A digital audio format, originally called R-DAT, for Rotating Digital Audio Tape. The format uses a rotating head, much like a VCR. The tape is contained in small plastic cassettes that look like miniature analog cassettes.

decay. The dying-away phase of a sound event.

decibel (dB). A standard unit for measuring the intensity of an audio event.

delay. The elapsed time between a sound and its echo.

demo. A recording made prior to beginning formal studio recording, usually made at home or in a rehearsal studio, that serves the purpose of a sketch.

digital audio. A representation of electrical audio signals in binary digits.

distortion. Technically, any alteration of a signal's waveform. In rock, the term usually denotes the rough, grainy sound quality produced by overloading an electronic system, producing high levels of harmonic distortion and changing the character of a sound.

dynamic microphone. A microphone that registers sound pressure magnetically using either a vibrating wire coil or a ribbon as the dynamic element. Dynamic microphones are very rugged but lack the frequency and transient response of condenser microphones.

envelope. The overall dynamic shape of a sound as it occurs over time.

equalization (EQ). The process of increasing or reducing the amplitude of selected frequency bands, which, in turn, alters the timbre of a sound.

expansion. A process by which the dynamic range of an audio signal is increased by a defined ratio, usually in a downward direction. The opposite of compression.

faders. The sliders on a console that control signal level.

flanging. A timbral effect that results from combining a sound with its delayed replica using a varying delay time of 1 to 20 milliseconds.

frequency. A particular rate of sound vibration. The frequency content of a sound affects the apprehension of pitch and timbre.

gain. The amount of power increase produced by an amplifier; the power difference between the amplifier's input and its output.

gating. A kind of expansion where sounds that fall below a selectable threshold of volume are immediately silenced, like an on/off switch.

groove. A piece's general rhythmic character.

head arrangement. A musical arrangement that is preserved in musicians' memories, rather than in musical notation.

headphone mix. The particular instrumental balance that is fed to a recording musician's headphones.

inches per second (ips). An expression denoting the speed at which magnetic tape moves across a tape recorder's heads.

lead sheet. A piece of sheet music containing song lyrics, melody, and chord symbols.

level. The intensity of an electronic audio signal.

limiting. A particular use of compression where a signal's dynamic peaks may not exceed a defined upward limit.

mix. The process of assembling multiple discrete musical parts and sounds into a composite whole. The proportional relationships among the elements of the mix are fixed in a mono, stereo, or 5.1 surround format.

monitor. A loudspeaker system.

multing. Routing a single audio signal to multiple destinations, into more than one console channel, for example.

multitrack. A tape or tape recorder that has several discrete parallel bands, each of which can store its own recorded sounds.

noise reduction. A process by which tape hiss is reduced.

overdub. Recorded material that is added to an existing recording; also, the process of doing this.

pan (panning). An adaptation of panorama. In stereo audio, "pan" refers to the position of a sound on the audio "horizon."

patch bay. A set of connectors providing access to the inputs and outputs of multiple devices in one centralized location. Studio equipment is connected to the patch bay, providing convenience and flexibility in the routing of signals.

polar pattern. The directional response pattern of a microphone that determines how it "hears" sound.

preamp. Short for "preamplifier." A device that raises the level of a weak signal before passing it along to subsequent devices in the signal path. A common use of a preamp is to amplify the signal produced by a microphone, hence "microphone preamp."

pre-delay. The delay between an initial sound and the onset of its reverberation.

pre-production. The stage of a recording project that precedes formal recording. It may include any or all of the following: songwriting, arranging, rehearsal, demo recording.

punch in/out (drop in/out). A kind of overdub that requires putting a tape recorder into or taking it out of record mode in the midst of previously recorded music. A wayward phrase, for example, might be re-recorded in this way, leaving the material on either side of it undisturbed.

remix. A mix created subsequent to a track's original mix and exhibiting some degree of difference from the original. Remixes may alter arrangements and sonic textures to the point of assuming their own identity independent of the original.

riding gain. Manually raising or lowering a signal's level as the music is playing. An engineer might ride gain on a vocal, for example, to keep it at the desired volume when fluctuations would otherwise make it too loud or too soft.

sample. A digitally recorded sound.

sequencer. A computer-based performance-data recorder that records all parameters of musical performance except sound (e.g., rhythm, pitch, dynamics, pedaling).

side chain. The input on a compressor or gate that allows the device to be controlled by a signal other than the one it is processing.

signal path. The route along which an electrical signal travels.

slapback. An echo whose delay time is approximately 70 milliseconds; characteristic of rockabilly style.

stereo. A system of sound localization relying on two-channel (right/left) audio recording and playback.

tape echo. A delayed repeat of a sound resulting from the time difference between recording and playback on a tape recorder with multiple heads.

tape head. An electromagnet in a tape recorder that translates electrical signals into patterns on the iron oxide coating of magnetic tape to record, erase, or play back audio signals.

track. An individual band of magnetic tape; or a finished mix.

transducer. A device that converts energy from one state to another. A microphone, for example, converts acoustic energy into electrical energy. A loudspeaker converts electrical energy into acoustic energy.

transient. A momentary high-level peak, such as the attack of a percussion instrument, the pluck of a guitar string, or certain consonants (e.g., "t").

VU meter. A meter that indicates the intensity level of a signal. VU meters are found on tape recorders, consoles, and many pieces of sound processing equipment.

Engineer and Producer Credits

This list is meant to give readers a representative context for engineers and producers cited in the course of the book. It is in no way a comprehensive listing, and it does not include songwriters/performers who produce their own recordings (e.g., Brian Wilson, Prince, George Clinton, Karl Wallinger). Also, the roles are not necessarily exclusive. Contributions by members of the recording team can always overlap, albums oftentimes have more than one engineer or producer, and credits are often incomplete, especially on older records. Moreover, very often the engineer and/or producer is also the mixer, though no additional credit is given. The list, then, should be taken as simply an indication of the kinds of projects these engineers and producers have worked on.

Record labels are those of the original release. Key: e—engineer, p—producer, m—mixer, re-m—remixer.

Ahern, Brian.
> Emmylou Harris, *Pieces of the Sky* (Reprise, 1975) e, p; David Bromberg, *Midnight on the Water* (Columbia, 1975) e, p; Rodney Crowell, *Ain't Living Long Like This* (Warner Bros., 1978) e, p; Johnny Cash, *Johnny 99* (Columbia, 1983) e, p; Ricky Skaggs, *Solid Ground* (Atlantic, 1995) p (with Skaggs).

Albini, Steve.
> The Pixies, *Surfer Rosa,* (4AD/Elektra, 1988) p; the Breeders, *Pod* (4AD/ Elektra, 1990) e; P. J. Harvey, *Rid of Me* (Island, 1993) p; Nirvana, *In Utero* (DGC, 1993) e; Jimmy Page and Robert Plant, *Walking into Clarksdale* (Atlantic, 1998) e, m.

Baker, Roy Thomas.
> T. Rex, *Electric Warrior* (Fly, 1971) e; Queen, *A Night at the Opera* (Hollywood, 1975) p (with Queen); the Cars, *The Cars* (Elektra, 1978) p; Devo, *Oh No! It's Devo* (Warner Bros., 1982) p; Ozzy Osbourne, *No Rest for the Wicked* (Epic, 1989) e, p.

Benitez, John "Jellybean."
> Madonna, *Madonna* (Sire, 1983) p, re-m; Hall and Oates, "Say It Isn't So" (RCA, 1983) re-m; the Bangles, "Walk Like an Egyptian" (Columbia, 1986) re-m; Whitney Houston, "So Emotional," *Whitney* (Arista, 1987) p; Sting, "If You Love Somebody Set Them Free" (A&M, 1987) re-m.

Blake, Tchad.
The Bangles, *Different Light* (Columbia, 1985) e; Los Lobos, *Kiko* (Slash, 1992) e; Tom Waits, *Bone Machine* (Island, 1992) e; Suzanne Vega, *Nine Objects of Desire* (A&M, 1996) e; Ron Sexsmith, *Other Songs* (Interscope, 1997) p (with Mitchell Froom).

Bottrill, David.
Joni Mitchell, *Chalk Mark in a Rain Storm* (Geffen, 1988) e; Peter Gabriel, *Us* (Geffen, 1992) e, m; Toni Childs, *The Woman's Boat* (Geffen, 1994) p (with Childs); Tool, *Aenima* (Volcano, 1996) e, p (with Tool); David Rice, *Green Electric* (Columbia, 1998) p (with Rice).

Brauer, Michael.
Luther Vandross, *Never Too Much* (Epic, 1981) e; Grace Jones, *Living My Life* (Island, 1982) m; Aretha Franklin, *Who's Zoomin' Who?* (Arista, 1985) m; Fishbone, *The Reality of My Surroundings* (Columbia, 1991) m; Regina Belle, *Passion* (Columbia, 1993) m.

Burn, Malcolm.
The Neville Brothers, *Yellow Moon* (A&M, 1989) e; Daniel Lanois, *Acadie* (Opal/Warner Bros., 1989) e; Chris Whitley, *Living with the Law* (Columbia, 1991) p; John Mellencamp, *Human Wheels* (Mercury, 1993) p (with Mellencamp, Mike Wanchic, and David Leonard); Lisa Germano, *Geek the Girl* (4AD, 1994) p (with Germano).

Cherney, Ed.
Ry Cooder, *Get Rhythm* (Warner Bros., 1987) e, m; Bonnie Raitt, *Nick of Time* (Capitol, 1989) e, m; Iggy Pop, *Brick by Brick* (Virgin, 1990) e, m; Bob Dylan, *Under the Red Sky* (Columbia, 1990) e, m; the Rolling Stones, *Bridges to Babylon* (Virgin, 1997) e.

Chiarelli, Rob.
Da Lench Mob, *Planet of Da Apes* (Priority, 1994) e; Adina Howard, *Do You Wanna Ride?* (EastWest, 1995) m; Coolio, *1, 2, 3, 4 (Sumpin' New)* (Tommy Boy, 1996) m; Will Smith, *Big Willie Style* (Columbia, 1997) m; Heavy D and the Boyz, *Waterbed Hev* (Uptown/Universal, 1997) e.

Chiccarelli, Joe.
Frank Zappa, *Joe's Garage: Acts 1–3* (Zappa, 1979) e; Lone Justice, *Shelter* (Geffen, 1986) e; Stan Ridgway, *Mosquitos* (DGC, 1989) p (with Ridgway); American Music Club, *Everclear* (Alias, 1991) m; the Verlaines, *Way Out Where* (Slash, 1993) p.

Clearmountain, Bob.
Roxy Music, *Avalon* (Reprise, 1982) e; Bruce Springsteen, *Born in the U.S.A.* (Columbia, 1984) m; Hall and Oates, *Big Bam Boom* (RCA, 1984) p (with Hall and Oates); the Pretenders, *Get Close* (Sire, 1986) p (with Jimmy Iovine); Aimee Mann, *Whatever* (Geffen, 1993) m.

Corsaro, Jason.
Madonna, *Like a Virgin* (Sire, 1984) e; the Power Station, *The Power Station* (Capitol, 1985) e; Public Image Limited, *Album* (Elektra, 1986) e; Bernie Worrell, *Funk of Ages* (Gramavision, 1991) m; Soundgarden, *Superunknown* (A&M, 1994) e.

Date, Terry.

Soundgarden, *Badmotorfinger* (A&M, 1991) e, p (with Soundgarden); Screaming Trees, *Uncle Anesthesia* (Epic, 1991) e, p (with Screaming Trees); Mother Love Bone, *Mother Love Bone* (Standog/Mercury, 1992) e, p; Pantera, *Far Beyond Driven* (EastWest, 1994) e, p; Limp Bizkit, *Significant Other* (Interscope, 1999) e, p (with Limp Bizkit).

Dickinson, Jim.

Big Star, *Third/Sister Lovers* (PVC, 1978) p; the Replacements, *Pleased to Meet Me* (Sire, 1987) p; Toots and the Maytals, *Toots in Memphis* (Mango, 1988) p; the Radiators, *Total Evaporation* (Epic, 1990) p; Mudhoney, *Tomorrow Hit Today* (Warner Bros., 1998) p.

Dixon, Don.

R. E. M., *Murmur* (I. R. S., 1983) p (with Mitch Easter); the Smithereens, *Especially for You* (Enigma, 1986) p; Matthew Sweet, *Inside* (Columbia, 1986) p; Marshall Crenshaw, *Mary Jean & 9 Others* (Warner Bros., 1987) p; Richard Barone, *Primal Dream* (Paradox/MCA, 1990) p.

Dodd, Richard.

George Harrison, *Cloud Nine,* (Dark Horse, 1987) e; Roy Orbison, *Mystery Girl* (Atlantic, 1989) e; Tom Petty and the Heartbreakers, *Into the Great Wide Open* (MCA, 1991) e; Wilco, *A. M.* (Sire/Reprise, 1995) m; Steve Earl, *I Feel Alright* (Warner Bros., 1996) e, p.

Douglas, Jack.

The New York Dolls, *New York Dolls* (Mercury, 1973) e; Aerosmith, *Toys in the Attic* (Columbia, 1975) p; Cheap Trick, *Cheap Trick* (Epic, 1977) p; John Lennon, *Double Fantasy* (Geffen, 1980) p; Graham Parker, *Another Grey Area* (RCA, 1982) p.

Dowd, Tom.

Ray Charles, *The Genius of Ray Charles* (Atlantic, 1959) e; Aretha Franklin, *I Never Loved a Man (the Way I Love You)* (Atlantic, 1967) e; Cream, *Disraeli Gears* (Atco, 1967) e; Derek and the Dominoes, *Layla* (Atco, 1970) p; Allman Brothers Band, *Idlewild South* (Atco, 1970) p.

Dust Brothers (John King, Mike Simpson).

Beastie Boys, *Paul's Boutique* (Capitol, 1989) p; Tone-Loc, *Loc-ed After Dark* (Delicious Vinyl, 1989) p; Beck, *Odelay* (DGC, 1996) p (with Beck Hansen); Hanson, *Middle of Nowhere* (Mercury, 1997) p; Sugartooth, *The Sounds of Solid* (Geffen, 1997) p (with Sugartooth).

Eaton, Al.

Too $hort, *Life Is . . . Too $hort* (Jive, 1988) p; Ice-T, *Cold as Ever* (Blue Dolphin, 1996) p; Mac Mall, *Untouchable* (Relativity, 1996) m; SWV, *Release Some Tension* (RCA, 1997) e; Rappin' 4-Tay, *Bigga Than Da Game* (Rag Top, 1998) p.

Edmonds, Kenneth "Babyface."

Bobby Brown, "Don't Be Cruel," *Don't Be Cruel* (MCA, 1988) p; Boyz II Men, "End of the Road," *Boomerang* soundtrack (LaFace, 1992) p; TLC, "Red Light Special," *Crazy Sexy Cool* (LaFace, 1995) p; Whitney Houston,

"Exhale (Shoop Shoop)" *Waiting to Exhale* soundtrack (Arista, 1995) p; Mary J. Blige, "Missing You," *Share My World* (MCA, 1997) p.

Edmunds, Dave.
  Brinsley Schwartz, *New Favourites of Brinsley Schwartz* (United Artists, 1974) e, p; Flamin' Groovies, *Shake Some Action* (Sire, 1976) p; Stray Cats, *Built for Speed* (EMI America, 1982) p; Everly Brothers, *EB '84* (Mercury, 1984) p; k. d. lang, *Angel with a Lariat* (Sire, 1987) p.

Emerick, Geoff.
  The Beatles, *Revolver* (Parlophone, 1966) *Sgt. Pepper's Lonely Hearts Club Band* (Parlophone, 1967) e; the Zombies, *Odyssey & Oracle* (1968) e; Split Enz, *Dizrhythmia* (Mushroom, 1977) e, p (with Split Enz); Elvis Costello and the Attractions, *Imperial Bedroom* (Columbia, 1982) p (with Costello).

Eno, Brian.
  Devo, *Are We Not Men* (Warner Bros., 1980) p; Talking Heads, *Remain in Light* (Sire, 1981) p; U2, *The Joshua Tree* (Island, 1987) p (with Daniel Lanois); Jane Siberry, *When I Was a Boy* (Reprise, 1993) p; James, *Laid* (Mercury, 1993) p.

Ett, Steven.
  LL Cool J, *Radio* (Def Jam, 1985) e; Run-D. M. C., *Raising Hell* (Profile, 1986) e; Danzig, *Danzig* (Def American, 1988) e; Public Enemy, *It Takes a Nation of Millions to Hold Us Back* (Def Jam, 1988) m; Mary J. Blige, *What's the 411?* (Uptown/MCA, 1992) e.

Flood (Mark Ellis).
  Nick Cave and the Bad Seeds, *The Firstborn Is Dead* (Mute, 1985) p (with Cave); U2, *Achtung Baby* (Island, 1991) e, m; Nine Inch Nails, *The Downward Spiral* (Interscope, 1994) p (with Trent Reznor); Smashing Pumpkins, *Mellon Collie and the Infinite Sadness* (Virgin, 1995) p (with Billy Corgan and Alan Moulder); P. J. Harvey, *To Bring You My Love* (Island, 1995) p (with Harvey and John Parish).

Flye, Tom.
  The Impressions, *Check Out Your Mind* (Curtom, 1970) e; Don McLean, *American Pie* (EMI America, 1971) e; Sly and the Family Stone, *Fresh* (Epic, 1973) e; the New Riders of the Purple Sage, *The Adventures of Panama Red* (Columbia, 1973) e; Mickey Hart and Planet Drum, *Supralingua* (Rykodisc, 1998) e.

Foster, David.
  Lionel Richie, *Can't Slow Down* (Motown, 1983) p (with Richie); Chicago, *Chicago 17* (Full Moon, 1984) p; Whitney Houston, "I Will Always Love You," *The Bodyguard* soundtrack (Arista, 1992) p; All-4-One, "I Swear," *All-4-One* (Blitzz/Atlantic, 1994) e; Toni Braxton "Un-Break My Heart," *Secrets* (LaFace, 1996) p.

Fox, Paul.
  XTC, *Oranges and Lemons* (Geffen, 1989) p; Robyn Hitchcock and the Egyptians, *Perspex Island* (A&M, 1990) p; 10,000 Maniacs, *Our Time in Eden* (Elektra, 1992) p; the Sugarcubes, *Stick Around for Joy* (Elektra, 1992) p; They Might Be Giants, *John Henry* (Elektra, 1994) p.

Froom, Mitchell.
    Del Fuegos, *The Longest Day* (Slash, 1984) p; Crowded House, *Temple of Low Men* (Capitol, 1988) p; Los Lobos, *Kiko* (Slash, 1992) p; Suzanne Vega, *Nine Objects of Desire* (A&M, 1996) p; Cibo Matto, *Viva! La Woman* (Warner Bros., 1996) p (with Cibo Matto).

Halee, Roy.
    Simon and Garfunkel, *Bookends* (Columbia, 1968), *Bridge over Troubled Waters* (Columbia, 1970) e, p (with Simon and Garfunkel); Laura Nyro, *New York Tendaberry* (Columbia, 1969) e, p (with Nyro); Rufus, *Street Player* (ABC, 1978) e, p; Paul Simon, *The Rhythm of the Saints* (Warner Bros., 1990) e.

Hall, Rick.
    Arthur Alexander, "You Better Move On" (Dot, 1962) e, p; Wilson Pickett, "Mustang Sally" (Atlantic, 1966) e, p (with Jerry Wexler); Clarence Carter, *The Dynamic Clarence Carter* (Atlantic, 1968) e, p; Etta James, *Tell Mama* (MCA/Chess, 1968) e, p.

Hardy, Joe.
    ZZ Top, *Afterburner* (Warner Bros., 1985) e; the Replacements, *Pleased to Meet Me* (Sire, 1987) e; Green On Red, *Here Come the Snakes* (Restless, 1989) e, p (with Jim Dickinson); Steve Earl and the Dukes, *The Hard Way* (MCA, 1990) e, p (with Earl); Tom Cochrane, *Mad Mad World* (Capitol, 1992) e, p (with Cochrane).

Harris, Jimmy Jam, and Terry Lewis.
    Janet Jackson, *Control* (A&M, 1986) p, *Rhythm Nation 1814* (A&M, 1989) p (with Jackson); Human League, *Crash* (A&M, 1986) p; Sounds of Blackness, *The Evolution of Gospel* (Perspective, 1991) p (with Gary Hines); Boyz II Men, "On Bended Knee," *II* (Motown, 1994) p; Mary J. Blige, "Love Is All We Need," *Share My World* (MCA, 1997) p.

Hodge, Steve.
    Shalamar, *Big Fun* (Solar, 1979) e; the Whispers, *Imagination* (Solar, 1981) e, m; Janet Jackson, *Control* (A&M, 1986) e, m; Shabba Ranks, *X-tra Naked* (Epic, 1992) e; Mariah Carey, *Rainbow* (Sony, 1999) e, m.

Horn, Trevor.
    The Buggles, *The Age of Plastic* (Island, 1980) p (with Geoff Downes); ABC, *The Lexicon of Love* (Mercury, 1982) p; Frankie Goes to Hollywood, *Welcome to the Pleasuredome* (ZTT/Island, 1983); Yes, *90125* (Atlantic, 1983) p (with Yes); Seal, *Seal* (Sire, 1991) p.

Jerden, Dave.
    Talking Heads, *Remain in Light* (Sire, 1980) e; the Call, *Scene Beyond Dreams* (Mercury, 1984) e; Jane's Addiction, *Ritual de lo Habitual* (Warner Bros., 1990) p (with Perry Farrell); Alice in Chains, *Dirt* (Columbia, 1992) p (with Alice in Chains); Biohazard, *Mata Leão* (Warner Bros. 1996) p (with Biohazard).

Johns, Glyn.
    The Rolling Stones, *Beggar's Banquet* (London, 1968) e; the Faces, *A Nod Is as Good as a Wink . . . to a Blind Horse* (Warner Bros., 1971) p; Joan

Armatrading, *Joan Armatrading* (A&M, 1976) p; Eric Clapton, *Slowhand* (Polydor, 1977) p (with Clapton); John Hiatt, *Stolen Moments* (A&M, 1990) p.

Johnston, Bob.
Bob Dylan, *Blonde on Blonde* (Columbia, 1966) p; Simon and Garfunkel, *Parsley, Sage, Rosemary, and Thyme* (Columbia, 1966) p; Leonard Cohen, *Songs from a Room* (Columbia, 1969) p; Michael Murphey, *Geronimo's Cadillac* (A&M, 1972) p; Loudon Wainwright III, *Attempted Moustache* (Columbia, 1973) p.

Jones, Quincy.
Lesley Gore, "It's My Party" (Mercury, 1963) p; Rufus, *Masterjam* (MCA, 1979) p; Patti Austin, *Every Home Should Have One* (Qwest, 1981) p; Donna Summer, *Donna Summer* (Geffen, 1982) p; Michael Jackson, *Thriller* (Epic, 1982) *Bad* (Epic, 1987) p.

Killen, Kevin.
Bryan Ferry, *Bête Noire* (Reprise, 1986) e; Peter Gabriel, *So* (Geffen, 1986) e; Sam Phillips, *Cruel Inventions* (Virgin, 1991) e, m; Lindsey Buckingham, *Out of the Cradle* (Reprise, 1992) e, m; Elvis Costello/Brodsky Quartet, *The Juliet Letters* (Warner Bros., 1993) e, p (with Costello and the Brodsky Quartet).

Lange, Robert "Mutt."
The Boomtown Rats, *Tonic for the Troops* (Columbia, 1978) p; AC/DC, *Back in Black* (Atco, 1980) p; Foreigner, *4* (Atlantic, 1981) p; Def Leppard, *Pyromania* (Mercury, 1983) p; the Cars, *Heartbeat City* (Elektra, 1984) p (with the Cars).

Lanois, Daniel.
Bob Dylan, *Oh Mercy* (Columbia, 1989) p; U2, *Achtung Baby* (Island, 1991) p (with Brian Eno); Peter Gabriel, *Us* (Geffen, 1992) p (with Gabriel); Emmylou Harris, *Wrecking Ball* (Elektra, 1995) p; Luscious Jackson, *Fever In Fever Out* (Grand Royal/Capitol, 1996) p (with Luscious Jackson).

Laswell, Bill.
Herbie Hancock, *Future Shock* (Columbia, 1983) p (with Hancock); Laurie Anderson, *Mister Heartbreak* (Warner Bros., 1984) p (with Anderson); Public Image Limited, *Album* (Elektra, 1986) p; Motörhead, *Orgasmatron* (Sinclair, 1990) e, p; Buckethead, *Monsters and Robots* (EMI, 1999) p.

Leckie, John.
Pink Floyd, *Meddle* (Harvest, 1971) e; the Stone Roses, *The Stone Roses* (Silvertone, 1989) p; the Posies, *Dear 23* (DGC, 1990) p (with the Posies); Radiohead, *The Bends* (Capitol, 1995) p; Kula Shaker, *K* (Columbia, 1996) e, p (with Chrispian Mills).

Leiber, Jerry, and Mike Stoller.
The Coasters, "Yakety Yak" (Atco, 1958) p; the Drifters, "There Goes My Baby" (Atlantic, 1959) p; Ben E. King "Spanish Harlem" (Atco, 1961) p;

the Exciters, "Tell Him" (United Artists, 1962) p; Peggy Lee, "Is That All There Is?" (Capitol, 1969) p.

Levine, Larry.

Bob B. Soxx and the Blue Jeans, "Zip-A-Dee-Doo-Dah" (Philles, 1963) e; the Crystals, "Da Doo Ron Ron" (Philles, 1963) e; the Ronettes, "Walking in the Rain" (Philles, 1964) e; the Checkmates, "Black Pearl" (A&M, 1969) e; the Ramones, *End of the Century* (Sire, 1980) e.

Lillywhite, Steve.

XTC, *Drums and Wires* (Virgin, 1979) p; Peter Gabriel, *Peter Gabriel* (Geffen, 1980) p; U2, *War* (Island, 1983) p; the Pogues, *If I Should Fall from Grace with God* (Island, 1988) p; Phish, *Billy Breathes* (Elektra, 1996) p (with Phish).

Lord-Alge, Tom.

Steve Winwood, *Back in the High Life* (Island, 1986) e, m; the Wallflowers, *Bringing Down the Horse* (Interscope, 1996) e, m; Big Head Todd and the Monsters, *Beautiful World* (Warner Bros., 1997) m; Grant Lee Buffalo, *Jubilee* (Warner Bros., 1998) m; Marilyn Manson, *Mechanical Animals* (Nothing/Interscope, 1998) m.

Marchand, Pierre.

Sarah McLachlan, *Fumbling towards Ecstasy* (Arista, 1995), *Surfacing* (Arista, 1997) e, p; Kate and Anna McGarrigle, *Heartbeats Accelerating* (Private Music, 1990) e, p; Greg Keelor, *Gone* (Warner Canada, 1997) e, p; Patty Larkin, *Strangers World* (High Street, 1995) m; the Devlins, *Waiting* (Uptown/Universal, 1997) e, p.

Mardin, Arif.

The Rascals, *I've Been Lonely Too Long* (Atlantic, 1967) p; Dusty Springfield, *Dusty in Memphis* (Atlantic, 1968) p (with Jerry Wexler and Tom Dowd); John Prine, *John Prine* (Atlantic, 1971) p; Donny Hathaway, *Extension of a Man* (Atlantic, 1973) p; Chaka Khan, *Chaka* (Warner Bros., 1978) p.

Martin, George.

Beatles albums (Parlophone, 1963–69) p; Jeff Beck, *Blow by Blow* (Epic, 1975) p; Jimmy Web, *El Mirage* (Atlantic, 1977) p; Ultravox, *Quartet* (Chrysalis, 1982) p; Paul McCartney, *Tug of War* (Columbia, 1982) p.

Massenburg, George.

Earth Wind and Fire, *That's the Way of the World* (Columbia, 1975) e, *All 'n All* (Columbia, 1977) e; 10,000 Maniacs, *In My Tribe* (Elektra, 1987) e, m; the Trio (Linda Ronstadt, Dolly Parton, Emmylou Harris) *Trio* (Warner Bros., 1987) e, p; Lyle Lovett, *Joshua Judges Ruth* (Curb/MCA 1992) e, p (with Lovett and Billy Williams); Jimmy Webb, *Suspending Disbelief* (Elektra, 1993) e, p.

Matassa, Cosimo.

Fats Domino, "Ain't It a Shame" (Imperial, 1955) e; Little Richard, "Tutti Frutti" (Specialty, 1955) e; Irma Thomas, "Ruler of My Heart" (Minit, 1962) e; Lee Dorsey, "Working in a Coal Mine" (Amy, 1966) e.

Meek, Joe.
    Screaming Lord Sutch and the Savages, "'Til the Following Night" (HMV, 1961) e, p; John Leyton, "Johnny Remember Me" (Top Rank) 1961, e, p; the Tornados, "Telstar" (Decca, 1962) e, p; Heinz, "Just Like Eddie" (Decca, 1963) e, p; the Honeycombs, "Have I the Right" (Pye, 1964) e, p.
Norberg, Bob.
    The Falla Trio, *Music for 3 Guitars* (Concord Jazz, 1986) e; Kathleen Battle, *A Christmas Celebration* (Angel, 1986) e; Christopher Parkening, *The Great Recordings* (Angel, 1993) e.
Nye, Steve.
    Bryan Ferry, *These Foolish Things* (Reprise, 1973) e; Japan, *Tin Drum* (Blue Plate, 1981) e, p (with Japan); XTC, *Mummer* (Geffen, 1983) p (with XTC); Clannad, *Macalla* (RCA, 1985) p; Robbie Robertson, *Storyville* (Geffen, 1991) e.
O'Brien, Brendan.
    Red Hot Chili Peppers, *Blood Sugar Sex Magik* (Warner Bros., 1991) e; Stone Temple Pilots, *Core* (Atlantic, 1992) p; the Jayhawks, *Hollywood Town Hall* (Def American, 1992) e; Pearl Jam, *Vitalogy* (Epic Associate, 1994) p (with Pearl Jam); Matthew Sweet, *100% Fun* (Zoo, 1995) p.
Offord, Eddie.
    Emerson, Lake & Palmer, *Emerson, Lake & Palmer* (Atlantic, 1970) e; Brian Auger, *A Better Land* (One Way, 1971) e; Yes, *Close to the Edge* (Atlantic, 1972) e, p (with Yes); Billy Squier, *A Tale of the Tape* (Capitol, 1980) p (with Squier); 311, *Music* (Capricorn, 1993) e, p.
Orbit, William.
    Bassomatic, *Set the Controls for the Heart of the Bass* (Virgin, 1990) p; Kraftwerk, "Radioactivity" (Elektra/Asylum, 1991) re-m; Torch Song, *Toward the Unknown Region* (DSV, 1996) p; Madonna, *Ray of Light* (Warner Bros., 1998) p (with Madonna); Blur, *13* (Virgin, 1999) p.
Organized Noize (Pat Brown, Ray Murray, Rico Wade).
    Xscape, *Hummin' Comin' at 'cha* (Columbia, 1993) p; OutKast, *Southernplayalisticadillacmuzik* (LaFace, 1994) p; Goodie Mob, *Soul Food* (LaFace, 1995) p; TLC, "Waterfalls," *Crazy Sexy Cool* (LaFace/Arista, 1995) p; Curtis Mayfield, "Here but I'm Gone," *New World Order* (Warner Bros., 1998) p.
Padgham, Hugh.
    Peter Gabriel, *Peter Gabriel* (Geffen, 1980) e; Phil Collins, *Face Value* (Atlantic, 1981) e, p (with Collins); XTC, *English Settlement* (Epic, 1982) e, p (with XTC); the Police, *Synchronicity* (A&M, 1983) e, p (with the Police); Melissa Etheridge, *Yes I Am* (Island, 1993) e, p (with Etheridge).
Petty, Norman.
    Buddy Holly and the Crickets, *The Chirping Crickets*, (Brunswick, 1957) e, p; Buddy Knox, "Party Doll" (Roulette, 1957) p; Jimmie Bowen, "I'm Stickin' with You" (Roulette, 1957) e, p; Buddy Holly, *Buddy Holly* (Coral, 1958) e, p; Jimmy Gilmer and the Fireballs, "Sugar Shack" (Dot, 1963) p.

Phillips, Sam.

Jackie Brenston with His Delta Cats, "Rocket '88' " (Chess, 1951) e, p; Howlin' Wolf, "Moanin' at Midnight" (Chess, 1951) e, p; Elvis Presley, "That's All Right" (Sun, 1954); Carl Perkins, "Blue Suede Shoes" (Sun, 1955) e, p; Jerry Lee Lewis, "Whole Lot of Shakin' Going On" (Sun, 1957) e, p.

Plotkin, Chuck.

Wendy Waldman, *Love Has Got Me* (Warner Bros., 1973) p; Andrew Gold, *Andrew Gold* (Asylum, 1975) p; Orleans, *Let There Be Music* (Asylum, 1975) p; Bruce Springsteen, *The River* (Columbia, 1980) m, *Born in the U.S.A.* (Columbia, 1984) p (with Springsteen, Jon Landau, and Steve Van Zandt); Dan Bern, *Dan Bern* (Work, 1993) p.

Rodgers, Nile.

Chic, *C'est Chic* (Atlantic, 1978) p (with Bernard Edwards); David Bowie, *Let's Dance* (EMI-America, 1983) p (with Bowie); Madonna, *Like a Virgin* (Sire, 1985) p; Thompson Twins, *Here's to Future Days* (Arista, 1985) p (with Tom Bailey); the B-52s, *Cosmic Thing* (Reprise, 1989) p.

Rubin, Rick.

Beastie Boys, *Licensed to Ill* (Columbia, 1986) p; Run-D. M. C., *Raising Hell* (Profile, 1986) p; Red Hot Chili Peppers, *Blood Sugar Sex Magik* (Warner Bros., 1991) p; Tom Petty, *Wildflowers* (Warner Bros., 1994) p (with Petty and Mike Campbell); Johnny Cash, *American Recordings* (American, 1994) p.

Ryan, Nicky.

Clannad, *Fuaim* (Atlantic, 1982) p; Altan, *Ceol Aduaidh* (Green Linnet, 1983) p; Enya, *Watermark* (Reprise, 1988), *Shepherd Moons* (Reprise, 1991) e, p.

Scheiner, Elliot.

Van Morrison, *Moondance* (Warner Bros., 1970) e, m; Steely Dan, *Aja* (MCA, 1977) e; Rickie Lee Jones, *Pirates* (Warner Bros., 1981) e; Ashford and Simpson, *Solid* (Warner Bros., 1984) e, p (with Ashford and Simpson); Bruce Hornsby and the Range, *The Way It Is* (RCA, 1986) e, p (with Hornsby).

Schmitt, Al.

The Astronauts, *Surfin' with the Astronauts* (RCA, 1963) e, p; Jefferson Airplane, *Volunteers* (RCA, 1969) e, p; Earth, Wind and Fire, *Last Days and Time* (Columbia, 1972) e; Jackson Brown, *Late for the Sky* (Asylum, 1974) p (with Browne); Doctor John, *Afterglow* (Blue Thumb, 1995) e.

Shipley, Mike.

A Flock of Seagulls, *A Flock of Seagulls* (Jive, 1982) e; Def Leppard, *Pyromania* (Mercury, 1983) e; Thomas Dolby, *The Flat Earth* (Capitol, 1984) m; Rodney Crowell, *Jewel of the South* (MCA, 1995) m; Joy Askew, *Tender City* (Private Music, 1996) m.

Shocklee, Hank.

Public Enemy, *It Takes a Nation of Millions to Hold Us Back* (Def Jam, 1988) p (with the Bomb Squad); Stop the Violence, "Self-Destruction" (Jive,

1989) p; Kid Panic, *Don't Be Alarmed* (MCA, 1991) p; Aaron Hall, *Truth* (Silas, 1993) p; Big Daddy Kane, *Looks Like a Job for Big Daddy* (Cold Chillin', 1993) p.

Shoemaker, Trina.

Iggy Pop, *American Caesar* (Virgin, 1993) e; Sheryl Crow, *Sheryl Crow* (A&M, 1996) e; Throwing Muses, *Limbo* (Rykodisc, 1996) e; Midnight Oil, *Breathe* (Sony, 1996) m; Victoria Williams, *Musings of a Creek Dipper* (Atlantic, 1998) e, p (with Williams).

Simon, John.

The Cyrkle, *Red Rubber Ball* (Columbia, 1966) p; The Band, *Music from Big Pink* (Capitol, 1968), *The Band* (Capitol, 1969) p; Leonard Cohen, *The Songs of Leonard Cohen* (Columbia, 1968) p; Big Brother and the Holding Company, *Cheap Thrills* (Columbia, 1968) p; Steve Forbert, *Jackrabbit Slim* (Nemperor, 1979) p.

Spector, Phil.

The Ronettes, "Be My Baby" (Philles, 1963) p; the Righteous Brothers, "You've Lost that Lovin' Feelin' " (Philles, 1964) p; Ike and Tina Turner, "River Deep—Mountain High" (Philles, 1966) p; George Harrison, *All Things Must Pass* (Apple, 1970) p (with Harrison); John Lennon, *Imagine* (Apple, 1971) p (with Lennon and Yoko Ono).

Stasium, Ed.

The Chambers Brothers, *Unbonded* (Avco Embassy, 1974) e; the Ramones, *Rocket to Russia* (Sire, 1977) e; Talking Heads, *Talking Heads '77* (Sire, 1977) e; Translator, *Translator* (415/Columbia, 1985) p; Living Colour, *Vivid* (Epic, 1988) e, p.

Stevens, Rob

The Golden Palominos, *A History (1982–1985)* (1992) e; Bill Laswell, *Destruction: Celluloid Recordings* (Enigma, 1993) e; Yoko Ono, *Rising* (Capitol, 1995) e, p (with Ono); Nina Hagen, *14 Friendly Abductions: The Best of Nina Hagen* (Columbia/Legacy, 1996) e; John Lennon, *Anthology* (Capitol, 1998) e, p.

Swedien, Bruce.

Jackie Wilson, "(Your Love Keeps Lifting Me) Higher and Higher" (Brunswick, 1967) e; the Chi-Lites, *A Lonely Man* (Brunswick, 1972) e; Michael Jackson, *Thriller* (Epic, 1983), *Bad* (Epic, 1987) e; Quincy Jones, *Back on the Block* (Qwest, 1989) e; the Isley Brothers, *Tracks of Life* (Warner Bros., 1991) e.

Thoener, David.

David Johansen, *David Johansen* (Blue Sky, 1978) e; J. Geils Band, *Freeze Frame* (EMI America, 1981) e; Was (Not Was), *Born to Laugh at Tornados* (Geffen , 1983) e, m; John Cougar Mellencamp, *Uh-Huh* (Mercury, 1983) e; the Hooters, *One Way Home* (Columbia, 1987) e, m.

Thomas, Chris.

Pink Floyd, *Dark Side of the Moon* (Harvest, 1973) m; Roxy Music, *Siren* (Reprise, 1975) p; the Sex Pistols, *Never Mind the Bollocks Here's the Sex*

Pistols (Warner Bros., 1977) p (with Bill Price); the Pretenders, *Pretenders* (Sire, 1980) p; INXS, *Listen like Thieves* (Atlantic, 1985) p.

Titlelman, Russ.
Randy Newman, *Sail Away* (Reprise, 1972) p (with Lenny Waronker); James Taylor, *Gorilla* (Warner Bros., 1975) p (with Waronker); Rickie Lee Jones, *Rickie Lee Jones* (Warner Bros., 1979) p (with Waronker); Paul Simon, *Hearts and Bones* (Warner Bros., 1983) p (with Waronker and Simon); Steve Winwood, *Back in the High Life* (Island, 1986) p (with Winwood).

Tucker, Tom.
Big Head Todd and the Monsters, *Sister Sweetly* (Giant, 1993) e; Prince, *Emancipation* (NPG/EMI, 1996) e; Greg Brown, *Slant 6 Mind* (Red House, 1997) e; Jonny Lang, *Wander This World* (A&M, 1998) e; Tuck and Patti, *Paradise Found* (Windham Hill, 1998) e.

Valentin, Val.
Ella Fitzgerald, *Sings the Johnny Mercer Song Book* (Verve, 1964) e; Bill Evans, *Trio '65* (Verve, 1965) e; the Animals, *Animalism* (MGM, 1966) e; the Mothers of Invention, *Freak Out!* (Verve, 1966) e; the Velvet Underground, *The Velvet Underground* (MGM, 1969) e.

Vig, Butch.
Nirvana, *Nevermind* (DGC, 1991) e, p (with Nirvana); Smashing Pumpkins, *Siamese Dreams* (Virgin, 1993) e, p (with Billy Corgan); Freedy Johnston, *This Perfect World* (Elektra, 1994) p; Helmet, *Betty* (Interscope, 1994) p (with Helmet); Garbage, *Garbage* (Almo, 1995) p (with Garbage).

Visconti, Tony.
Gentle Giant, *Gentle Giant* (Polydor, 1970) p; T-Rex, *Electric Warrior* (Fly/Reprise, 1971) p; David Bowie, *Low* (RCA, 1977) p (with Bowie), *Heroes* (RCA, 1977) e, p (with Bowie), *Scary Monsters . . . and Super Creeps* (RCA, 1980) e, p (with Bowie); Thin Lizzy, *Bad Reputation* (Mercury, 1977) e, p (with Phil Lynott and Thin Lizzy).

Wallace, Andy.
Slayer, *Reign in Blood* (Def American, 1986) e; Nirvana, *Nevermind* (DGC, 1991) m; Jeff Buckley, *Grace* (Columbia, 1994) e, p (with Buckley); Blind Melon, *Soup* (Capitol, 1995) e, p; Ben Folds Five, *Whatever and Ever Amen* (Sony, 1997) m.

Wallace, Matt.
Faith No More, *The Real Thing* (Slash, 1989) e, p; the Spent Poets, *The Spent Poets* (Geffen, 1992) p (with the Spent Poets); School of Fish, *Human Cannonball* (Capitol, 1993) p (with School of Fish); Paul Westerberg, *14 Songs* (Sire, 1993) e, p (with Westerberg); Train, *Train* (Aware, 1998) e, p (with Train).

Was, Don.
Bonnie Raitt, *Nick of Time* (Capitol, 1988) p; Ringo Starr, *Time Takes Time* (Private Music, 1992) p; Willie Nelson, *Across the Borderline* (Columbia, 1993) p; Jackson Browne, *I'm Alive* (Elektra, 1993) p (with Browne);

the Rolling Stones, *Voodoo Lounge* (Virgin, 1994) p (with the Glimmer Twins).

Way, Dave.

Toni Braxton, "Breathe Again," *Toni Braxton* (LaFace, 1993) m; TLC, "Red Light Special," *Crazy Sexy Cool* (LaFace, 1995) m; Fiona Apple, "Across the Universe," *Pleasantville* soundtrack (Sony, 1998) m; Christina Aguilera, "Genie in a Bottle," *Christina Aguilera* (RCA, 1999) m; Macy Gray, *On How Life Is* (Epic, 1999) e.

Wexler, Jerry.

Ray Charles, "What'd I Say Parts I & II" (Atlantic, 1958) p (with Ahmet Ertegun); Solomon Burke, "Got to Get You off My Mind" (Atlantic, 1965) p (with Bert Berns); Wilson Pickett, "In the Midnight Hour" (Atlantic, 1965) p; Aretha Franklin, "I Never Loved a Man (the Way I Love You)" (Atlantic, 1969) p; Delaney and Bonnie, *To Delaney from Bonnie* (Atco, 1970) p.

Yakus, Shelley.

The Band, *Music from Big Pink* (Capitol, 1968) e; Van Morrison, *Moondance* (Warner Bros., 1970) e; Tom Petty and the Heartbreakers, *Damn the Torpedoes* (MCA, 1979) e; Lone Justice, *Lone Justice* (Geffen, 1985) e; Suzanne Vega, *Solitude Standing* (A&M, 1987) m.

Recordings Cited

This list is intended to help readers locate recordings mentioned in the book. Thus, while dates are for the original releases, labels—and for some older recordings the album titles as well—are those that are currently available.

ABC. "Many Happy Returns," *The Lexicon of Love*. Mercury, 1982.

The Band. "I Shall be Released," "Chest Fever," *Music from Big Pink*. Capitol, 1968.

———. *The Band*. Capitol, 1969.

The Bangles. "If She Knew What She Wants," *Different Light*. Columbia, 1985.

The Beach Boys. "God Only Knows," *Pet Sounds*. Capitol, 1966.

———. "Good Vibrations." Capitol, 1966.

The Beatles. *Please Please Me*. Parlophone, 1963.

———. "Long Tall Sally" (1964), *Past Masters*. Vol. 1. Parlophone, 1988.

———. "Words of Love," *Beatles for Sale*. Parlophone, 1964.

———. *Rubber Soul*. Parlophone, 1965.

———. "Yesterday," *Help*. Parlophone, 1965.

———. "Eleanor Rigby," "I'm Only Sleeping," "Tomorrow Never Knows," "Love You To," "Taxman," *Revolver*. Parlophone, 1966.

———. "A Day in the Life," *Sgt. Pepper's Lonely Hearts Club Band*. Parlophone, 1967.

———. "Hello Goodbye," "Blue Jay Way," "Strawberry Fields Forever," *Magical Mystery Tour*. Parlophone, 1967.

———. "Back in the U.S.S.R.," "Ob La Di, Ob La Da," *The Beatles*. Parlophone, 1968.

———. *Anthology*. Vol. 1. Capitol, 1995.

———. *Anthology*. Vol. 2. Capitol, 1996.

Beck. "The New Pollution," *Odelay*. DGC, 1996.

Big Country. *The Crossing*. Mercury, 1983.

Björk. "The Hunter," *Homogenic*. Elektra, 1997.

Blondie. "The Tide Is High," *Autoamerican*. Chrysalis, 1980.

Bob B. Soxx and the Blue Jeans. "Zip-A-Dee-Doo-Dah" (1962), *Back to MONO*. Phil Spector Records/ABKCO, 1991.

Boogie Down Productions. "Illegal Business," *By All Means Necessary*. Jive, 1988.

Boone, Pat. "Long Tall Sally," "Tutti Frutti" (1956), *Fifties: Complete*. Bear Family, 1997.

Bowie, David. "Speed of Life," *Low*. Virgin, 1977.

———. "Fashion," *Scary Monsters . . . and Super Creeps*. Virgin, 1980.

———. "Let's Dance," *Let's Dance*. Virgin, 1983.

Brenston, Jackie. "Rocket '88' " (1951), *Rocket '88'*. Charly, 1991.

The Buggles. "Video Killed the Radio Star," *The Age of Plastic*. Island, 1980.

The Byrds. "Mr. Tambourine Man," *Mr. Tambourine Man*. Columbia, 1965.

Collins, Phil. "In the Air Tonight," *Face Value*. Atlantic, 1981.

Colvin, Shawn. "Diamond in the Rough," *Steady On*. Columbia, 1989.

Crosby, Stills, Nash, and Young. "Ohio," *Four Way Street*. Atlantic, 1971.

Crowded House. "Kill Eye," *Temple of Low Men*. Capitol, 1988.

Def Leppard. *Pyromania*. Mercury, 1983.

Dire Straits. "Money for Nothing," *Brothers in Arms*. Warner Bros., 1985.

Dream Academy. *The Dream Academy*. Reprise, 1985.

Dylan, Bob. *Blonde on Blonde*. Columbia, 1966.

———. "All along the Watchtower," *John Wesley Harding*. Columbia, 1967.

———. "To Be Alone with You," *Nashville Skyline*. Columbia, 1969.

———. "Man in the Long Black Coat," *Oh Mercy*. Columbia, 1989.

———. *Under the Red Sky*. Columbia, 1990.

Dylan, Bob, and The Band. *The Basement Tapes*. Columbia, 1975.

The Eagles. *Hotel California*. Asylum, 1976.

Eno, Brian. *Discreet Music*. EG, 1975.

———. *Ambient 1: Music for Airports*. EG, 1978.

Fleetwood Mac. *Rumours*. Warner Bros., 1977.

Franklin, Aretha. "I Never Loved a Man (the Way I Love You)," "Respect," *I Never Loved a Man (the Way I Love You)*. Atlantic, 1967.

Frida. *Something's Going On*. Epic, 1982.

Gabriel, Peter. "The Intruder," *Peter Gabriel*. Geffen, 1980.

———. "Digging in the Dirt," "Love to Be Loved," *Us*. Geffen, 1992.

Garbage. "Supervixen," "Stupid Girl," *Garbage*. Almo, 1995.

Gaye, Marvin. "What's Going On," *What's Going On*. Motown, 1970.

Harris, Emmylou. "Goodbye," *Wrecking Ball*. Elektra, 1995 .

Harrison, George. "Isn't It a Pity," *All Things Must Pass*. Capitol, 1970.

Hendrix, Jimi. "Hey Joe," "Purple Haze," *Are You Experienced?* MCA, 1967.

———. "All along the Watchtower," *Electric Ladyland*. MCA, 1968.

Hiatt, John. "Through Your Hands," *Stolen Moments*. A&M, 1990.

Holly, Buddy. "Peggy Sue," "Words of Love," "Not Fade Away," "Everyday" (1957–58), *Buddy Holly: From the Original Master Tapes*. MCA, 1985.

Jackson, Janet. "Control," *Control*. A&M, 1986.

Jackson, Michael. "Beat It," *Thriller*. Epic, 1983.

The Kingsmen. "Louie Louie," *The Kingsmen in Person*. Sundazed, 1963.

Lanois, Daniel. "Amazing Grace,"*Acadie*. Opal/Warner Bros., 1989.

Led Zeppelin. "Whole Lotta Love," "Ramble On," *Led Zeppelin II*. Atlantic, 1969.

———. *ZOSO [IV]*. Atlantic, 1972.

Lennon, John. "Happy Xmas (War Is Over)," *The John Lennon Collection.* Capitol, 1971.

Little Richard. "Long Tall Sally," "Tutti Frutti" (1956), *Georgia Peach.* Specialty, 1991.

Los Lobos. "Angels with Dirty Faces," *Kiko.* Slash, 1992.

Madonna. *Ray of Light.* Warner Bros., 1998.

Manson, Marilyn. *Antichrist Superstar.* Nothing/Interscope, 1996.

McCartney, Paul. "Kreen-Akrore," *McCartney.* Capitol, 1970.

McMurty, James. *Too Long in the Wasteland.* Columbia, 1989.

The Neville Brothers. *Yellow Moon.* A&M, 1989.

Nirvana. "Smells like Teen Spirit," *Nevermind.* DGC, 1991.

———. *In Utero.* DGC, 1993.

O'Connor, Sinéad. "I Want Your (Hands on Me)," "Drink before the War," "Just Call Me Joe," *The Lion and the Cobra.* Ensign/Chrysalis, 1987.

Page, Jimmy and Robert Plant. *Walking into Clarksdale.* Atlantic, 1998.

The Paragons. "The Tide Is High" (1967), *On the Beach with the Paragons.* Jet, 1999.

Paul, Les and Mary Ford. "How High the Moon" (1951), *Love Songs by Les Paul and Mary Ford.* Ranwood/EMI-Capitol, 1997.

Pell Mell. *Star City.* Matador, 1997.

Petty, Tom. "Don't Come Around Here No More," *Southern Accents.* MCA, 1985.

———. *Full Moon Fever.* MCA, 1989.

———. *Wildflowers.* Warner Bros, 1994.

———. "Echo," *Echo.* Warner Bros., 1999.

Pickett, Wilson. "In the Midnight Hour," "Mustang Sally" (1965–66). *The Very Best of Wilson Pickett.* Rhino, 1993.

Pink Floyd. "Echoes," *Meddle.* Capitol, 1971.

Presley, Elvis. "Blue Moon," "Baby Let's Play House," "Blue Moon of Kentucky," "Heartbreak Hotel," "Hound Dog" (1954–56), *The King of Rock 'n' Roll: The Complete 50s Masters.* RCA, 1992.

Prince. "Starfish and Coffee," *Sign O' the Times.* Paisley Park/Warner Bros., 1987.

Public Image Ltd. *Album.* Elektra, 1986.

Queen. "Now I'm Here," *Sheer Heart Attack.* Hollywood, 1974.

The Ramones. "Teenage Lobotomy," *Rocket to Russia.* Sire, 1977.

———. *End of the Century.* Sire, 1980.

Redding, Otis. "Respect" (1966), *The Very Best of Otis Redding.* Rhino, 1993.

The Red Hot Chili Peppers. "Under the Bridge," *Blood Sugar Sex Magik.* Warner Bros., 1991.

Reed, Lou. *Mistrial.* RCA, 1986.

———. *Set the Twilight Reeling.* Warner Bros., 1996.

R. E. M. "Tongue," *Monster.* Warner Bros., 1994.

The Righteous Brothers. "You've Lost that Lovin' Feelin' " (1964), *Back to MONO.* Phil Spector Records/ABKCO, 1991.

Robertson, Robbie. "Fallen Angel," *Robbie Robertson.* Geffen, 1987.

The Rolling Stones. "(I Can't Get No) Satisfaction," *Out of Our Heads.* ABKCO, 1965.

———. "As Tears Go By," *December's Children (and Everybody's),* ABKCO, 1966.

———. "Wild Horses," *Sticky Fingers.* Virgin, 1971.

———. "Tumbling Dice," *Exile on Main Street.* Virgin, 1972.

The Ronettes. "Be My Baby" (1963), *Back to MONO.* Phil Spector Records/ABKCO, 1991.

Roxy Music. *Stranded.* Reprise, 1973.

———. "Love Is the Drug," *Siren.* Reprise, 1975.

The Sex Pistols. "Anarchy in the U.K.," *Never Mind the Bollocks Here's the Sex Pistols.* Warner Bros., 1977.

Simon, Paul. "Proof," *Rhythm of the Saints.* Warner Bros., 1990.

Soft Cell. "Where Did Our Love Go?" *Non-Stop Ecstatic Dancing.* 1982, Polygram.

Springsteen, Bruce. "She's the One," "Born to Run," *Born to Run.* Columbia, 1975.

———. "Atlantic City," *Nebraska.* Columbia, 1982.

———. "Working on the Highway," *Born in the U.S.A.* Columbia, 1984.

Steely Dan. *Aja.* MCA, 1977.

Stone, Sly. *There's a Riot Goin' On.* Epic, 1971.

———. "In Time," *Fresh.* Epic, 1973.

The Stooges. *Raw Power.* Columbia, 1973; remix, 1997.

The Supremes. "Where Did Our Love Go?" (1964), *Diana Ross and the Supremes: The Ultimate Collection.* Motown, 1997.

Sweet, Matthew. "Sick of Myself," *100% Fun.* Zoo, 1995.

The Thompson Twins. "Doctor! Doctor!" *Into the Gap.* Arista, 1984.

TLC. "Red Light Special," "Waterfalls," *Crazy Sexy Cool.* LaFace, 1995.

U2. *War.* Island, 1983.

———. *The Unforgettable Fire.* Island, 1984.

———. "Zoo Station," *Achtung Baby.* Island, 1992.

———. *Zooropa.* Island, 1993.

The Velvet Underground. "Heroin," *The Velvet Underground and Nico.* Polydor, 1967.

———. *White Light/White Heat.* Polydor, 1968.

———. "Candy Says," "I'm Beginning to See the Light," *The Velvet Underground.* Polydor, 1969.

Winwood, Steve. "Higher Love," *Back in the High Life.* Island, 1986.

World Party. "Way Down Now," *Goodbye Jumbo.* Ensign/Chrysalis, 1990.

———. "Is It like Today?" "Sunshine," *Bang!* Ensign/Chrysalis, 1993.

———. *Egyptology.* 1997.

Wray, Link. "Rumble" (1958), *Rumble! The Best of Link Wray.* Rhino, 1993.

Yes. "Siberian Khatru," *Close to the Edge.* Atlantic, 1972.

Young, Paul. "Everytime You Go Away," *The Secret of Association.* Columbia, 1985.

Bibliography

Much of the background source material to which I am indebted is not included here. This is a list of sources cited, excepting periodicals and liner notes.

Amburn, Ellis. *Dark Star: The Roy Orbison Story*. New York: Carol Publishing Group, 1990.

Babbitt, Milton. *Milton Babbitt: Words about Music*. Edited by Stephen Dembski and Joseph N. Straus. Madison: University of Wisconsin Press, 1987.

Ballou, Glen, ed. *Handbook for Sound Engineers: The New Audio Cyclopedia*. 2d ed. Carmel, Minn.: SAMS, 1991.

Barthes, Roland. *Image, Music, Text*. Translated by Stephen Heath. New York: Hill and Wang, 1977.

Bartók, Béla. *Béla Bartók Essays*. Edited by Benjamin Suchoff. Lincoln: University of Nebraska Press, 1976.

Belz, Carl. *The Story of Rock*. New York: Oxford University Press, 1969.

Benjamin, Walter. *Illuminations*. Translated by Harry Zohn, edited by Hannah Arendt. New York: Schocken Books, 1969.

Bennett, H. Stith. *On Becoming a Rock Musician*. Amherst: University of Massachusetts Press, 1980.

Berliner, Paul F. *Thinking in Jazz: The Infinite Art of Improvisation*. Chicago: University of Chicago Press, 1994.

Blum, Stephen. "Theory and Method: Analysis of Musical Style." In *Ethnomusicology: An Introduction*, edited by Helen Myers. New York: W. W. Norton, 1992.

Bonds, Mark Evan. *Wordless Rhetoric: Musical Form and the Metaphor of the Oration*. Cambridge: Harvard University Press, 1991.

Boretz, Benjamin. "Nelson Goodman's *Languages of Art* From a Musical Point of View." In *Perspectives on Contemporary Music Theory*, edited by Benjamin Boretz and Edward T. Cone. New York: W. W. Norton, 1972.

Brackett, David. *Interpreting Popular Music*. Cambridge: Cambridge University Press, 1995.

Buelow, George J. "Rhetoric and Music." In *The New Grove Dictionary of Music and Musicians*, edited by Stanley Sadie, vol. 15. London: Macmillan, 1980.

Chavez, Carlos. *Toward a New Music: Music and Electricity*. Translated by Herbert Weinstock. New York: Da Capo Press, 1937.

Copland, Aaron. *Music and Imagination.* Cambridge: Harvard University Press, 1952.

Cunningham, Mark. *Good Vibrations: A History of Record Production.* London: Sanctuary Publishing, 1998.

Dahlhaus, Carl. *Nineteenth-Century Music.* Translated by J. Bradford Robinson. Berkeley: University of California Press, 1989.

Daniel, Oliver. *Stokowski: A Counterpoint of Views.* New York: Dodd, Mead and Co., 1982.

Dixon, Robert M. W. and John Godrich. *Recording the Blues.* New York: Stein and Day, 1970.

Eisenberg, Evan. *The Recording Angel: Explorations in Phonography.* New York: McGraw-Hill, 1987.

Eisenstein, Sergei. *Film Form: Essays in Film Theory.* Translated and edited by Jay Leyda. San Diego: Harcourt Brace Jovanovich, 1949.

Erickson, Robert. *Sound Structure in Music.* Berkeley: University of California Press, 1975.

Everett, Walter. *The Beatles as Musicians: Revolver through the Anthology.* New York: Oxford University Press, 1999.

Fast, Susan. "Music, Contexts, and Meaning in U2." In *Expression in Pop-Rock Music: A Collection of Critical and Analytical Essays,* edited by Walter Everett. New York: Garland Publishing, 2000.

Finnegan, Ruth. *The Hidden Musicians: Music-Making in an English Town.* Cambridge: Cambridge University Press, 1989.

Flanagan, Bill. *Written in My Soul: Conversations with Rock's Great Songwriters.* Chicago: Contemporary Books, 1987.

———. *U2 at the End of the World.* New York: Delacorte Press, 1995.

Floyd, Samuel A. *The Power of Black Music: Interpreting Its History from Africa to the United States.* New York: Oxford University Press, 1995.

Fox, Ted. *In the Groove: The People behind the Music.* New York: St. Martin's Press, 1986.

Frith, Simon. *Sound Effects: Youth, Leisure and the Politics of Rock.* London: Constable, 1983.

Gillett, Charlie. *Making Tracks: Atlantic Records and the Growth of a Multi-Billion-Dollar Industry.* New York: E. P. Dutton, 1974.

———. *The Sound of the City: The Rise of Rock and Roll.* Rev. and exp. ed. New York: Pantheon Books, 1984.

Goehr, Lydia. *The Imaginary Museum of Musical Works: An Essay in the Philosophy of Music.* Oxford: Clarendon Press, 1992.

Goodman, Nelson. *Languages of Art: An Approach to a Theory of Symbols.* 2d ed. New York: Hackett, 1976.

Gould, Glenn. *The Glenn Gould Reader.* Edited by Tim Page. New York: Alfred A. Knopf, 1984.

Gracyk, Theodore. *Rhythm and Noise: An Aesthetics of Rock.* Durham: Duke University Press, 1996.

Guralnick, Peter. *Lost Highway: Journeys and Arrivals of American Musicians.* New York: Harper and Row, 1989.

———. *Last Train to Memphis: The Rise of Elvis Presley.* Boston: Little, Brown and Co., 1994.

Hanslick, Eduard. *Hanslick's Music Criticisms.* Translated and edited by Henry Pleasants. New York: Dover, 1950.

———. *On the Musically Beautiful: A Contribution towards the Revision of the Aesthetics of Music.*Translated and edited by Geoffrey Payzant. Indianapolis: Hackett, 1986.

Harrington, John. *The Rhetoric of Film.* New York: Holt, Rinehart and Winston, 1973.

Hegel, G. W. F. "Aesthetik," in *Werke (Jubiläumsausgabe).* Excerpted in "Georg Wilhelm Friedrich Hegel," in *Music and Aesthetics in the Eighteenth and Early-Nineteenth Centuries,* translated and edited by Peter le Huray and James Day. Cambridge: Cambridge University Press, 1981.

Hitchcock, H. Wiley, ed. *The Phonograph and Our Musical Life.* Brooklyn: Institute for Studies in American Music, 1980.

Hoffman, E. T. A. "Beethoven's Instrumental Music." In *Source Readings in Music History,* selected and annotated by Oliver Strunk. New York: W. W. Norton, 1950.

Hopkins, Jerry. *Elvis: A Biography.* New York: Simon and Schuster, 1971.

Hoskyns, Barney. *Across the Great Divide: The Band and America.* New York: Hyperion, 1993.

Ingarden, Roman. *The Work of Music and the Problem of Its Identity.* Translated by A. Czerniawski. Berkeley: University of California Press, 1986.

Ives, Charles. "Essays before a Sonata." In *Essays before a Sonata, The Majority, and other writings of Charles Ives,* edited by Howard Boatwright. New York: W. W. Norton, 1970.

Jablonski, Edward, and Lawrence D. Stewart. *The Gershwin Years: George and Ira.* New York: Da Capo Press, 1996.

Jones, Quincy. "Producing Records." In *Making Music: The Guide to Writing, Performing and Recording,* edited by George Martin. London: Pan Books, 1983.

Jones, Steve. *Rock Formation: Music, Technology, and Mass Communication.* Newbury Park, Calif.: Sage Publications, 1992.

Kahn, Douglas, and Gregory Whitehead, eds. *Wireless Imagination: Sound, Radio, and the Avant-Garde.* Cambridge: MIT Press, 1992.

Katz, Mark. "The Phonograph Effect: The Influence of Recording on Listener, Performer, Composer, 1900–1940." Ph.D. dissertation, University of Michigan, 1999.

Kealy, Edward. "The Real Rock Revolution: Sound Mixers, Social Inequality, and the Aesthetics of Popular Music Production." Ph.D. dissertation, Northwestern University, 1974.

Keil, Charles, and Steven Feld. *Music Grooves: Essays and Dialogues.* Chicago: University of Chicago Press, 1994.

Koch, Heinrich Christoph. *Versuch einer Anleitung zur Composition.* 3 vols. Rudolstadt and Leipzig (1782–1793). Facsimile, Hildesheim: Georg Olms,

1969. Partial translation in Nancy Kovaleff Baker, *Introductory Essay on Composition*. New Haven: Yale University Press, 1983.

Kostelanetz, Richard, ed. *Moholy-Nagy*. New York: Praeger, 1970.

Langer, Susanne. *Feeling and Form*. New York: Scribner, 1953.

Leaf, David. *The Beach Boys*. Philadelphia: Courage Books, 1985.

Lewisohn, Mark. *The Beatles Recording Sessions*. New York: Harmony Books, 1988.

Lippman, Edward. *A History of Western Musical Aesthetics*. Lincoln: University of Nebraska Press, 1992.

Marcus, Greil. *Mystery Train: Images of America in Rock 'n' Roll Music*. New York: E. P. Dutton, 1976.

Marsh, Dave. *Glory Days: Bruce Springsteen in the 1980s*. New York: Pantheon Books, 1987.

Martin, George. *All You Need Is Ears*. London: MacMillan, 1979.

————, with William Pearson. *Summer of Love: The Making of Sgt. Pepper*. London: Macmillan, 1994.

————, ed. *Making Music: The Guide to Writing, Performing and Recording*. London: Pan Books, 1983.

McFarland, Thomas. *Originality and Imagination*. Baltimore: Johns Hopkins University Press, 1985.

Meyer, Leonard B. *Style and Music: Theory, History, and Ideology*. Philadelphia: University of Pennsylvania Press, 1989.

Mezzrow, Mezz, with Bernard Wolfe. *Really the Blues*. London: Flamingo, 1993.

Middleton, Richard. *Studying Popular Music*. Milton Keynes, U. K.: Open University Press, 1990.

Millard, Andre. *America on Record: A History of Recorded Sound*. Cambridge: Cambridge University Press, 1995.

Moholy-Nagy, Laszlo. *Vision in Motion*. Chicago: Paul Theobald, 1969.

Moore, Allan F. *Rock, The Primary Text: Developing a Musicology of Rock* (Milton Keynes, U. K.: Open University Press, 1993.

Moore, Scottie, and James Dickerson. *That's Alright, Elvis*. New York: Schirmer Books, 1997.

Olsen, Eric, with Paul Verna and Carlo Wolff. *The Encyclopedia of Record Producers*. New York: Billboard Books, 1999.

Panofsky, Erwin. *Meaning in the Visual Arts*. Garden City, N.Y.: Doubleday Anchor Books, 1955.

Pareles, John, and Patricia Romanowski, eds. *The Rolling Stone Encyclopedia of Rock & Roll*. New York: Rolling Stone Press/Summit Books, 1983.

Pruter, Robert. *Doowop: The Chicago Scene*. Urbana: University of Illinois Press, 1996.

Read, Oliver, and Walter L. Welch. *From Tin Foil to Stereo: Evolution of the Phonograph*. Indianapolis: Howard W. Sams, 1959.

Repsch, John. *The Legendary Joe Meek: The Telstar Man*. London: Woodford House, 1989.

Reynolds, Roger. "Thoughts on What a Record Records." In *The Phonograph and Our Musical Life,* edited by H. Wiley Hitchcock. Brooklyn: Institute for Studies in American Music, 1980.

Ribowsky, Mark. *He's a Rebel.* New York: E. P. Dutton, 1989.

Rolling Stone Editors, comps. *The Rolling Stone Interviews.* 2 vols. New York: Warner Paperback Library, 1971.

Schaffner, Nicholas. *Saucerful of Secrets: The Pink Floyd Odyssey.* New York: Harmony Books, 1991.

Schaughnessy, Mary Alice. *Les Paul: An American Original.* New York: William Morrow, 1993.

Schoenberg, Arnold. "New Music, Outmoded Music, Style and Idea." In *Style and Idea: Selected Writings of Arnold Schoenberg,* translated by Leo Black, edited by Leonard Stein. New York: St. Martin's Press, 1975.

Selvin, Joel. *Sly and the Family Stone: An Oral History.* New York: Avon Books, 1998.

Sessions, Roger. *The Musical Experience of Composer, Performer, Listener.* Princeton: Princeton University Press, 1974.

Sontag, Susan. *Against Interpretation and Other Essays.* New York: Doubleday Anchor Books, 1990.

Stern, Chip. "The Serious Metafoolishness of Father Funkadelic, George Clinton." In *The Rock Musician,* edited by Tony Scherman. New York: St. Martin's Press, 1994.

Sting. "Songwriting." In *Making Music: The Guide to Writing, Performing and Recording,* edited by George Martin. London: Pan Books, 1983.

Stone, Terri, ed. *Music Producers: Conversations with Today's Top Record Makers.* Winona, Minn.: Hal Leonard, 1992.

Stravinsky, Igor. *An Autobiography.* New York: Simon and Schuster, 1936.

———. *Poetics of Music in the Form of Six Lessons.* Cambridge: Harvard University Press, 1974.

Szatmary, David P. *Rockin' in Time: A Social History of Rock-and-Roll.* 3d ed. Upper Saddle River, N.J.: Prentice Hall, 1996.

Tamm, Eric. *Brian Eno: His Music and the Vertical Color of Sound.* Boston: Faber and Faber, 1989.

Théberge, Paul. *Any Sound You Can Imagine: Making Music/Consuming Technology.* Hanover, N.H.: University Press of New England, 1997.

Walser, Robert. *Running with the Devil: Power, Gender, and Madness in Heavy Metal Music.* Hanover, N.H.: University Press of New England, 1993.

Walton, Kendall L. "The Presentation and Portrayal of Sound Patterns." In *Human Agency: Language, Duty, and Value,* edited by Jonathan Dancy, J. M. E. Moravcsik, and C. C. W. Taylor. Stanford: Stanford University Press, 1988.

Weill, Kurt. "Radio and the Restructuring of Musical Life." In *Writings of German Composers,* translated and edited by Michael Gilbert, Jost Hermand, and James Steakly. New York: Continuum, 1984.

Wexler, Jerry, and David Ritz. *Rhythm and the Blues: A Life in American Music.* New York: Alfred A. Knopf, 1993.

Wicke, Peter. *Rock Music: Culture, Aesthetics and Sociology.* Translated by Rachel Fogg. Cambridge: Cambridge University Press, 1990.

Williams, Richard. *Out of His Head: The Sound of Phil Spector.* New York: Outerbridge and Lazard, 1972.

Wilson, Brian, with Todd Gold. *Wouldn't It Be Nice: My Own Story.* New York: Harper Collins, 1991.

Woolf, Virginia. *Collected Essays.* Vol. 2. London: Hogarth Press, 1966.

Woram, John. *Sound Recording Handbook.* Indianapolis: Howard W. Sams, 1989.

Zappa, Frank, with Peter Occhiogrosso. *The Real Frank Zappa Book.* New York: Poseidon Press, 1989.

Index

A&R Studios, 106

A and Z energy, 133–34; and live backing track, 136; and mixing, 161

ABC, 152

AC/DC, 197

Abba, xvii, 197

Abbey Road Studios, 71, 134

absolute music, 39

Acadie, 163

Ace, Johnny, 185, 190

Achtung Baby, 67–69

"Against Interpretation," 44

Ahern, Brian, 102

Aja, 79

Albini, Steve, 163; use of microphones, 111

Album, 100

"All Along the Watchtower," 48–49

Allison, Jerry, 102

allographic media, 21–22. *See also* autographic media

All Things Must Pass, 59

All You Need Is Ears, 97

"Amazing Grace," 94–96

ambience, xiv; 49, 76–85, 119, 128, 168, 186, 190; Beatles use of, 78–79; and compression, 80, 120, 127; distancing effect of, 147; drum, 79–82; and echo, 70, 76; and gates, 80–81, 126–27; lack of 84–85; and limiting, 125; and linked processors, 120; and microphone placement, 76, 80; in multichannel recording, 16; and multiple sound spaces, 82–84; (reverb) simulator, 101, 107; and spatial dimension, 145; and studio space, 100–2; and timbre, 81; and vocal sound, 112, 160. *See also* association

ambient chamber, 70; Buddy Holly's use

of, 81–82, 101; Phil Spector's use of, 78, 101

ambient image, 46, 160, 190; definition, 77; and echo, 74; and mixing, 142; multiple, 83–84

"ambient music." *See* Eno, Brian

Ampex, 14. *See also* tape recorder

amplifier, 107

amplitude, 160; and console, 118; and echo, 70; and foreground sound, 143; and frequency range, 155; and prominence, 156–57; rhythm and texture, 85, 87, 89–90, 91–92; and stereo spectrum, 147; and vocal sound, 112

amplitude modulator. *See* timbral processor

analog/digital debate, 113–15

analog recording, 112–15

"Anarchy in the U.K.," 178

"Angels with Dirty Faces," 33

Antichrist Superstar, 183

Aristotle, 187

Aronoff, Kenny, 52

arrangement, 32–37, 43, 153, 154, 169, 192; developed in performance, 33; developed in pre-production, 33, 137; echo in, 74; electronic versus traditional, 152; and frequency range, 151; head, 32, 34; and mixing, 37, 141, 155; and narrative, 161; as principal element of record, 17, 24–25, 164; and producer, 170, 172, 174–77; in rehearsal, 53; shaping, 28; and sound processing, 151–52; stereo placement in, 149; techniques, 86; and timbre, 151; written, 59. *See also* association; Bartholomew, Dave; Beatles; Spector, Phil; string quartet

Compositor: BookMatters, Berkeley
Text: 10/13 Palatino
Display: Palatino